S0-BRS-672

WAGNER AND THE EROTIC IMPULSE

WAGNER AND THE EROTIC IMPULSE

LAURENCE DREYFUS

HARVARD UNIVERSITY PRESS
Cambridge, Massachusetts
London, England
2010

Copyright © 2010 by the President and Fellows of Harvard College
All rights reserved

Library of Congress Cataloging-in-Publication Data
Dreyfus, Laurence, 1952–
    Wagner and the erotic impulse / Laurence Dreyfus.
        p.   cm.
    Includes bibliographical references and index.
    ISBN 978-0-674-01881-5 (alk. paper)
    1. Wagner, Richard, 1813–1883—Criticism and interpretation.   2. Opera—19th
century.   3. Sex in opera.   I. Title.
    ML410.W13D74 2010
    782.1092—dc22   2010011118

Need I add that Wagner also owes his *success* to his sensuality?

Habe ich noch zu sagen, daß Wagner seiner Sinnlichkeit *auch seinen Erfolg verdankt?*

—Friedrich Nietzsche, *Nachlaß* **(1888)**

Contents

Preface   ix

Abbreviations   xv

1. Echoes   1
   Music and Eros—Søren Kierkegaard—Suggestive Music—
   Peculiarities of Musical Erotics—Charles Baudelaire—Friedrich
   Nietzsche and Malwida von Meysenbug—Édouard Schuré and
   Hans von Bülow—Ludwig Schnorr von Carolsfeld—Gabriele
   D'Annunzio and Thomas Mann—Wagner's critics—
   Clara Schumann

2. Intentions   40
   *Julius Kapp and Ernest Newman—*Das Liebesverbot*—*
   Salvation from Arousal—Wilhelmine Schröder-Devrient—
   Arthur Schopenhauer—Opera, Not Philosophy

3. Harmonies   73
   Der Fliegende Holländer—Tannhäuser—*Erotics in the*
   Literary Sources—A Tour of the Venusberg—Love in the Ring
   Poem—Die Walküre—Tristan und Isolde—*The* Tristan
   Chord—*Musical Paradigms in the* Tristan Prelude—Tristan,
   *Act II—Renunciations of Love—*Die Meistersinger *and*
   Götterdämmerung—Parsifal

4. Pathologies   117
   Theodor Puschmann—Nietzsche the Pathologist—Worries
   about Masturbation—Pink Satin and Rose Perfumes—Wagner

*and His Milliners—Judith Gautier—Julius Cyriax—Fetishism
and Cross-dressing—Fabric and Perfumes in the Operas—
Flower-Maidens—Kundry—James Gibbons Huneker—Paul Lindau,
Max Kalbeck, and Paul Heyse—Berthold Auerbach and Daniel
Spitzer—Max Nordau and Theodor Herzl—Otto Weininger—
Effeminacy and Jewishness*

5. Homoerotics   175
    *Paul von Joukowsky and Pepino—Henry James—Richard von
    Krafft-Ebing and Oscar Panizza—Hanns Fuchs and the
    "Homosexual in Spirit"—Homosexual Sensibilities in German
    Literature—Ludwig II of Bavaria—Rejection of Pederasty—
    Signs of Romantic Friendship—Brangäne—Kurwenal—
    King Marke—Parsifal—Wagner and His Romantic Friends*

    Epilogue   218

    Appendix: Musical Examples   225

    Notes   243

    Index   261

PREFACE

All books about Richard Wagner are acts of love or hate, often a strange mixture of the two. While Wagner is an easy man to hate, he has become increasingly difficult to love, and his well-deserved reputation as unrepentant anti-Semite has prejudiced several generations of listeners against enjoying his music, predisposing them to hearing in it a harmful ideology. My own love of Wagner's music will be obvious to readers of this book, and I give relatively short shrift to twentieth-century ideologies and politics, as my goal was to survey what I take to be one of Wagner's most important contributions to music—what I call his erotics.

I first came to know Wagner's *Ring* in 1969–70 while studying the cello at Juilliard. My roommate, the pianist Jeffrey Swann—who went on to win the Queen Elizabeth Competition—barred me from joining his equally talented friends David Golub and Robert Black in a 24-hour extravaganza (including breaks), during which they listened in darkness to Georg Solti's *Ring* recordings. Since I hadn't ever studied the leitmotives, this trio of Wagnerians felt justified in banning me from their communal reverie and drove me from my apartment. Provoked, I began my own study of the *Ring*. A more generous Juilliard pianist, Steven Mayer, offloaded an unwanted copy of Solti's *Götterdämmerung*—a prohibitively expensive purchase for a student in those days—and I was hooked, collecting scores, books, and vintage records and supplementing the latter with a regular diet of Wagner at the Metropolitan Opera in New York. While teaching at Yale, I became fascinated by the first conductor of *Parsifal*, Hermann Levi, son of a rabbi, and began investigating the origins of his Wagnerism, a project which included a visit to the archives at Bayreuth. Hoping to hear Wagner in his native habitat, I wrote to the grandson of the composer, Wolfgang Wagner, who helped me obtain tickets in 1987. There, in the *Festspielhaus*, I attended several operas along with my wife and daughter, the latter still *in utero* at the time. Since then, a multitude of students at Yale, Stanford, King's College London, and Oxford have put up with my passion for Wagner, sometimes bewildered, but often enough enthused.

Not all the journey has been smooth sailing, and like the rocky sea voyage that inspired Wagner's *Flying Dutchman*, my travels were nearly shipwrecked by the tidal wave of Wagner literature, which overwhelms the inexperienced Wagner researcher with its clashing currents and dangerous undertow. In attempting to master the scholarship and sources—not to mention coming to terms with the composer's anti-Semitism—I am sure to have come up short, though not for lack of trying. As an undergraduate at Yeshiva University in 1973 studying politics and Jewish theology—having briefly abandoned music for religion—I wrote a breezily researched essay on Wagner as forerunner of the Nazis and was about to submit it when I put on a recording of *Tristan und Isolde*. The shock of the musical experience forced me to admit that my denunciation was hypocritical. Much to the dismay of my professor—Ruth Bevan—I appended an "afterword" challenging my own conclusions and was rewarded by a curt note suggesting I articulate a coherent argument about Wagner and stick to it. This book tries to do just that.

Writing about Wagner and sex wasn't imaginable when I was a graduate student in musicology at Columbia (1973–1980). It wasn't because the music historians who taught me were prudes, but because they would have considered erotics, like politics, demeaning to scholarly discourse. Times have changed in both regards. Having held a Chair in London (1995–2005) honoring the scholar and performer Thurston Dart, I was interested to learn—thanks to Margaret Bent—that in 1967 the editors of a trade press asked Dart whether they should commission a translation of a book defending Wagner against charges of indecency and perversity. Although the original exposé of Wagner's fabric fetish had appeared in 1877, and everyone from Brahms and Nietzsche to Thomas Mann knew about it, this wasn't a subject appropriate for scholarly treatment over much of the twentieth century, much less fit to be linked to the composer's music. Dart's private response was typical for the time: "My own feeling is against [an English translation of *Wagner und die Putzmacherin* (Wagner and his

Milliner)]," he wrote, "simply because there is no end to the correspondences of composers' laundresses and wine merchants (cf. G[eorge]
F[rederick] H[andel]) and these usually tell one absolutely s[od] f.- a. new."
As it turns out, Dart was wrong, though his coded obscenity turns out to
contain more than a grain of truth.

The five chapters in the current book began life as a series of public
lectures delivered at the British Library in 2003–2004, which have since
spun off in unexpected directions. In their final form, the five chapters
tell a story that requires a brief preamble. Chapter 1, Echoes, introduces
Wagner's musical erotics by surveying important nineteenth-century reactions to Wagner that have often been marginalized in contemporary
scholarship. I contend that these "receptions"—both glowing and
scathing—do not merely record subjective responses but actually help
identify intrinsic components of Wagner's practice. Chapter 2, Intentions, investigates whether Wagner knew what he was doing in composing music representing "sensuality." It seems he knew exactly what he was
doing, even if—given the mores of the time—he must be classed as a re-
luctant if obsessive eroticist. Chapter 3, Harmonies, surveys the key musical techniques Wagner developed for his erotics and focuses especially on
Tannhäuser, *Die Walküre*, and *Tristan und Isolde*. With *Tristan*, Wagner
revealed the fundamental outlines of his erotico-musical world, and
though I could have gone further in discussing *Die Meistersinger*, *Siegfried*, *Götterdämmerung*, and *Parsifal*, I believe the subtle variants of erotic
experience found in these later operas are better treated in specialized
studies. Chapter 4, Pathologies, considers late nineteenth-century receptions of Wagner's "diseased" erotics to show how critics like Nietzsche
unwittingly identify positive values in Wagner's erotics at the same time
that they expose the composer's unconventional masculinity. The link
between the composer's silk and perfume fetishes and their representations in his operas seems remarkable in this light, as is the absence of his
interest in "sexualizing" anti-Semitism. Finally, Chapter 5, Homoerotics,
treats Wagner's surprising regard for same-sexual love (*Männerliebe* or
Freundesliebe) as a complementary aspect to his personality: Wagner encouraged a spate of younger, sometimes "homophile," men to become
passionately attached to him and this sensibility, too, surfaces in his
operas.

Throughout the book, I aim to understand musicians and critics from their own vantage points, and try to traffic in concepts and categories contemporary with them. Although twentieth- and twenty-first-century critical theories may be pulling strings behind the scenes, I don't advocate any particular theoretical position beyond pursuing what I'd call a radical historicism, seeking out relevant documentary and musical evidence wherever I can find it. I also favor the extended quotations of documents by and about Wagner (often in fresh translation) so as to sample undiluted flavors from the past. We can still easily empathize with these vivid experiences even when our attitudes have changed, above all because the music that unites us is the same and has helped form our sensibilities. Biography needs to play an unembarrassed role in linking life and art, for to talk erotics but ignore a person's own special brew of desires is historically irresponsible: The evidence in the case of Wagner is simply too compelling to drive a skeptical theoretical wedge between compositional intention and its realization. Nor can an aesthetic response to Wagner's operas be left out of the concoction, for our own sensibilities provide a gauge by which we measure the intensity of our musical experiences. The astounding quality of Wagner's music is the reason I wrote this book, and a good reason to read it as well. Appreciation comes in many forms, and by unraveling Wagner's intentions as well as their significance I hope to enlarge critical comprehension and enhance musical pleasure.

The Music Department of Royal Holloway kindly invited me to give the British Library Lectures in Musicology: I'm grateful to colleagues at both institutions—David Charlton, Timothy Day, Katharine Ellis, John Rink, Jim Samson and Andrew Wathey—for their candid responses. Arvid Vollsnes asked me to repeat the talks at the University of Oslo, where challenging questions forced me to refine my views. Robert Baldock of Yale University Press first helped me devise the theme of Wagner's eroticism as a book-length subject, and Margaretta Fulton—the editor of my two previous books on Bach—persuaded me to remain with Harvard University Press. Sharmila Sen, her successor, together with Ian Stevenson, provided just the right spurs for me to reach the final stage, and I'm grateful for their keen interest.

Other friends and colleagues I'd like to thank include: Roger Allen, Avigdor Arikha, Anne Atik, Michael Beckerman, George Benjamin, Margaret Bent, Reinhold Brinkmann, Felix Budelmann, Carlo Caballero, Martin Crimp, Jonathan Cross, John Deathridge, Huguette Dreyfus, Reidar Due, Michael Fend, Christine Ferdinand, Peter Franklin, Jonathan Freeman-Attwood, Marigold Freeman-Attwood, Nicola Gardini, Malcolm Gerratt, Thomas Grey, Frithjof Haas, Clare Harris, Tobias Janz, James Kennaway, Daniel Leech-Wilkinson, Barry Millington, Silvina Milstein, Anna Papaeti, Hilary Pattison, Ian Partridge, Daniel-Ben Pienaar, Curtis Price, Lawrence Rosenwald, Rhian Samuel, Alberto Sanna, Robert Saxton, Stewart Spencer, Oliver Taplin, David Trendell, Jacqueline Waeber, Arnold Whittall, and Claudia Zenck. King's College London, the University of Oxford and Magdalen College, Oxford supported me with research funds and sabbatical leave, and the Klassik Stiftung Weimar graciously permitted an image from their collection to be reproduced. Martin Suckling engraved the musical examples with ingenuity and aplomb, and I am especially grateful to Karol Berger, Eric Clarke, and J. P. E. Harper-Scott, whose penetrating criticisms on the manuscript I've tried to address, if not always successfully. Christian Stier saved me from numerous infelicities, and Jonathan Oddie's perceptive suggestions clarified my argument and citation of the evidence. Irene Auerbach combed the copy-edited manuscript for errors and inconsistencies: my debt to her is simply enormous. All remaining blunders are my own.

George and Rita Dreyfus bequeathed a love of great music and continue to inspire me with their unflagging enthusiasm. Nancy Elan shared her passion for Wagner over many years, and Orhan Memed's interest in my work was a great boon during the period of initial research. Most recently, Bilal Iqbal Avan offered unstinting support, even if he refuses all thanks. The baby who absorbed *Parsifal* in the womb at Bayreuth, Emily Dreyfus, has since developed her own taste for Wagner and cast a critical if always sympathetic eye over the manuscript. This book, like the last, is dedicated to her.

Abbreviations

BB   Richard Wagner, *Das Braune Buch: Tagebuchaufzeichnungen 1865 bis 1882*, ed. Joachim Bergfeld (1975; Munich, 1988)

CD   *Cosima Wagner's Diaries*, ed. Martin Gregor-Dellin and Dietrich Mack, trans. Geoffrey Skelton, 2 vols. (London, 1978)

CT   Cosima Wagner, *Die Tagebücher*, ed. Martin Gregor-Dellin und Dietrich Mack, 4 vols., rev. ed. (Munich, 1982)

EC   Barbara Eichner and Guy Houghton, "Rose Oil and Pineapples: Julius Cyriax's Friendship with Wagner and the Early Years of the London Wagner Society," *The Wagner Journal* 1 (2007), 19–49

FH   Hanns Fuchs, *Richard Wagner und die Homosexualität: mit besonderer Berücksichtigung der sexuellen Anomalien seiner Gestalten* (Berlin, 1903)

GE   Claire von Glümer, *Erinnerungen an Wilhelmine Schröder-Devrient* (1862; Leipzig, 1904)

GV   Susanna Großmann-Vendrey, *Bayreuth in der deutschen Presse: Beiträge zur Rezeptionsgeschichte Richard Wagners und seiner Festspiele*, 2 vols. (Regensburg, 1977, 1983)

GW   Carl Friedrich Glasenapp, *Das Leben Richard Wagners in sechs Büchern* (Leipzig, 1896–1911)

HS   E. T. A. Hoffmann, *Die Serapions-Brüder*, ed. Walter Müller-Seidel and Wulf Segebrecht (Munich, 1976)

HT   Magnus Hirschfeld, *Die Transvestiten* (Leipzig, 1910), trans. Michael Lombardi-Nash as *The Transvestites: The Erotic Drive to Cross-Dress* (Amherst, NY, 1991)

HW   Heinrich Heine, *Werke und Briefe in zehn Bänden*, ed. Hans Kaufmann (1961; Berlin, 1972)

JA   Richard Wagner, *Dichtungen und Schriften: Jubiläumsausgabe*, ed. Dieter Borchmeyer, 10 vols. (Bayreuth, 1983)

JL   Henry James, *Letters*, ed. Leon Edel, 4 vols. (London, 1975)

KB   *König Ludwig II. und Richard Wagner: Briefwechsel*, ed. Otto Strobel, 5 vols. (Karlsruhe, 1936)

KSA   Friedrich Nietzsche, *Sämtliche Werke: Kritische Studienausgabe*, ed. Giorgio Colli and Mazzino Montinari, 15 vols. (Berlin, 1980)

LK   Berthold Litzmann, *Clara Schumann: Ein Künstlerleben nach Tagebüchern und Briefen* 3 vols. (Leipzig, 1923)

LN   Georges Liébert, *Nietzsche and Music*, trans. David Pellauer and Graham Parkes (Chicago, 2004)

ML   Richard Wagner, *Mein Leben: Jubiläumsausgabe*, ed. Martin Gregor-Dellin (Munich, 1963)

MR   Mildred Adams, ed., *Rebel in Bombazine: Memoirs of Malwida von Meysenbug*, trans. Elsa von Meysenbug Lyons (New York, 1936)

MW   *Richard Wagner an Mathilde Wesendonk: Tagebuchblätter und Briefe, 1853–1871*, ed. Wolfgang Golther (Berlin, 1910)

MWE   *Richard Wagner to Mathilde von Wesendonck*, trans. William Ashton Ellis (London, 1905)

NB   Friedrich Nietzsche, *Briefwechsel: Kritische Gesamtausgabe*, ed. Giorgio Colli and Mazzino Montinari (Berlin, 1981)

ND   Max Nordau, *Degeneration* (1893; London, 1895)

NL   Ernest Newman, *The Life of Richard Wagner*, 4 vols. (London, 1933, 1937, 1941, 1946)

NM   Ernest Newman, *Wagner as Man and Artist* (1914; London, 1924)

NW   Friedrich Nietzsche, *Der Fall Wagner: Ein Musikanten-Problem* (1888), trans. Walter Kaufmann as *The Case of Wagner* in *Basic Writings of Nietzsche* (New York, 1967)

PH   Oscar Panizza, "Bayreuth Und die Homosexualität," in *Die Gesellschaft: Monatsschrift Für Literatur, Kunst Und Sozial politik* 11 (1895) 88–92; English trans. as "Bayreuth and Homosexuality," *Wagner* 9 (1988), 71–75

PS   Theodor Puschmann, *Richard Wagner: eine psychiatrische Studie* (Berlin, 1873)

PW   *Richard Wagner's Prose Works*, trans. William Ashton Ellis, 8 vols. (1899; London, 1966)

SB   Richard Wagner, *Sämtliche Briefe*, ed. Gertrud Strobel and Werner Wolf (Leipzig, 1967)

SF   Gustave J. Stoeckel, "The Wagner Festival at Bayreuth," *The New Englander* 36 (1877), 258–293

SL   *Selected Letters of Richard Wagner*, trans. and ed. Stewart Spencer and Barry Millington (London, 1987)

SM   Nicolas Slonimsky, *Lexicon of Musical Invective* (New York, 1953)

SS   Richard Wagner, *Sämtliche Schriften und Dichtungen*, 16 vols., 6th ed. (Leipzig, 1911–1914)

SW   Arthur Schopenhauer, *The World as Will and Representation*, 2 vols., trans. E. F. J. Payne (Clinton, Mass., 1958)

TW   Ludwig Tieck, *Werke in einem Band*, ed. Richard Alewyn (Hamburg, 1967)

WC   Otto Weininger, *Sex and Character* (1903; London 1906)

WE   Eliza Wille, *Erinnerungen an Wagner* (1894; Munich, 1935)

WS   Richard Wagner, *Skizzen und Entwürfe zur Ring-Dichtung: mit der Dichtung* Der junge Siegfried, ed. Otto Strobel (Munich, 1930)

WWV   *Wagner Werk-Verzeichnis: Verzeichnis der musikalischen Werke Richard Wagners und ihrer Quellen*, ed. John Deathridge, Martin Geck, and Egon Voss (Mainz, 1986)

WAGNER
AND THE
EROTIC
IMPULSE

CHAPTER ONE

Echoes

To treat eroticism in music might seem an exercise in vain speculation since—tempting as it is to draw connections—most composers leave, at best, only a hazy trace in their music. Not so Richard Wagner (1813–1883), who more than anyone else in the nineteenth century made plain his relentless fixation on sexual desire, a fixation documented in private correspondence, personal diaries, published essays, and, of course, in his operas and music dramas. Wagner's obsession with sex also sparked a remarkable reaction to his works, which, in its public parade of the issue, changed the course of European music history. An explicit theme in *Das Liebesverbot* (1836), *Der fliegende Holländer* (1843), the four operas of the *Ring* (1853–1876), and *Die Meistersinger* (1868), Eros is elevated to a central concern in *Tannhäuser* (1845), *Tristan und Isolde* (1859), and *Parsifal* (1882). As a kind of biographical leitmotive echoing incessantly throughout the composer's life, Wagner's erotics cemented one of the most enduring images of high Romantic music, that of the love-sick artist in whom listeners invest their most intimate desires and private suffering.

While contemporary scholarship on Wagner is rich in historical research and analysis, most writers have steered clear of tackling what has long been blatantly obvious—that Wagner was the first to develop a detailed musical language that succeeded in extended representations of erotic stimulation, passionate ecstasy, and the torment of love.[1] Beyond academic groves, on the other hand—whether in popular dictionary entries on Wagner, record reviews, or essays accompanying recordings of the operas—writers point without fail to long stretches of the composer's music that pulsate with an acute and unforgettable eroticism: the voluptuous harmonies of the Venusberg in *Tannhäuser,* the fevered pitch of the duet between Siegmund and Sieglinde in *Die Walküre,* the ecstatic exchanges between Walther and Eva in *Die Meistersinger,* the haunting entreaties in Kundry's seduction of Parsifal, and virtually all of *Tristan und Isolde.* In these scores, Wagner distinguishes himself from his operatic predecessors who, for all their wonderful music, observe sexual desire from a safer aesthetic distance. If one thinks of suggestive scenes in, say, *Poppea, Dido, Don Giovanni, Le Comte Ory, Norma,* or *La Traviata,* the dramatic effect depends on listeners' belief in a character's libido, though the music can scarcely be said to fuel an audience's libidinal drives. It may be that Monteverdi, Purcell, Mozart, Rossini, Bellini, and Verdi crafted their music without wishing to arouse spectators, or else depicted characters who merely displayed their own eroticized states of minds. Or perhaps, because tastes have changed, we no longer respond to an intended allure these works once possessed. But whatever the aspirations of earlier operas, it is Wagner's erotic scenes that have sparked the most intense audience reactions up to and including the present day, which is why they ought to claim our critical attention.

The descriptive language of listeners shaken by Wagner's erotics follows predictable paths, and it matters little if a reaction is positive or negative. Consider a review from 1877 by the critic Gustave Stoeckel (born *ca.*1830) who emigrated to the United States from Germany, later becoming the first Professor of Music at Yale. Stoeckel attended the premiere of the *Ring* at Bayreuth in 1876, and in describing the Finale of the First Act of *Die Walküre* captures the eroticized state experienced by many spectators:

All the scene seems to tremble under the wild glow of sensual love. As the air of the spring night is penetrated through and through by the pale moonlight, so are the listener's senses captivated by this scene. It is impossible to criticize, while hearing it. All aesthetics, theory and morals, are chased out of one; one's breath is bated and the beating of the heart seems to stand still, the whole soul bewitched by an irresistible power. . . . During the performance, all that is sensual in human nature is wrought up to its wildest activity by the alluringly tempting music.[2]

While it is true that *Die Walküre* still today can cause bated breath and a fluttering heartbeat, the moral context for these remarks is peculiar to the nineteenth century. For it turns out that Stoeckel was appalled by his own arousal:

It is true . . . that after the intoxicating enjoyment is over, you perceive the ethical anarchy of the whole scene, which upsets all the holy emotions of a pure soul, defies the teachings of all morality and is in direct antagonism to established rules and customs. [For] the curtain closes upon a scene [of incest] which offends Morality and Religion, wakes up those sleeping passions in human nature which a refined and cultivated taste must abhor and detest. The masterly treatment is all the more offensive, because of its influence upon a sensitive nature. (*SF*, 276)

The "sensitive nature" offended by *Die Walküre* is none other than Stoeckel's own, and he assumes that serious listeners share his delicate constitution. In fact, as we shall see, his essay echoes the widely held nineteenth-century view that Wagner's music provokes an explicit erotic charge (signaled by the term "sensual love"—*sinnliche Liebe* or simply *Sinnlichkeit*) that should be condemned.

How different it is, Stoeckel writes, with that other great Romantic figure, Beethoven, who also wrestles with the human heart, but who, by aiming "high" and shunning ignoble impulses, defends music's nobility of the spirit. No one, Stoeckel implies, would dream of linking Beethoven's

works with erotic thoughts, so pure is the space in which his music
dwells:

> So does the music of Beethoven subdue the instincts of ferocity, bru-
> tality, and sensuality. He, by the power of his art, softens the heart
> and ennobles it; he pours his harmonies over the contradictory ele-
> ments in the soul of man, and awakens, encourages, and strengthens
> all that is noble in human nature; his melodies, like bright shining
> lights, lead upward and on to higher spheres, where low appetites and
> vulgar desires cannot be admitted. (*SF*, 261)

As against the high-minded bliss of Beethoven, *Die Walküre* induces a
critical stupor which, like the blind obedience of the flesh to carnal desires, so dazes the faculties that you recognize only after the curtain has
fallen how Wagner has betrayed your morals. The aesthetic transgression
is grave because music aroused sexual thoughts, and both the stimulus and
response are out of place in an opera house. Although a German, Stoeckel
wrote in English for American readers, but the same stock phrases mark
a review of the same performances by the twenty-seven-year-old Max Kalbeck (1850–1921), later to become Brahms's biographer. The music to the
final scene of *Die Walküre*, Act I may be a masterstroke of the highest genius, but the offense against ethics is severe:

> Here Wagner's art reaches its culmination point. Everything he has
> written until now to glorify sensuous love [*zur Verherrlichung der sinn-
> lichen Liebe*] is mere child's play when compared with this scene which
> quivers with the most raging heat in every fiber [*gegen diese von wildester
> Glut in allen Fibern erzitternde Scene*]. Like oppressive perfume [*wie
> schwüler Duft*] the spring night wafts over us, drunk with moonlight.
> Against this achievement, theory, aesthetics, criticism—morality—
> are all drowned in the moment of enjoyment. From the intoxication
> of the senses which begins with the transitional chords introducing
> Siegmund's love song until the outrageous ending there is only one
> breath and heartbeat. One can rebut someone who created such a
> thing with mere turns of phrase. Only in the future can a more loftier
> act of justice decide whether the more purified aesthetic sense restores

truth and quashes adoration. For once the effect of the fleeting sensual drug subsides, moral scruples start exercising their claims in a long queue. As beautiful and gripping as is the whole First Act—on a par with the most sublime creations ever devised by human art and ingenuity—it slaps in the face all the holy stirrings of the soul as outrageous and provocative signs of ethical anarchy.[3]

It was a different matter for the conductor Bruno Walter (1876–1962) whose reaction to *Tristan und Isolde* sparked an adolescent love affair with Wagner. Born into a middle-class Jewish family named Schlesinger, Walter heard his first *Tristan* in 1889 at the tender age of fourteen and recalls how his family and teachers at the Stern Conservatory in Berlin tried to put him off Wagner, but to no avail. Beyond the supposed formal and aesthetic weaknesses of Wagner's music, "there was," young Bruno was told, "something very wicked and unclean [*sehr Verruchtes, Unreines*]" about it, namely, its "sensuality" [*Sinnlichkeit*]. It was just this sensuality, however, that Bruno "found interesting and not at all wicked." For him, as for countless others before and since, Wagner's erotics sparked a quasi-religious conversion:

> So there I sat in the uppermost gallery of the Berlin Opera House, and from the first entry of the cellos my heart contracted as in a spasm. . . . Never before had my soul been deluged with such floods of sound and passion, never before had my heart been consumed by such suffering and yearning, by such holy bliss, never before had such heavenly transfiguration transported me away from reality. I felt myself no longer of this world, afterwards I wandered aimlessly in the streets—when I got home, I recounted nothing and asked not to be questioned. My ecstasy sang further within me through half the night, and when I awoke the next morning I knew that my life had changed. A new epoch had begun: Wagner was my god, and I wanted to become his prophet.[4]

More than a few writers noticed the link between religion and erotics in the appreciation of Wagner. As the writer and essayist Vernon Lee [Violet Page] (1856–1935) observed in 1911, Wagner has "his votaries and blasphemers," and Bayreuth is "described by some as a Grail-Church, and by others as a Venusberg." Lee was far from a Wagner admirer, however, and—developing critical thoughts from the late Nietzsche—decries his music as "static" and "going nowhere," wearing down the semi-literate listener with tedium. Yet she admits that the power of Wagner's leitmotives makes him "a genius and a wizard":

> the greatest, perhaps, of dramatic geniuses, one of the most marvelous of musical wizards. I am alluding to his passages, often lasting pages and pages, of musical imitation of the symptoms of emotional conditions: grief, joy, despair, terror, but, most of all, mystic or erotic self-surrender and ecstasy. Take as example the great scenes in *Tristan*. The music . . . becomes the most masterly and unmistakable translation of a series of emotional crises: it gives the equivalent of . . . all that the actors can represent for our eyes, and a good deal more which they refrain from exhibiting.

For Vernon Lee, Wagner's musical wizardry reenacts the bodily experience of sexual climax thought previously to have been beyond art's power of depiction: "The music quivers and throbs and droops and dissolves and reels and dies; the music imitates what no words have ever imitated . . . the languors and orgasms within the human being."[5] For the public domain in 1911, this is exceptionally vivid prose, attesting to a confessional urge to convey in words what the Wagnerian experience—whether excoriated, applauded or merely respected—was all about.

Music and Eros

There are continuities and ruptures in the story of how Wagner has been heard, but it has been especially difficult to pin down the *musical* essence of his erotics. For it is fundamentally music—both played and sung—that is heard as erotic. Of course, with Wagner, music is aligned with words and concepts, and accompanied in the opera house by bodily gestures, costumes, and scenic design. Yet the bodies of opera singers— not to put too fine a point on it—rarely seduce on their own, and no one in good faith imagines a Wagner libretto kindling sensual ecstasies without the music. Indeed, Wagner's detractors have had an easy time ridiculing the erotic babble of *Tristan and Isolde*—Eduard Hanslick was fond of this stratagem—not to mention that critics have always poked fun at the theatrical gesticulations of singers. All very unsexy, it seems. But if certain music is "erotic," as the differing testimonies of Stoeckel, Kalbeck, and Lee make clear, what is it in the notes and sounds—in their melodies, harmony, orchestration, rhythm, and texture—that arouse thoughts of sexual desire? By comparison with the other arts, the answer isn't straightforward.

In the visual arts, the nude and semi-nude stare one plainly in the face as an arousing stimulus, which since Classical times has made routine references to the erotic unavoidable. It is true, of course, that some writers on art try to detach erotic reactions from erotic subject matter. In a celebrated essay of 1933, for example, the philosopher Samuel Alexander claimed that if a nude "raises in the spectator ideas or desires appropriate to the material subject, it is false art and bad morals." But it isn't easy to wear such a straitjacket for long, which is why the art historian Kenneth Clark "labor[ed] the obvious" in his classic study of 1956 to assert, on the contrary, "that no nude, however abstract, should fail to arouse in the spectator some vestige of erotic feeling." Indeed, "if [a nude] does not do so," he goes on to say, "it is bad art and false morals."[6] For Clark, the erotic response to a nude encapsulates a universal "desire to grasp and be united with another human body," which is "dragged into the foreground" when we observe the naked form, irrespective of which sex is observing or depicted. With this liberal attitude in mind, Clark goes on to catalog—with some intellectual detachment, it has to be said—paintings, drawings, and sculptures crafted in various erotic forms: from the cultic depictions of Apollo and male athletes from the time of the Greeks up to the pathos-laden godliness of the male body as found in Michelangelo; together with images of idealized female beauty in the classical Venus; through to Ingres's nude bathers; and even further, on to the abstract representation of female nudes by Matisse and Picasso. One axiom of Clark's study—though he is quiet about it—is that we recognize the potential for the erotic even when we don't share an artist's particular tastes. Our common humanity, in other words, allows us to cross borders that in ordinary life might never be traversed. Such was the case when the philosopher Arthur Danto championed Robert Mapplethorpe's photography, to cite just one striking example.[7]

All the same, viewers' reactions to visually arousing images depend on how they respond to particular erotic themes. One might savor the intent of Manet's *Déjeuner sur l'herbe* of 1863 (Paris, Musée d'Orsay) without being drawn to its object of arousal—in this case, the ample female nude who shares a picnic with a pair of fully clothed men and who looks out quizzically from the foreground of the canvas. Or one may choose to ignore the thrusting postures and rippled thighs of the male nudes in Ingres's *Envoys of Agamemnon* of 1801 (Paris, École Nat. Sup. B.-A), chalking them up to mere historicist conventions, yet recognize their likely attraction to women and other men, at least once the possibility is raised.[8] Images, moreover, not only reflect entrenched tastes but also configure and expand one's erotic repertoire, which is why visual culture plays such an obvious role in developing established norms.

Similar limits on erotic effects operate within literature, where a reader needs to be attracted by characters and the suggestive situations in which they are enmeshed. The most extreme form of literary eroticism—pornography packaged as such—shifts the boundaries to the furthest extreme because it depends on a market of distinct tastes: one false move, one reaction of disgust rather than titillation, and a reader will dismiss a work out of hand. (Equally, the same criteria apply to visual pornography, irrespective of debates about the presence of a clear dividing line between art and pornography.)[9] The power of market forces and requirement of immediate arousal, moreover, explain why pornography tends to date quickly, thereby diluting its repeated effect. Still, if one compares literary novels—erotically tinged rather than erotically saturated—with painting, the written word enjoys a slight advantage over an image in creating an erotic aura. For in prose forms like the novel, which introduce characters with whom readers identify, the very absence of a visual dimension, no matter how meticulous the physical descriptions, allows readers to appreciate erotic experiences that extend beyond their repertoire of attractions. The talent inherent in everyone to play a variety of imaginary roles helps here, as do doses of selective amnesia that filter out unsavory literary details hindering an attraction or hampering the success of a fantasy. In fact, the fewer details supplied, the wider the potential sensual reach, which is why lyric poetry, the literary form that feels closest to music, so readily captures an erotic mood.

The definitions of eroticism in literature, film, or sculpture, moreover, have traditionally proceeded from a stylistic hierarchy reflecting operative views about idealized love, sexual behavior and public decency. In any age, erotic art will be found beneath forms devoted to "higher" kinds of love but above those denounced as crudely "low" and pornographic. Within works devoted to romantic love, artists shun even oblique references to carnal desires so as not to compromise the high style and elevated subject matter. In works considered erotic, on the other hand, artists cultivate a more "middling" style that alludes to sexual objects and desires but stops short of arousing the spectator's or reader's sexual feelings. Below this erotic threshold are works whose lurid designs and graphic methods of depiction target both explicit sexual arousal and its gratification. As Peter Webb put it, pornography signifies "any material whose sole purpose is to excite sexual appetite with no concern for aesthetic response."[10] And despite an always fluid line of demarcation between a higher eroticism and a debased pornography—which has become ever less discernible since the time of *Lady Chatterley's Lover* (1928) by D. H. Lawrence, Genet's *Our Lady of the Flowers* (1943), or Mapplethorpe's *Mark Stevens* (1976)—the division between a high and a low erotic remains crucial to the reception of art and literature interested in sexuality.

Implicit in genre criticism since the Greeks, the relative high- or lowness of erotic forms seems, in some primitive sense, to gauge the distance of subject matter away from the genitalia, which, from the primal vantage point of our eyes and ears, are located far beneath the emotive heart and reasoning brain, not to mention miles below the aspiring soul. High and low styles also reinforce our primitive sense of difference between the clean and the dirty. This linkage between art and moral behavior can be seen early on, as when Plato notes in the *Republic* that his "purge" of the city must include a ban on the instruments of the satyr Marsyas, as his coarsely blown *aulos* is associated with debauchery and drunkenness.[11] A Red-figure plate (Paris, Bibliothèque nationale) by the Athenian painter Epiktetos (fl. *ca.* 520–*ca.* ?480 B.C.) even depicts a satyr holding a double *aulos* in both hands with its carrying case suspended from his erect penis: "the analogy," according to Peter Wilson, "between two 'instruments' so difficult to control is inescapable."[12] Accordingly, the further we situate an artwork away from the sexual organs, the "higher" its form of eroticism.

By contrast, the more closely we approach them, the "lower" and more pornographic its effect. To put it another way, eroticism in the arts captures experiences connected with sexual desire short of physical arousal. Eroticism wants to arouse, just not too much.

Turning finally to music, it is easy to see how its eroticism poses a special analytical problem different from that of literature or the visual arts. Lacking predefined objects of representation, music seems only to grope ambiguously toward sexual lust and desire: No musical gesture functions as vividly as a poetic simile about a lover's breast or as graphically as a brush stroke caressing a desirable nude. At the same time, one can argue that music—*pace* formalist aestheticians—has never occupied a space sealed off from verbal and visual concepts, which is why, when brought into their proximity, music absorbs the values of these related arts, despite lacking a lexicon of simple correspondences. We seem, in fact, to possess a "tacit knowledge" about the link between music and sexual arousal even without an explicit literature on the subject. Although music's patterns and processes can be heard to mirror virtually any human activity one could name—film soundtracks routinely engage in this kind of *mimesis*—it is music's much-vaunted "sensuality" and its role in creating an enveloping or imaginary aura for lovemaking that lead it into the realm of Eros. Music acts as an aphrodisiac in life as much as it can arouse in art.

Søren Kierkegaard

For many people, exactly how music incites sexual passion remains a mystery. Søren Kierkegaard devotes much of the first volume of *Either/Or* (1843) to establishing a "musical erotic" without once naming what it is in music that prompts his extreme reaction. The cause of the philosopher's infatuation, he claims, is Mozart's "sensuous immediacy" in *Don Giovanni*, by which he means a process of experienced desire spun out over time. "Music can naturally express many other things," Kierkegaard writes, but sensuousness "is its absolute subject." Observing how Don Juan embodies desire within music characterized as "victorious, triumphant, irresistible and demonic," Kierkegaard—or at least his imaginary author named "A"—enters an irrational state of heightened stimulation and admits succumbing to his sensual urges:

Mozart's music did not inspire me to great deeds, but turned me into a fool, who lost through him the little reason I had, and spent most of my time in quiet sadness humming what I do not understand, haunting like a specter day and night what I am not permitted to enter. Immortal Mozart! Thou, to whom I owe everything; to whom I owe the loss of my reason, the wonder that caused my soul to tremble. . . . Thou, to whom I offer thanks that I did not die without having loved, although my love became unhappy.[13]

What is it, though, in the "sensuous immediacy" of the music that spurs on the author to feel "like a young girl in love with Mozart"? Is it no more than the lusty tunefulness that the Danish philosopher finds so inspiring? He cites all of *Don Giovanni* as the emblem of the third and highest immediate stage of his "musical-erotic," but ignores the musical depiction of a character demonically "intoxicated in himself." Instead, he appeals to the self-evidence of "the music." Citing the so-called champagne aria, "Fin ch'han dal vino," Kierkegaard claims that the music shows Don Giovanni's "inner vitality" as it "breaks forth in him." The breathless comedic patter of this arietta, the lightning quickness of its delivery, the outrageous echo of the "universal" taunt of children (beginning with the falling minor third), the obsessive fun of the repeated melodic lines that begin with the same syncope—Kierkegaard responds tacitly to all these features so as to eroticize the freedom they represent, savoring the way they thumb their noses at social conventions about morality just as the Don sings of leading girls from the piazza into disorderly dancing so he can conquer them sexually. There is little doubt, I think, that Mozart injected his setting with a short-lived erotic tinge, encouraging us to observe and identify with the Don's arousal. What has changed are the musical tropes that have lost their erotic appeal: Since the works of Wagner, their effect is raucous and amusing, if also tuneful and puerile, rather than sensuous and libertine. Yet Kierkegaard discovered something important about music's "immediate sensuousness." Whereas erotic arousal in life depends on visual, gustatory, olfactory, and tactile sensations, it is the absence of sight, taste, smell, or touch that accounts for music's effect as an aphrodisiac. That is, once a composer decides to tap this source, the invisibility of erotic objects fuels music's seductive power. In suggesting sexual desire or experience by audible if ambiguous signs, moreover, music remains "high" and "pure," free from the charge of baseness or the taint of pornography.

Suggestive Music

As will become clear from reactions to Wagner, music's freedom from clear erotic depictions permitted his early advocates to skirt around the issue, at least in their public utterances, and espouse his "higher" ideals and values. It was more often the outraged critics who disclosed the frank details and name, in a kind of litany, the composer's transgressions against decency. Then there was Wagner himself, who, as we shall see, veers self-consciously between a horror of confronting erotic desire and the obsessive need to portray it with a nearly religious zeal. Gustave Stoeckel's description of "alluringly tempting music" that stirs up "all that is sensual in human nature . . . to its wildest activity" comes close to the mark in characterizing not only a widespread audience reaction to Wagner's erotics but their underlying intention as well.

Compositional processes that shape Wagner's musical erotics will be discussed in Chapter 3, but even at this introductory point, one might consider how nineteenth-century art music is well placed to suggest erotic phenomena and feelings. Music can, for example, suggest (1) gender as well as bodily position through high and low instruments and their tessituras, (2) the desirable drawing out of an erotic encounter through harmonic prolongation, or (3) the intertwining of bodies through melodic combinations and invertible counterpoint, (4) the curves of bodies or the act of touching them through melodic contour, (5) the sensations of bodily texture through the timbre of various instruments, (6) the thwarting and fulfillment of desires through chromatic voice-leading, (7) the alternating stages of lovemaking through cadential deceptions, (8) the sense of breathlessness through pauses and caesuras, (9) the performing of obsessive actions through repeated rhythmic patterns, (10) the sensation of shivering through string tremolos, (11) the heightening of pleasure through dynamic crescendos, (12) the allusion to erotically charged animal sounds (nightingales, doves, fauns) through instruments symbolizing these associations, and (13) the enactment of sexual climaxes through tonal closure and percussive explosions. Offered half the chance, most musicians could surely supply a far longer list of further correspondences, though it is worth recalling that musical suggestions or allusions differ from depictions dependent on verbal texts and contexts.

As many of these musical techniques have formed part of a composer's toolbox since about the sixteenth century, it is frankly impossible that these connections didn't dawn on musicians and their sensitive listeners long before the arrival of Wagner. Poets, for example, have for centuries relied on erotic musical metaphors. Just to cite Shakespeare, there is music as "the food of love" (in *Twelfth Night*, I, i), or music that "doth ravish like enchanting harmony" (in *Love's Labour Lost* I, i), or music that "penetrates" [her] "o'mornings" (in *Cymbeline*, II, iii), or "the lascivious pleasing of a lute" (in *Richard III*, I, i) or music, the "moody food/of us that trade in love (*Antony and Cleopatra*, II, v). The sensuous appeal of music likewise attracted painters, and references to musical instruments enhance erotic scenes such as Titian's *Venus and the Organ Player* (Prado, Madrid), Caravaggio's *Young man playing a lute* (Hermitage, St. Petersburg), and Watteau's *Scale of Love* (National Gallery, London). Yet in critical discourse about music, the subject is rarely aired. Musical eroticism seems to have offended traditional notions of propriety, and was a subject too private—or too pleasurable—to raise in public. The result was a conspiracy of silence about an intimate sphere of life, not only because naming the phenomenon elicited condemnation but also because music's seemingly "arbitrary signs" freed it from charges of obscenity. *Doubles entendres* in love sonnets can be hidden from the uneducated, and erotic images painted for aristocratic consumption can be viewed in private apartments. An elevated musical eroticism requires the same highly-developed sensibility, but even then cannot be named and shamed with any great assurance. Why, moreover, should anyone have invited trouble in an age obsessed with proscription when music's immateriality exempted it from censure? The lack of evidence over many centuries of an explicit musical eroticism doesn't mean it didn't exist, just that its presence is harder to identify.

It is much the same with the "high styles" of twentieth-century dance, despite the obvious presence of intermingled bodies. Even the most "abstract ballets" of George Balanchine (1904–1983) are drenched in the steamiest eroticism, yet one would be hard pressed to find the issue discussed in the relevant literature. Euphemism is still the rule, even in this seemingly liberated age. Balanchine himself is rather coy in characterizing his choreography: "A *pas de deux* is always a kind of romance," he writes in the 1950s. "The man is tender and admiring as he lifts the woman and supports her in order to display her beauty, while she, in her reliance on his strength and assurance, admires him in return."[14] The fact that in depicting "romance" the dancers intertwine their bodies and mime the gestures of idealized lovers in endless states of desire and arousal is not seen fit to mention. But as art rarely depends on saying things outright to make its point, the problem may have more to do with formulating an adequate explanatory language so as to cope—decently—with erotic experience.

Peculiarities of Musical Erotics

In contrast with writings on music, contemporary literary and art-historical studies boast a multitude of authors treating eroticism. In the case of literature, one can read up on erotic styles in Chaucer's "Miller's Tale," Shakespeare's *Sonnets*, or Goethe's *Venetian Epigrams*. One learns, too, how erotic styles that deal with the physical aspects of passion differ from the so-called "nobler manifestations of love."[15] Or one can consult *The Grove Dictionary of Art*, for example, which includes a substantial essay on "Erotic Art" that surveys longstanding research in the field: The first contribution to a study of eroticism was Eduard Fuchs's multi-volume *History of Erotic Art* (1912–1926).[16] After lengthy art-historical disquisitions on autoeroticism and individual erotic goals, Fuchs (1870–1940) supplies a succession of lavishly illustrated chapters on clothed nudity; crescendo in lovemaking; lesbian love; female sodomy; and the orgy leading to treatments of various kinds of fetishism in art, sadism, masochism, flagellantism, and even anal eroticism. (One notable blind spot is male homoeroticism, which the author—emblematically—ignores.) To be sure, Fuchs's publishers took precautions to avoid censorship and made it clear that this learned study was not for everyone by enclosing it in a box and admonishing on each title page of the three weighty volumes: "This volume is only to be distributed to scholars, collectors, and libraries."

It is no coincidence that in a work from 1912, Wagner comes in for a mention as an artist whose musical style reflects his erotic attachments. As Eduard Fuchs puts it:

Because the creative artist satisfies himself in the process of artistic production—whether he writes verse, composes, paints, sculpts or configures space—it is entirely logical that the individual artist, during the creative process, acts out a role corresponding to his sexual life [*Triebleben*] when he feels the most stimulated. Or to cite quite a concrete example, it is hardly surprising that Richard Wagner sported sexually ambiguous [*zwitterhaft*] lace-stockings while composing. This is a thoroughly appropriate covering for his distinctly masochistic character, and likewise covers up the heatedly bisexual character [*den brünstig-zwitterhaften Character*] of his art which dispenses with any authentic masculinity.

I return to Wagner's cross-dressing in Chapter 4, but it is interesting to note how, in Fuchs's view, even elevated erotic forms stand in an ineluctable relation to biological-driven sexuality. "All eroticism," he writes:

is only a translation of a more or less transparent disguise of both [the sexual organs], these primary bearers of sexuality and its functions. As a result, they form not only the sole and direct subjects of the Lower or Primitive Erotic but also the actual, if secret, content of the Erotic Sublime."[17]

Musical studies miss such colorful authors. Neither *The New Grove Dictionary of Music* nor *Die Musik in Geschichte und Gegenwart* includes any articles on "eroticism"—nor do they even refer to Kierkegaard and his "Musical Erotic"—although the *New Grove* (2000) editors commissioned a short essay on "Sex, sexuality" in which Jeffrey Kallberg suggests how "music and its attendant realms emerge not only as mirrors of the sexual currents and ideologies of an age, but also as producers of these very modes of discourse." While this formulation challenges music's passivity, it is striking that no charted history of musical erotics could be cited that would identify both its reflective "mirrors" and illuminating "lamps." In fact, Kallberg seems overanxious not to overplay music's links with sexuality, whose categories, we are reminded, are always unstable, and "constructed according to power relations and discursive practices prevailing in every society." Wagner's *Tristan* shows up—not to explain to us what a "constructed" view of sexuality might be but instead to warn against overly hasty assessments of its eroticism. "Steeped in the ubiquitous sexual content of popular music," Kallberg writes:

> and conditioned by apparently transparent representations of sexual desire in the canonic classical repertory (the love duet from *Tristan und Isolde*, the opening bars of *Der Rosenkavalier*), modern listeners can readily misconstrue convergences of sex and music from earlier eras.[18]

It is unclear how we might "misconstrue" the "convergence of sex and music" in *Tristan*, but Kallberg seems to think that the opera's ability to awaken erotic feelings today differs markedly from the way it did in the mid-nineteenth century: One must be vigilant, therefore, in supposing any common ground between contemporary and historical forms of arousal. While it is legitimate to question our aesthetic perceptions of the past, it is worth noting how, at least in musical studies, we have become a bit hamstrung in treating historical phenomena such as Wagner's erotics for which there is in fact ample (if anecdotal) psychological evidence from the present day suggesting that our responses *haven't* changed much over the last 150 years. We may wish to enter into theoretical debates about premises and methods of treating such evidence, but there is a danger that one misses what can be learned from history. As knowledge about the human heart isn't noticeably improving all the time, Wagner and the nineteenth century may have something to teach us that will still be of value.

In this book, I prefer to listen to what historical voices—including Wagner's own—have to say, and tread a pragmatic path in treating Wagner and his "erotic impulse." Though some may feel disadvantaged by not being offered a clear definition of what "erotic" might mean, the benefit is a more historically nuanced account of Wagner—not to mention one that I hope will be vastly more entertaining. Instead of worrying about misreading our reactions to *Tristan*, we can consider all the evidence to form a view of his erotics, both in his stated intentions as well as in their wide-ranging effects on acolytes, critics and enemies. Everyone recognizes the vast but not limitless range of human sexual attractions, while also acknowledging that certain patterns of desire recur again and again. A quick stroll around the *gabinetto segreto* at the National Archaeological Museum in Naples, for example, shows how little the erotic objects of antiquity can shock us: What has delighted viewers since the eighteenth century are the subtly different sets of accents that emerge from this remote yet wholly recognizable ancient world of desires. When Nijinsky in Debussy's *L'après-midi d'un faune* simulated masturbation (and sparked an uproar in the theater), its particular meaning might be read as historically contingent, but its representation would be clear to anyone, irrespective of time or culture. Wagner's Venusberg ballet and the climax in the *Tristan* Prelude are really no different.

Naturally, some erotic art from the past no longer attracts us even if we can understand the source of its original allure. Yet it cannot be pure accident that some texts and images from sixteenth-century London or Florence held to be erotic then are still considered so today, or that even those from seventeenth-century Kyoto might still exert a magnetic pull in the West four centuries later. What we mustn't do is switch off our own erotic sensibilities when responding to art—a syndrome that, depressingly, appears far too often in academic discourse. As soon as we do so, we impoverish aesthetic experience and deprive ourselves of the blindingly obvious. If anything, we might follow Kenneth Clark and remain open to that "vestige of erotic feeling" that in Wagner's music is so often "dragged into the foreground" so as to consider how an artist poured old ideas into new molds. If there is a fundamental premise underlying the idea of an "erotic impulse," it is the truism that one misses something important when ignoring human sexual urges.

Charles Baudelaire

The first serious author to notice Wagner's erotics—and hear their peculiar echoes—was none other than the poet Charles Baudelaire (1821–1868), who, in his only published essay on music, certifies Wagner's credentials as the quintessential European modernist. While Baudelaire treats other matters beyond eroticism in "Richard Wagner and *Tannhäuser* in Paris" (1861)—such as the relation between theory and practice, the nature of the musical sign, along with his pet theory of correspondences, or synesthesia—the notion of *la volupté* (sensuality or voluptuousness) makes a frequent enough appearance to warrant a special look, not least because Baudelaire himself had faced a lawsuit on charges of immorality [*un procès en moralité*] for his *Fleurs du Mal* of 1857. Not only were he and his publisher found guilty and fined as a result of the legal proceedings, but six poems had to be amended or removed before a second, corrected edition could be issued.

Baudelaire became a convert to Wagner's music almost spontaneously in January and early February 1860, when he attended three performances of orchestral and choral excerpts conducted by the composer in the Salle Ventadour of the Théâtre-Italien. In each concert, the first half began with the Overture to the *Flying Dutchman*, followed by several selections from *Tannhäuser*: the Procession of the Nobles, the Introduction to the Third Act and Pilgrims' Chorus, and the Overture to the First Act. Somewhat incongruously from a contemporary point of view, the Prelude to *Tristan und Isolde* opened the second half of the program, after which came the *Lohengrin* Prelude, the Betrothal Procession from *Lohengrin*'s Second Act, and the first section of the Third Act, ending with the famous Bridal Chorus.

Right at the first concert, Baudelaire was gripped with an aesthetic fever. He had undergone, he writes:

> a spiritual operation, a revelation. My sensuous desire [*ma volupté*] was so strong and terrible that I couldn't help wishing to return to it over and over again. . . . [There] was something new . . . that I experienced which I was helpless to define and this helplessness [*impuissance*] caused an anger and a curiosity mixed with a bizarre delight. For several days and for a long time I said to myself: "Where can I hear some Wagner this evening?" Those of my friends who owned a piano became more than once my victims [*martyres*]. Soon afterwards Wagner's symphonic pieces, as they were a novelty item, were blaring every evening in the all-night casinos for a crowd inclined toward trivial erotic pleasures [*une foule amoureuse de voluptés triviales*]. The dazzling majesty of this music struck like thunder in an evil place. Noise quickly pervaded the venue and one enjoyed the amusing spectacle of serious and sensitive men enduring the unsuitable tumult just to relish, in anticipation of better days, the solemn march

of the guests to the Wartburg, and the grandiose wedding music from *Lohengrin*.

Baudelaire's wit should not blind us to his sincerity, for in a remarkable letter sent to Wagner a week after the last performance, the poet waxes lyrical about the performances without the slightest trace of irony:

> Above all, I want to tell you that I owe you *the greatest musical pleasure I have ever experienced* [*underlining in the original*]. I've reached an age when one rarely writes to famous men any more, and I should still have hesitated a long time to describe to you my admiration, if it were not the case that my eyes alight daily on scurrilous and absurd articles, in which every possible effort is made to defame your genius. You're not the first man, Monsieur, about whom I've had the occasion to blush and be ashamed of my country. My indignation has finally induced me to show you my gratitude: to myself I say I wish to be distinguished from all these imbeciles.

Despite his disinclination to appreciate Wagner's music, Baudelaire had been "smitten at once" [*vaincu tout de suite*]:

> What I experienced is indescribable, and if you deign not to laugh, I'll try to interpret it for you. At first, it seemed as if I knew this music, and later, in thinking about it, I understood where this mirage came from: it seemed this music was my own [*la mienne*] and I recognized it as anyone recognizes the things they are destined to love.

Not only destined to love Wagner's music, he felt both "abducted and subjugated" [*enlevé et subjugué*]:

> And another thing: I often experienced a feeling of a rather bizarre kind, the pride and pleasure of understanding, of letting myself be penetrated, invaded, a truly sensual voluptuousness [*une volupté vraiment sensuelle*], which resembles that of ascending into the atmosphere or of riding the waves. . . . One more time, Monsieur, I thank

you. You've recalled me to myself and to noble thoughts [*au grand*] during the bad hours.[19]

A final postscript reads: "I'm not adding my address because you might think I had something to ask of you." Baudelaire's extraordinary letter boasts an unalloyed *Schwärmerei*—that untranslatable German term for gushing idol-worship that evokes fervent enthusiasts swarming toward their mentor. Of particular interest is the homoerotic imagery, almost a staple of this kind of *Schwärmerei* for Wagner's music on the part of men: We read of the noble defense of the composer's honor, the vanquishing of the admirer by superior force, his Ganymede-like kidnap and ascent into the higher spheres where surprisingly pleasurable penetration and invasion take place, followed by a rapturous aftermath and the bliss of self-recognition.

There is also a striking change of literary persona between the private letter and the published essay, from a same-sexual sensibility to a more conventional self-representation emphasizing the writer's interest in women. Baudelaire was too great a poet not to be acutely aware of his contrasting set of metaphors. Having delivered the revised edition of his controversial *Fleurs du Mal* to the publisher (without its banned "Lesbian" poems) two weeks after attending the Wagner concerts, he surely thought it prudent to recast the account of his Wagnerizing when it came to drafting the *Tannhäuser* essay the following year, as when he described what he calls "the erotic section [*la partie voluptueuse*] of the [*Tannhäuser*] overture." His argument was revolutionary enough without—given his legal troubles three years before—laying himself open to an unwarranted charge of perversity and unnaturalness. The letter was unusual enough that Wagner himself recalled its contents when dictating his autobiography to Cosima, noting that Baudelaire's opinions were "expressed with conscious boldness in the most peculiar flights of fancy [*in der seltsamsten Phantastik*]."[20] Other homoerotic attachments to Wagner are treated in the last chapter, but the issue becomes unavoidable, so often does it make unexpected appearances.

It is all the more amusing today to consider that Baudelaire's infatuation was caused by "bleeding chunks" from the Romantic operas rather than from the later, so-called music dramas. For although Wagner cleverly smuggled the challenging *Tristan* Prelude onto the second half of the program just after the interval—the opera itself wasn't premiered for another five years—Baudelaire could not, it seems, make it out at all: At least *Tristan* does not rate more than a passing mention in the 1861 essay. Yet it is surely *Tristan* Baudelaire means when he notes that "many things remained obscure without a doubt," and he quotes Berlioz so as to assert that "impartial spirits" would have to await the appearance of this music on the stage where "matters not sufficiently defined will be explained" by theatrical three-dimensionality, by *la plastique.*

One can forgive Baudelaire his bewilderment at the music of *Tristan* since even a sophisticate such as Berlioz was famously mystified, not to say distressed, by its Prelude when he attended the same programs. Berlioz received the Breitkopf full score of *Tristan* from Wagner several days before the first performance, but even an intense study of the notes on the page was to no avail. "I have read and reread this strange page," he writes of the opening of the Prelude. "I have listened to it with the most profound attention and a healthy desire to discover its sense. And now I must confess that I have yet to discover the least idea of what the author wishes to do."[21] Wagner himself was well aware of the difficulties posed by *Tristan* for listeners, but by the time of the third Paris performance, even he was pleased with the rendition and thought the audience "thoroughly stirred by it; for when an opponent ventured to hiss—after the applause—such a storm broke forth, and so intense, protracted and continually renewed, that poor I . . . had to motion people to leave off . . . , but that sent the temperature up again, and once more the storm broke loose. In short, I never passed through such a thing before."[22] Incited no doubt by the suggestive text that Wagner distributed, the more receptive listeners grasped *Tristan*'s erotic message without being put off by its arcane chromatic idiom.

Baudelaire's reaction to Wagner's erotics stems only in part from a work that treats sensuality, namely, *Tannhäuser* with its Venusberg themes. In fact, he was equally entranced—almost by a process of osmosis—by the overwhelming effect of the *Lohengrin* Prelude and the set pieces from *Tannhäuser*'s Second Act. The poet was well aware of this tension, for he admits that there are two Wagners, "the ordered man and the impassioned man," arguing that "the artist has . . . devoted as much energy" to "the depiction of that mystical quality which characterizes the *Lohengrin* overture" [*sic*] as to "the voluptuous and orgiastic section of the *Tannhäuser* overture." Yet it is the second man who interests him most. For what is most "unforgettable," he writes, "is the nervous intensity, the violence in the passion, and the conviction [*la volonté*], music that "expresses by the most suave or the most shrill voice all that is hidden in the heart of man," expresses in fact the "truest representative of the modern being." Noting that critics will cite these qualities as outrageous, Baudelaire admits that "he loves these excesses of health, these willful overflows [*ces débordements de volonté*]."

Although far from a moralist, Baudelaire grapples with the ethics of Wagner's eroticism and muses on the irony of the composer being hounded from Paris not by philistines or moralists, but by libertines. Following on the hissing, hooting, and whistling that virtually destroyed the Paris *Tannhäuser* the year after the orchestral concerts, Baudelaire criticizes the "keepers [*entreteneurs*] of girls," members of the Jockey Club, and others whose mistresses were dancers at the Opéra and on whose behalf, he believed, the claque had decided to demonstrate. What they failed to understand, he writes, is that the opening scene of Wagner's opera isn't "a bad ballet with music ill-suited to dancing," but rather "a bacchanal, an orgy, as indicated by the music, and which sometimes is able to be represented at theaters"—he names several—"but not at the Opéra, where they don't know how to present anything at all."

The problem of Wagner's eroticism in Paris was that its musical style was too high for libertines only interested in "vulgar hymns to love." Rather than treating something trivial, Baudelaire writes, Wagner unveils

> an unbridled love, immense, chaotic, elevated to the height of a counter-religion, a satanic religion. Thus the composer, in his musical representation [*traduction*], has escaped the vulgarity which too often accompanies the depiction of the most popular feeling—I was about to say "of the rabble" [*populacier*]—and for this reason his task was to depict the surplus of desire and energy, the indomitable and unrestrained drive within the sensitive soul who has taken the wrong path. Similarly in the theatrical representation of the idea, he has thankfully disposed of the irritating crowd of victims, the countless Elviras. The pure idea, embodied in the unique Venus, conveys a

much higher aspiration [*parle bien plus haut*] and with much greater eloquence.[23]

Tannhäuser is no "ordinary libertine, turning from beauty to beauty" (as does Don Juan), but rather depicts "man in general, universal, living in a morganatic state with the absolute ideal of the erotic [*la volupté*], with the queen of all the she-devils, . . . the indestructible and irresistible Venus." The elevation of music as a vehicle of dark feelings also figures in Baudelaire's own poetry. Already in "La Musique" from *Les Fleurs du Mal*, the poet identified music not only as a vibrating agent of all the passions of a vessel that suffers [*Je sens vibrer en moi toutes les passions/d'un vaisseau qui souffre*], but also as a great mirror of poetic despair [*grand miroir/de mon désespoir*]. In Wagner and his music, Baudelaire seems to have recognized not only a likeminded modernist who dares to depict the destructive chaos of erotic urges, but an artist whose music indulges in this peculiar form of suffering.

A writer who speaks so forcefully on Wagner's erotics is rare among Wagner's supporters, who more often resorted to euphemism in treating the obvious. Significantly, even writers from the Wagner circle known for their loose living, such as Judith Gautier and Catulle Mendès—the latter himself an author of erotic short stories—never broach the subject. Neither does Édouard Dujardin, founder in 1885 of *La Revue wagnérienne* nor his mentor Stéphane Mallarmé, who contributed to the journal.[24] Instead, one often has to read between the lines to imagine the first inklings of an ecstatic reception of Wagner's erotics.

Friedrich Nietzsche and Malwida von Meysenbug

Friedrich Nietzsche (1844–1900), for example, first converted to Wagnerism at the age of sixteen when his local Germania Debating Society scraped together the funds to buy a piano-vocal score to *Tristan*. Eight years later, he is still enthusing about the *Tristan* Prelude in a letter to a friend: "I simply cannot bring myself to remain critically aloof from this music; every nerve in me is a-twitch, and it has been a long time since I had such a lasting sense of ecstasy."[25] In his *Birth of Tragedy* (1870–71), moreover, it is the "bond of brotherhood" between Apollonian luminosity and Dionysian intoxication that makes *Tristan* the ideal tragedy; in fact, *Tristan* is the only musical work named in a study originally entitled *The Birth of Tragedy out of the Spirit of Music*, and accounts for Nietzsche's "Preface to Richard Wagner" in the first edition. Yet Nietzsche ensures that "ecstasy" in the *Birth of Tragedy* is not given a lower, sexual reading: It is rather a spiritual state of intoxication that is "the very antithesis" of similar festivals celebrated by ancient peoples where "the center of the cult lay in the absence of all sexual discipline, in the destruction of all family life by unrestrained hetaerism" or free concubinage.[26] To "genuine musicians" Nietzsche directs the "question whether they can imagine someone able to hear the Third Act of *Tristan* without any aid of word or image purely as a tremendous symphonic movement without expiring in a spasmodic release of all the wings of the soul [*ohne unter einem krampfartigen Ausspannen aller Seelenflügel zu veratmen*]?"[27] This figurative spasm is the closest Nietzsche comes in 1872 to capturing what was obviously a cipher for the opera's erotics. Yet even after his disenchantment with Wagner sets in, Nietzsche was still calling *Tristan* "the real *opus metaphysicum* of all art" with its "insatiable and sweet craving for the secrets of night and death"—this in *Richard Wagner in Bayreuth* of 1876.[28] One needs therefore, to tease out what transpired in the minds of Wagner's supporters who failed to engage publicly with what was a topic of conversation for several decades.

A key figure to consider in this regard is Nietzsche's friend, the pacifist, essayist, and women's rights advocate, Malwida von Meysenbug (1816–1903), to whom he wrote in 1888 of his "deep hatred for the repugnant sexuality of Wagnerian music" (*LN*, 252). Von Meysenbug was a lifelong ardent admirer of Wagner—she was also close to Giuseppe Mazzini and Romain Rolland—and attended the same three concerts as did Baudelaire, in addition to the Paris premiere of *Tannhäuser* thirteen months later. In fact, Wagner invited her to the final dress rehearsal of the opera where she reports being "affected as by something sublime and sacred and touched as by some great truth." Like Baudelaire, she addresses the issue of libertinage among Wagner's enemies as something to scorn:

> It was a known fact [she writes in her memoirs] that the ladies of the ballet had their wages increased by [the young Paris lions, the men of the Jockey Club], and that the latter were accustomed to go to the

Opéra after dining, not to hear beautiful harmonies, but to see the most unnatural and most terrible production of modern art, the ballet. After the performance, they became better acquainted with the dancing nymphs behind the scenes. What did these aristocratic rakes care about a performance of a chaste work of art, which celebrated the victory of sacred love over the frenzy of emotions? Not only did they not care but they must hate and condemn it even before hearing it. It was the divine judgment on their boundless depravity.[29]

Wagner remains blameless because the "higher love" of Elisabeth triumphs over the lower form offered by Venus. Very far from a prudish bourgeoise, von Meysenbug had been forced to leave Germany for her political associations, and lived during the 1850s in London in the house of Alexander Herzen, the Russian liberal, raising his youngest daughter, Olga. So it is all the more interesting to see her defense of Wagner's high-mindedness in his victory *over* the "frenzy of emotions." For von Meysenbug, unlike for Baudelaire, "all's well that ends well," and it is tacitly assumed that the composer needed to represent the wildest desires so as to surmount his psychological struggles to form a "chaste work of art." What was unchaste and unnatural were the lower forms of eroticism: the ogling of women's bodies at the ballet and the negotiation of sexual favors with which, she believes, they must be connected.

What lay behind von Meysenbug's view was the strong influence of Arthur Schopenhauer (1788–1860), whose "negation of the will to live" Wagner had enthused about at a Hampstead dinner party she attended in 1855.[30] Raised in Frankfurt, Malwida had grown up watching Schopenhauer walk his dog every day on the quay of the River Main and had been told even by trustworthy people, she reports, that "he was an absolute idiot" (*MR*, 212). Hearing now about Schopenhauer from Wagner, whose texts (though not yet his music) she knew intimately, she was drawn to the philosopher's critique of optimism, causing her even to question her socialist principles. Instead of "directing the will toward uninterrupted moral perfections and action as the final goal of existence," she now sensed that Schopenhauer provided "the key to a gate toward which my life was tending and behind which the light of final perception would appear to me." It doesn't come as any surprise that von Meysenbug omits any reference to Schopenhauer's lengthy discussion of the "metaphysics of sexual love" [*Metaphysik der Ge-schlechtsliebe*], especially as it manifests itself within music, but the chapter by the same name in *The Will as World and Representation* surely made a deep impression on her, along with everyone else who read it.

For these reasons, the depiction of seething desire in *Tristan* failed to dent von Meysenbug's enthusiasm for Wagner—on the contrary—although it is difficult to know how much her change of heart was due to Schopenhauer's writings as apart from Wagner's ringing endorsement of them. Malwida heard *Tristan* for the first time in Paris in a private run-through when Karl Klindworth played the piano and Wagner sang the vocal parts. Not surprisingly, considering her already advanced case of *Schwärmerei*, she felt "gripped with an overwhelming force." Not one word in her memoirs about the unusually frank subject matter; only an oblique reference to what she calls "the peculiarities which would lead most people to throw stones at [Wagner]." "These notwithstanding," she writes:

> I realized that he could count on me unto death, and that his genius would be one of the few brilliant lights which would make my life worth living. In this primitive power of perception, in the force of their passion, in the broad human scope of their characters, I could only compare these works with Shakespeare's, but here one has also the music which enfolds the course of tragic action in its transfigur-ing cloud. Now I completely understood the man whose powerful daemon forced him to create such great and marvelous things. From that time on I knew that nothing would make me lose confidence in him, that I would understand him even in his dark moods, in the vio-lent outbreaks of his sensitive nature. (*MR*, 294–295)

Meysenbug was true to her word. Her first volume of *Memoirs of an Idealist* ends in 1861 following the *Tannhäuser* performances, a season in which she "again became absorbed in Schopenhauer," calling that period "the crowning epoch of my life." In deciding to take on full responsibility for bringing up Herzen's daughter Olga as her own, she had "found the goal and task to which my life from now on was to be devoted: to raise a human being to the highest degree of perfection of which she was capable." And this practical feminism was very much connected to the person of Richard

Wagner, "an artist," she writes, "whose labors revealed to me a new ideal and confirmed my belief that the ideal is to be found in art":

Even the greatest achievement in the political sphere must, like all else which is bound by earthly limitations, fall short of perfection. It was clear to me that the German mind especially seeks perfection in an ideal world. This very thing with which I had reproached the Germans, I now recognized to be their true greatness, their original sphere, and it was a German genius who was pointing this out to me. (*MR*, 310)

Von Meysenbug was aware of the reproaches aimed at Wagner as "sensualist," especially while living in London for eight years where critics repeated this charge continually. That a nineteenth-century feminist chose to rebut these accusations in a circuitous fashion signals a self-conscious attempt to keep to the rhetorical high ground. Years later, she was still stressing the "idealist" nature of Wagner's works: after hearing ten performances [*sic*] of *Parsifal* at the 1882 Bayreuth Festival, she writes to Carolyne von Sayn-Wittgenstein that "every time I feel more captivated, and discover new and sublime beauties. It is truly *ein Weihefestspiel* [a consecrated festival-play] and whoever in their heart fails to sink to his knees when hearing the first and last acts doesn't deserve to hear it."[31] It was only the Second Act, with its sweet-smelling Flower-Maidens and Kundry's domineering kiss that did not rate an explicit mention—not even in her account of the opera in her memoirs[32]—but presumably even the female seductresses formed part of the ideal world of the spirit that von Meysenbug ascribed to Wagner.

As for other Wagnerians of the 1860s, there were none as explicit as Baudelaire in treating Wagner's eroticism, though naming it was superfluous because Wagner had already let the cat out of the bag in his prose description of the *Tristan* Prelude. The text, distributed at the Paris concerts, will be examined in detail in Chapter 3, but consider just a snippet:

He therefore caused insatiable yearning to swell upwards in a long patterned breath, from the most timid confession, and the most tender hesitation, through anxious sighs, hopes and fears, moans and

wishes, joys and torments, until the mightiest blast, the most violent
effort to find the rupture which unlocks for the boundlessly craving
heart the path into the sea of unending sexual bliss [*Liebeswonne*].[33]

The literary merit of the passage may be dubious, but the fact remains
that none of the early Wagnerians would have dared traffic in the imagery
of mighty blasts, craving hearts, and endless bliss.

Édouard Schuré and Hans von Bülow

Given such suggestive language, not to mention the unusual music it
accompanies, it is not surprising that nineteenth-century Wagnerians
might be the last ones to extol the link between music and sexual arousal.
Édouard Schuré (1841–1929), a Wagnerian from Alsace, attended the 1865
Munich premiere of *Tristan und Isolde* and first celebrated Wagner's Dionysian spirit in a lengthy journal article in 1869 without the slightest
mention of *Tristan*'s eroticism. Only in the second volume of *Le Drame
musical* (1875) does he devote an entire chapter to *Tristan* that identifies its
greatness precisely in terms of its particular erotics. Eros, Schuré writes:

> that flamboyant and terrible god, who elsewhere only appears in
> flashes of lightning, has filled this drama with his glowing torch. The
> tragic and sublime effects of ecstatic love [*du grand amour*] have been
> painted before, but what hasn't before been expressed is the essence of
> love with such intensity, and such perseverance of passion. Novelists,
> moralists, painters, poets and musicians have described the raptures,
> the dangers, the turnabouts and the catastrophes. What hasn't ever
> been rendered to such an extent is the complete commixture of two
> souls, this fusion of two beings attracted by the most subtle means.

It is clear to Schuré that the ebb and flow of Wagner's music feed the emotive stream of *Tristan*'s eroticism:

> The untiring wave of this melody never ceases; it rumbles and widens
> until the silences and lovers' lulls [*accalmies des amants*], but we feel on
> the other hand that in a few bars it could pass from an imperceptible

shiver to the unleashing of every storm. Harmony and melody in this
music resemble a deep river of passion which now laps up against its
banks [*se redresse contre ses bords*] or boils over in spume onto the reefs,
now broadens into an immense expanse, now rushes in roaring tor-
rents so as lose itself with Isolde's last melody in the silence and majesty of the ocean.[34]

Despite Wagner's strained relations with the French after the Franco-
Prussian War, Schuré was close enough to the family to have visited
Bayreuth in 1873, when he read out from the draft of his manuscript for
Le Drame Musical. Cosima Wagner, for one, commented approvingly on
his approach: "Schuré's work, apart from a few bits of Alsatiana," she writes,
"is very interesting—he really has understood R[ichard]."[35]

In a later memoir of the performance from the turn of the century,
Schuré becomes even more explicit in paraphrasing Wagner's own sexual-
ized program, describing the musical progression at the climax of the
Prelude as one that "ascends to the final fury of an exasperated passion
and immediately falls back into a mortal exhaustion so as to lapse into a
sigh." Schuré also recalls how his emotional state mirrored those of Wagner's characters:

> The interior of the characters became *transparent* for me. The may-
> hem which agitates the impassioned soul: the indignation, the irony,
> the desperation, love changed into hate clamoring for suicide and
> death, all the currents and undercurrents of thought insinuated them-
> selves into me in such an enveloping manner and with such irresist-
> ible violence—*that everything that occurred within Isolde also occurred
> within me.*

"No drama," Schuré continues:

> has ever given such a powerful expression to the malady of love with
> its fevers, its fatigue, its hallucinations and its hysterics [*ses frénésies*].
> In this formidable progression, one remains suspended with the hero
> between life and death. But the arrival of Isolde, her last embrace of
> Tristan as he dies, the transfiguration and supreme demise of the

lover leave you in the atmosphere of apotheosis, in a sort of ecstasy, and divine calm.[36]

There is no reason to think that Schuré misrepresented his ecstasy only with hindsight, for he drew the line of acceptable Wagnerian erotics at *Parsifal*, which left him with a "morbid impression barely concealed by the grandeur of the spectacle," noting—rightly—that "there is more thirst for eternal rest than for eternal life."[37] His earlier ecstatic—rather than erotic—reaction to *Tristan* is probably best read in light of what wouldn't have been prudent to say openly in the 1860s.

In similar fashion, one might read Hans von Bülow's praise of *Tristan* in 1859 as signifying more than a panegyric on its sublime achievement. Von Bülow wrote an open letter about *Tristan* in 1859 to Franz Brendel, editor of the *Neue Zeitschrift für Musik*, and in assessing Wagner's change of style between *Lohengrin* and *Tristan*, admits:

> to have been moved from surprise to rapture. If there is a musician who doesn't hear that this is progress he hasn't any ears. . . . After *Tristan* there can only be two parties: those who have learned something and those who have learned nothing. Anyone not converted by this opera hasn't a musical bone in his body. . . . You know me too well to suspect that I might dissolve into extravagant idol-worship [*Schwärmerei*]: you know that my heart asks permission of the authority of my head before filling with enthusiasm. Now it is my head that is given unconditional approval. *Tristan and Isolde* can scarcely become popular, but every poetically talented lay person will be seized with the sublimity and force of genius which reveal themselves in this work. Apart from every other consideration: I assure you, the opera is the summit of all music hitherto.[38]

Given the hyperbolic metaphors of rapture [*Entzücken*], dissolution, conversion, seizure, and the attainment of a climactic summit, one might infer a rather more suggestive story, one to which von Bülow is happy to allude as long as it is not spelled out.

Ludwig Schnorr von Carolsfeld

As for private reactions to *Tristan*, it was long assumed that the opera's erotics even caused the death of its first protagonist, Ludwig Schnorr von Carolsfeld. At least Wagner thought his music drove the singer to an early grave when Schnorr died suddenly at the age of twenty-nine, just weeks after the first performances in 1865. Even a month later, Wagner is still lamenting the loss of his first and favorite tenor in his diary, the so-called *Brown Book*:

> My Tristan! My beloved!—I drove you to the abyss! I was used to standing there. I don't suffer from vertigo. But I can't bear to see anyone standing at the edge: I am seized with frenzied sympathy. I catch hold so as to hold on, to pull back, and push over, just as we kill the sleep-walker we shout at when startled.—So I pushed him over. And myself?—I don't suffer from vertigo.—I look down—indeed, it pleases me to—But my friend? It is him I lose.
>
> My Tristan! My Beloved! [*Mein Trauter!*][39]

Schnorr made a point of denying that he fell ill from the vocal and emotional exertions of the operatic role. In a moment of lucidity before his death, the tenor's "chief worry"—Wagner was told after the funeral—"was to refute the false view that Schnorr had met his death as a result of his over-exertions in *Tristan*":

> "No! No!" he then called out. "All of you bear witness to this, that *Tristan* hasn't caused my death. I'm dying in the most unbroken strength succumbing to an ailment which can strike anyone. . . . Oh! my Richard loved me! How contentedly I die: He loved me![40]

Even in Schnorr's protestations of Wagner's innocence, it is clear from his enthused proclamations that the erotic intensity of the opera had forged a strong bond to the composer at the same time that it exacted a terrible toll.

There is, in fact, a revealing link between Schnorr's death and Wagner's depiction of love's torment in the future *Parsifal;* for only three days thereafter Wagner begins drafting a new prose narrative for *Parzifal* [*sic*] in which the themes of a character being "driven to the abyss" by a form of love-sickness and a frenzied sympathy of one man for another's erotic torment play a crucial role. The draft, prepared for Ludwig II, begins by naming Anfortas [*sic*] who "lies stricken of a spear-wound received in some mysterious love adventure, which will not heal" (*KB*, 46). It also describes Parzifal's reaction to Kundry's kiss: "Transferred wholly into the soul of Anfortas, he feels Anfortas's enormous suffering, . . . the unspeakable torments of yearning love" (*KB*, 57). For Wagner, Schnorr's Parzifal [*sic*] understands the suffering of Wagner's Anfortas almost as much as Wagner's Parzifal empathizes with Schnorr's deathbed torments, the draconian result of having sung *Tristan*.

Gabriele D'Annunzio and Thomas Mann

More explicit tributes to *Tristan*'s eroticism had to await the so-called decadent writers of the 1890s, such as Gabriele D'Annunzio, whose protagonist in *Trionfo della Morte* (1894), Giorgio Aurispa, recalls a performance of *Tristan* at Bayreuth in a long description that closely shadows the music and poem of the opera.[41] For the climax of the First Act, D'Annunzio describes the "rising and swelling," the "panting and sobbing" of the "love motive" as it "soared irresistibly towards the heights of undreamt-of ecstasy, towards the summits of supreme voluptuousness." The second act "swept triumphantly upwards to the supreme heights of spasmodic ecstasy" until a "brutal attack interrupts the ecstatic embrace."[42] A brutal attack also marks the end of the novel when Aurispa murders his lover before killing himself.

Then there is Thomas Mann's decadent *Tristan* (1902), in which Detlev Spinell induces the fragile and consumptive Gabriele Klöterjahn, another patient at the Einfried sanatorium, to play through *Tristan* at the piano in the salon. The narrator portrays the music of the Prelude, where "two beings strove towards each other in transports of joy and pain where they embraced and became one in delirious yearning after eternity and the absolute." And then, after she has completed the prelude, he dares to make a more suggestive request:

"The Second Act," he whispered, and she turned the pages and began. . . . thine and mine at one forever in a sublimity of bliss. To him who has looked upon the night of death and known its secret sweets, to him day never can be aught but vain, nor can he know a longing save for night, eternal, real, in which he is made one with love.[43]

Three years later, in 1905, Mann played yet another erotic card when he wrote the astounding *Blood of the Volsungs* [*Wälsungenblut*]. In this Wagnerian novella, the Jewish twins Siegmund and Sieglind Aarenhold attend a performance of *Die Walküre*, which inspires them to come home and repeat the act of incest they have witnessed at the opera. In the only moments in which Mann offers the haughty and unlikable protagonists a moment of authenticity, his formerly alienating descriptions and petulant conversational style give way to a strikingly erotic diction. The implicit, if ironic, musical accompaniment goes even further than did Wagner, whose postlude to Act I famously brings the curtain down before the lovemaking becomes visible: The Aarenhold twins succumb to "caresses which became a hasty tumult and finally were only a sobbing." It is Wagner's musical erotics which fire Mann's imagination to translate them into language.[44]

Wagner's Critics

It would be an exaggeration to see all Wagnerians as so sex-obsessed: Most of them between 1860 and 1890 occupy a ground so lofty that they are rarely seen to peer down onto the facts of fleshly love named by more courageous literary libertines. Wagner's critics display no such timidity, however, and beginning with the Munich premiere of *Tristan* in 1865, they make a veritable profession of attacking Wagner's perilous sensuality. In one sense the assault on Wagner's erotics was a long time in coming, as can be seen from a conservative critic writing in the Leipzig *Allgemeine musikalische Zeitung* who sees *Tristan* foreshadowed by Senta's infatuation with the *Dutchman:*

What the hysterical Senta veils in a mysterious aura [he writes] now reveals itself unambiguously in the new musical drama *Tristan und*

Isolde—it is, to call something by its proper name, the glorification of sensual lust outfitted with every kind of thrilling stimulation device [*mit allem aufregenden Apparat*]. It is the most dismal kind of materialism, according to which people have no loftier goal than to "expire [*verhauchen*] in sweet fragrances"!

Not only does Wagner fail to exemplify a Nordic hero's life, which would stimulate and edify the German mind, but he shows a heroism at the moment of its depraved descent into sensuality. He professes a point of view long ago overcome, that of the lascivious, French approach to life of Wolfram von Eschenbach's enemy, Gottfried von Strassburg, who makes *sensuality itself* the subject of his drama. To serve this purpose music is enslaved to words: the most absolute of the sister arts becomes the paint-grinder for obscene canvasses [*zur Farbenreiberin für unsittliche Malerei*]. Dissolute above all (in our view) is the adaptation of the poem "Tristan und Isolde" for the contemporary stage.[45]

This kind of criticism had made occasional appearances in the decade before, mostly by English critics, as when H. F. Chorley writes in the *Athenaeum* that "here is comfort . . . in thinking that beyond Herr Wagner in his peculiar manner it is hardly possible to go" and that the "saturnal of licentious discord must have here reached its climax."[46] Or when a writer in the *Musical World* reviews Wagner's London concerts and speaks of "the true basis of harmony, and the indispensable government of modulation cast away for a reckless, wild, extravagant and demagogic cacophony, the symbol of profligate libertinage!"[47]

Reacting to *Tristan*, the denunciations of Wagnerian erotics become entrenched to a degree never before seen in music criticism, migrating from the world of *feuilleton* in newspapers and journals even to scholarly tomes such as an eight-volume *History of Drama* published in Leipzig in 1871, which attacks

the wild Wagnerian corybantic orgy, . . . this lewd caterwauling, scandal-mongering, gun-toting music, with an orchestral accompaniment slapping you in the face. . . . Hence, the secret fascination that makes it the darling of feeble-minded royalty, the plaything of the camarilla, of the court flunkeys covered with reptilian slime, and of the blasé hysterical female court parasites who need this galvanic stimulation by massive instrumental treatment to throw their pleasure-weary frog-legs into violent convulsion.[48]

Predictably, *Tristan* sparked renewed attacks on the love scene between Siegmund and Sieglinde in Act I of *Die Walküre* as when a French critic in 1888 commented on "the repugnant spectacle of incestuous love" that follows "the sensuous amours to the point of a delirium tremens of Tristan, gorged with aphrodisiac drugs."[49] Even more mild-mannered negative reviews of the 1876 *Walküre* note that "brutality and sensuality are never quite so bad in epic as they in drama, because the narration of an immoral plot never reaches the clarity of that acted out onstage."[50] "Never," writes Karl Frenzel in the *Nationalzeitung*, "is there a moral barrier [*sinnliche Schranke*] to sensuality: not only are Siegmund and Sieglinde siblings who embrace each other in the most savage passion of love—but they also have to be fornicators."[51]

Rather than dignifying such effusions with reasoned debate, Wagnerians either stuck their heads in the sand, or as Wilhelm Tappert did in 1876, collected the nastiest bits of criticism into a hugely successful lexicon of Wagner-invective, alphabetically ordering the crimes and misdemeanors with which the Master was charged. *A Dictionary of Impoliteness* in the words of the subtitle, *Richard Wagner in the Mirror of Criticism* contains "coarse, scornful, spiteful and defamatory expressions" that are "for the delectation of the spirit in idle hours." As for "immorality":

> What stands out strikingly in Wagner is that his aim is to depict the wild frenzy of lust, which he also understands how to do as a virtuoso, and with faunic delight he revels in such stimulating tone-pictures. It is through this, however, that his art becomes immoral and noxious, an ideal only for hysterical wenches and nervously effeminate men [*für hysterische Weiber und nervös erschlaffte Männer*].[52]

By 1915, Tappert's *Lexikon* boasted a third edition.

Although Chopin had been the victim of prurient scandal-mongering as a result of his affair with George Sand, and Verdi's *Traviata* had faced charges of immorality, it is Wagner criticism that ensured that the charge of musical perversion became commonplace in the treatment of modernists who dared to take up erotic themes. After 1850, the perceived loosening of morals saw similar assaults on naturalist drama and literature, such as the attacks on Ibsen, and in the visual arts, such as the denunciations of Degas. In music, the public was predictably shocked by erotic references that exposed the hypocritical *cordon sanitaire* that had insulated nineteenth-century Romanticism, excluding eroticism from aesthetic propriety. It then became outrageous (or titillating) to experience Carmen as voluptuous gypsy, Violetta as loose-living courtesan, to savor Chopin's salon melodies draped in immorality, or even wink back at Berlioz's lustful desires in his *Symphonie Fantastique.*

What nineteenth-century critics found appalling in the case of Wagner was the pretence that his music was not designed to titillate or arouse, but proposed a philosophy of life and art. As an undeniable fact of human experience, the erotic invaded precisely where it was least welcome; that is, within the realm of Romantic love. Wagner's sensuality raised the stakes of the game, suggesting that artists could treat previously forbidden subjects as long as they avoided the taint of cheapness and wantonness, thereby enabling a new kind of spiritualized erotics which some then chastised as threatening and socially disruptive. This perspective helps explain why anti-Wagnerians, even among professional musicians, found Wagner's music so deserving of repudiation: The shift of the aesthetic ground to embrace an explicit reappraisal of the effects of carnal desire signaled an attack on an official ideology of high musical expression, which preached that composers and performers served the chaste goddess of Art who was never sullied by the association to erotic love. Naturally, this supposed distance between high musical values and lowly sex asserted an untenable point of view; one that many poets, for example, had safely ignored. But musicians of an idealistic bent clung to this illusion well into the twentieth century, perhaps to secure their hard-won social acceptance as much as to protect their sometimes questionable calling from charges of indignity.

There were other objections to Wagner beyond that of his "sensualism." A basic lexicon includes the following: that Wagner was a dangerous revolutionary; that he was personally arrogant, especially in writing his own opera librettos; that the music of the future was nonsense; that he was compositionally inept; that his music was too noisy; that it was too cacophonous; that it flouted accepted standards of good taste; that it was chaotic and formless; that it was destitute of melody and lyricism; that it repeated themes obsessively; that it made dramatic nonsense; that it was tedious, boring, and enervating; that it was pompous or too common; or that it constituted a monstrous assault on the senses. The historical validity of these views is beyond doubt, but—as important as they were in the reception of Wagner—it is important to note that many of them show up in music criticism of the period, attacking a wide swathe of composers. Other claims, indeed, are consonant with accusations of unashamed eroticism and sexual degeneracy. The point, then, is that Wagner's erotics represent a special nodal point that brought together both advocates and critics, and the high pitch of the attack on sensualism signals widely shared social anxieties. Certainly it was a charge not leveled at anyone else's music before Wagner's.

Clara Schumann

Perhaps the most telling rejection of Wagner's erotics issued from a musician of the first rank: Clara Wieck Schumann (1819–96). Her reaction not only records her obvious distress but even helps us understand the affective content in the music to which she was committed. Clara had first met Wagner in the 1840s, and loathed both him and his music from the start. In September 1875, she traveled to Munich to hear her late husband's *Manfred*, steeling herself to hear *Tristan* after ten years of critical outcry. She was then in her mid-fifties and belonged to the very same generation as Malwida von Meysenbug. In her diary, she explodes as follows:

> In the evening we went to see *Tristan und Isolde*. It was the most repulsive thing [*das Widerwärtigste*] I have ever seen or heard in my life. To be forced to see and listen to such sexual frenzy [*einen solchen Liebeswahnsinn*] the whole evening, in which every feeling of decency is violated and by which not just the public but even musicians seem to be enchanted—that is the saddest thing I have experienced in my entire artistic life.

Given such a reaction, Clara might have been expected to exit the theatre at the first opportunity. In fact, she was glued to her seat:

> I endured it to the end since I wanted to hear the whole thing. During the entire Second Act the two of them sleep and sing; through the entire last act—for fully forty minutes—Tristan dies. They call that dramatic!!! . . . . Levi says Wagner is a much better musician than Gluck! And Joachim doesn't have the courage to speak up against the others. Are they all fools, or am I? I find the subject matter so wretched [*elend*]; sexual frenzy precipitated by a potion; can one be in the least interested in the lovers? This isn't a matter of feelings, it is a sickness, which rips the heart in pieces out of the body, and which the music sensualizes [*versinnlicht*] with the most loathsome sonorities [*widerlichsten Klängen*]! Oh, how I never tire of moaning about this, wailing "woe is me."[53]

A month later she is still railing against Wagner in a letter to Brahms, though she tones down her moral outrage when writing to someone from the "younger" generation who subscribed to a less upright set of moral standards than she:

> Unfortunately the pleasure I had [hearing Robert Schumann's *Manfred*] was marred by the evening that followed, for, being in Munich, one had no choice but to see *Tristan*. The Vogl couple are certainly a magnificent pair of singers, but I cannot remember ever having heard or seen anything more repulsive than this opera. Anyone who can hear and—see!—it with pleasure must surely lack all moral feeling. That they should dare to offer such a piece to a cultivated public, or to a public desirous of culture, is a terribly sad sign of the demoralization of our age. But even to think about this makes me boil with indignation [*es empört sich in mir alles*], so I shall say no more about it.[54]

Clara Schumann hadn't invented the notion of Wagner's "sick" sensualism, but from the 1870s the idea took on a life of its own, culminating in Max Nordau's *Degeneration* (1893) and Friedrich Nietzsche's late writings, both discussed in Chapter 4. Clara returns to the idea repeatedly, however. She even refers to it in the midst of an altercation with an old friend, the Munich conductor Hermann Levi (an intimate of Brahms turned Wagnerian) to whom she writes in 1880 that Wagnerism is "a serious illness to which you have succumbed with body and soul" (*LK* III, 409). Few disputes in the history of music were as bitter as the one over Wagner, and it shouldn't surprise us that at its heart lay the issue of sex and its role within music.

Thereafter, when Liszt is slated with composing "erotic-flagellant music," when Tchaikovsky is accused of "vulgar, obscene phrases," when Debussy's *Afternoon of a Faun* is blamed for its "erratic and erotic spasms," when Richard Strauss is condemned for "prostitut[ing] music to . . . the purposes of pornography," when Berg is charged with a "highly diseased eroticism,"[55]—the debt owed is to Richard Wagner. And not only the critics have him to thank but also the composers so charged; for it was Wagner who opened the flood gates representing sexual desire within music. To what extent he intended to wreak such havoc is the subject of the following chapter.

CHAPTER TWO

Intentions

So both admirers and detractors of Wagner's erotics observed in the composer's music an intoxication with sexual desire, or "sensualism," as the nineteenth century referred to it. Whether by depicting orgiastic voluptuousness in *Tannhäuser* or by painting the "wild glow of sensual love" in *Die Walküre*, or by exposing the "insatiable and sweet craving" for physical union in *Tristan*, Wagner earned both praise and contempt for daring to treat such themes in a venue unused to them, namely, an opera house elevated into an altar for High Art. It is a curious fact that everyone within this menagerie of conflicting views assumed that Wagner set out to stir up trouble, that he intended his work to be sexually provocative, and that, in one way or another, he succeeded. In fact, Wagner was far from a libertine, although throughout his career a preoccupation with sexual love was never far from the surface. Describing his early opera, *Das Liebesverbot* or *The Ban on Love* (1836) in an autobiographical sketch from 1843, Wagner notes that its subject was "the victory" of "free and open sensuality" (*SS* I, 10). Forty years later, on February 13, 1883, the day he died, Wagner was drafting an essay entitled "On the Feminine within the Human" in which the final footnote, the last text he ever penned, reads cryptically: "The process of emancipation of the female only takes place amid ecstatic convulsions. Love—Tragedy."[1]

For all the continuity of interest, Wagner never claimed eroticism as one of his central achievements: Such an accolade would surely have been beneath him. One notes with some amusement, for example, his panicked reaction in 1872 when introducing some of his early writings in which he had made liberal use of the word "sensuality" [*Sinnlichkeit*]. Fearful lest readers misunderstand him as invoking the "coarse meaning of sensualism" [*übler Bedeutung des "Sensualismus"*] or even "the submission to lustful desires" [*der Ergebung an die Sinnenlust*], Wagner goes out of his way to say that he had intended purely a philosophical meaning—a kind of physicalism or materialism—and that no reference to the erotic was intended (*SS* III, 4). At the same time, it is clear that many of the leading themes in his voluminous prose writings hover around the issue of sex: One thinks of the panacea of Love, Drama as the union of the masculine spirit of poetry with the feminine spirit of music, the redemption of a woman's love, or the resignation of the Schopenhauerian Will. To form a view of Wagner's ideas on sexual love, one needs therefore to inspect the passing references to the erotic in his various autobiographies, his correspondence, and in his published works as a background to ideas put forward in his operas. And, of course, one also needs to consider the role of the erotic in his own life, a rather weighty subject, as it turns out, for which there is substantial evidence.

Although most nineteenth-century artists lived in dread of intimate revelations about their persons that might be seen to motivate their creations, Wagner, to the contrary, never tired of pointing out the inseparable connection between his life and work. A particularly categorical statement is found in *Eine Mitteilung an meine Freunde* [*A Communication to my Friends*] (1851): "I can't hold with those who claim to love me as an artist, but deny me their sympathy as a person," and he goes on to claim that "the dissociation of the artist from his person is as foolish a thought as the divorce of the soul from the body," that "an artist will never have his art understood . . . unless he was also loved" (*JA* VI, 199). As much as Wagner hid the most embarrassing aspects of his biography from his public, he certainly leaves posterity in no doubt that his aesthetic ideas were rooted in lived experience.

Julius Kapp and Ernest Newman

Although his widow, Cosima Liszt von Bülow Wagner (1837–1930), attempted to sanitize the Master's image after his death by controlling the flow of information about his personal life, biographers beyond the Bayreuth circle of acolytes realized early on the importance of studying Wagner's love life. The first major achievement in this area was a monograph of 1912 by Julius Kapp (1883–1962) entitled *Richard Wagner and Women: An Erotic Biography,* based on a careful survey of original documents. "Avoiding all idle rumor and cheap sensationalism," Kapp based his "simple chronicle exclusively on available source material" that "rounds out a complete biography of the Master on an erotic basis."[2] Rejecting the uncritical hero-worship engaged in by Glasenapp and Ashton Ellis, Kapp included lengthy citations from unpublished correspondence so as to recount Wagner's attractions to an assortment of women, from "trifling entanglements—some tragic, some ludicrous"—to his "profound passion" for Mathilde Wesendonck, always emphasizing, if not detailing, the erotic links with his creative output.[3] The book is far from the romanticized whitewash that one sees in biographical works on Byron and Goethe from about the same time, which sought to portray the poets as larger-than-life lovers of women.[4]

Kapp revised his book twice—for the first time after the author obtained access to the Burrell Collection—and completed a second expanded edition in 1951, thus crowning a research effort of more than forty years. In the 1951 edition, Kapp goes so far as to assert that "Eros is the fundamental force in all creative art and no more valid proof of this thesis can be found in the whole cultural history of mankind than the life of Richard Wagner." The model of a circumspect but critical Wagnerian, Kapp never shied away from painting what is an essentially truthful psychological portrait, one focused on what he calls Wagner's "unheroic effeminate nature, so prone to self-pity, [which] reveled in all the torments of disappointed love."[5] As if to excuse his inattention to the operas, he notes that "a biography of Wagner centering round Eros therefore becomes automatically a history of his creative achievement."

Ernest Newman's first large-scale biographical study, which appeared in 1914, *Wagner as Man and Artist*, represents another zealous effort to get at the truth of Wagner's love life. But whereas Kapp excuses the great artist for his peccadilloes because of his "imperishable" masterpieces, especially *Tristan und Isolde*, Newman paints a far more modern picture of Wagner as an obsessed and selfish man "who stands naked and unashamed before us, equally capable of great virtues and of great vices, of heroic self-sacrifice and the meanest egoism, packed with a vitality too superabundant for the moral sense always to control it." Invoking an armchair acquaintance with Freud, Newman diagnoses Wagner as hopelessly "neurotic," someone who mistreats virtually everyone with whom he comes into intimate contact.[6]

Yet Newman refrains from psychoanalyzing Wagner's works. Although he views "the enormous part the erotic played in his life" as "the key to his whole nature" (*NM*, 128), he argues that this role can ultimately be reduced to a simple "oscillation between desire and the slaying of desire":

> In the *Flying Dutchman* Vanderdecken-Wagner is redeemed by the woman who loves and trusts him unto death. Tannhäuser-Wagner fluctuates between the temptress and the saint. Lohengrin-Wagner seeks in vain the woman who shall love him unquestioningly. Wieland the Smith . . . is again Wagner, lamed by life, but healed at last by another "redeeming" woman. Tristan-Wagner finds love insatiable, and death the only end of all our loving. Sachs-Wagner renounces love. Parsifal-Wagner finds salvation in flight from sensual love. (*NM*, 272)

On the whole, this is a fair résumé of the operas' central preoccupations, but Newman's wit blinds him to the very different sets of erotic charges found in the various operas. In his inimitable no-nonsense way—here, and throughout his majestic four-volume biography that followed in the 1930s and 40s—he warns his readers against taking Wagner's views on sex, or indeed, any of Wagner's thinking seriously.[7] "There is no need, no reason," he writes, "to discuss the 'philosophy' of such a mind. He is no philosopher: he is simply a perplexed and tortured human soul and a magnificent musical instrument. All that concerns us today is the quality of the music wrung from the instrument under the torture" (*NL*, 273). Newman is right to reject Wagner as a philosopher, but as he repeatedly shows, too much of the person is audibly enmeshed in the work for us to ignore the composer as we hear the music. The question is rather how the thinking of such a "perplexed and tortured human·soul" resulted in the specific musical qualities of his works.

Not surprisingly, both Kapp and Newman, scrupulous as they were, appeal to the moral standards of their time in their biographical work, and in both writers there is an unspoken sense that Wagner must be judged adversely against the example of normal men, whose desires, fantasies, and sexual behavior are predictably monochrome. The precise complexion of Wagner's musical eroticism is therefore never addressed, for the simple reason that it exposes too many skeletons in the post-Victorian closet. As a result, Newman believes his account of Wagner's miseries and erotic sufferings is best seen away from music. On the other hand, it becomes famously difficult to locate this non-Wagnerian, non-neurotic, sexually conventional male as soon as one tries to identify him, not to mention that sexually conventional specimens among artists and musicians are not exactly encountered in high concentrations. What is more, the separation of the personal from the musical domain suppresses yet another key question: Why in heaven's name should *we* be attracted to music crafted by someone so obviously aberrant and perverse? As will be shown in the final chapter, some writers at the turn of the last century were savvy enough to forge a link between Wagner's erotic tastes and the rest of humanity, but could advance their case only from the intellectual margins.

It makes more sense to jettison ideas of aberrance and perversion and take a closer look at Wagner to see what he reveals about his music as well as what his predilections suggest about us, those who love, hate, or are indifferent to his music. A deciphering of Wagner's erotic intentions, spanning a lifetime, opens up a huge number of questions, which even a book-lengthy study can scarcely begin to address. Instead of attempting to provide an exhaustive account of the biographical and documentary evidence, I intend to capture some salient images from the historical record that recount the story of Wagner's increasing involvement of music in his erotic conundrums. Though incomplete, this narrative helps lay the groundwork for a more concrete consideration of Wagner's musical erotics in the following chapters.

Das Liebesverbot

The story of Wagner's erotics begins with his early opera *Das Liebesverbot* [*The Ban on Love*] of 1836, in which the composer, still in his early twenties, reacted against the moral standards of his Biedermeier age, an epoch dominated by mass-produced knick-knacks above the hearth, hypocritical middle-class pieties, and the brutal suppression of social dissent. Writing about the opera for an autobiography destined for a journal in 1843 while sketching out ideas for *Tannhäuser*, Wagner says that he adapted Shakespeare's *Measure for Measure*, "only with the difference, that I took away its prevailing seriousness and modeled it on *Das junge Europa* [by Heinrich Laube]: in this way free and forthright sensuality won the purest victory over puritanical hypocrisy" (*SS* I, 10). Newman paraphrases the opera's theme with great acuity: "The older men were mercilessly ridiculed as pedants, and a newer and more sprightly art was to hustle the ponderous old one off the stage" (*NM*, 157). Wagner is still sticking to this story in 1871, when, in a passage that prefigures *Mein Leben*, he writes that "the basis of my view [in *Das Liebesverbot*] had been directed against puritanical hypocrisy and consequently led to a bold glorification of 'free love' [*der freien Sinnlichkeit*]" (*SS* I, 21).

In fact, the glorification of "free love" is in short supply in *Das Liebesverbot*, and it is fascinating to observe how the exposé of Puritanical hypocrisy in *Das Liebesverbot* interests Wagner to the virtual exclusion of any real plea for hedonism. At least in musical terms, the motive representing the hypocritical ban acts as an effective apodictic statement rather to the detriment of the routine Italianate frothiness representing the frolics of the freedom-loving libertines. In one sense, the victory over the "German" ban on love at the end of the opera is pyrrhic, in that Wagner has invested his musical efforts in representing a German's castigation of sinful sex and precious little in celebrating the Italians' joyous libertinage. It is difficult to avoid thinking that Wagner, despite all his political protestations, actually identifies with Friedrich, the German prig, rather than the Sicilian hedonists.

One hears this stark contrast of musical registers in the opening scene of Act I, in which a Donizetti-tinged patter of forced laughter ("ha-ha-ha") echoes the bacchanal of revelers enjoying the carefree milieu of Danieli's wine bar and brothel outside Palermo. Luzio, a young and dissolute aristocrat, has been enjoying an evening of wine, women, and song when his party is attacked by the secret agents [*die Sbirren*] of Friedrich, the German Viceroy of Sicily, who has ordered a general prohibition on illicit sex and alcohol. Carnival is due to begin, and has been cancelled, to the general dismay of the assembled crowd. Luzio and the chorus of drinkers, libertines, barmaids, and pimps shout back at Friedrich's emissary Brighella:

LUZIO:

Was, keine Liebe, keinen Wein,
und endlich gar kein Karneval!

ALLE [AUßER BRIGHELLA]:

Der deutsche Narr, auf, lacht ihn
     aus,
das soll die ganze Antwort sein;
schickt ihn in seinen Schnee nach
     Haus,
dort laßt ihn keusch und nüchtern
     sein.

LUZIO:

What, no Love, no wine,
and not even Carnival in the end!

EVERYONE [BUT BRIGHELLA]:

The German fool, just laugh at
     him,
that should be our whole reply;
send him home to his snow,

And let him stay there chaste
     and dry.

Here and throughout the opera, the chorus, expressing the "free and forthright sensuality" that Wagner wishes to promote, sings in precisely the same Franco-Italian style that he was later to tarnish as trivial and immoral. When Isabella, who abandons her cloistered retreat to save her brother's life, states a version of the opera's slogan—"O, how barren life would be/if God had not given us love and love's desire"—the music evokes the sickly sweet banality of the most conventional four-square cavatina. In no way does Wagner's music take his subject matter seriously.

When, on the other hand, Friedrich's henchman Brighella taunts Pontio Pilato, a pimp who works at Danieli's, about his professional duties, the music, by contrast, strikes a serious pose that will endure through to the *Dutchman* and sounds the chromatic "Ban" motif first heard in the overture. As for the text, Wagner the librettist wildly overdoes the puritanical characterization of debauchery that, like the title of the opera, has the unintentionally amusing effect of showing his underlying preference for condemning, not recommending, free love. Indeed, the title of the opera irked the local authorities in Magdeburg so much that Wagner was forced to change it to *The Novice of Palermo* before the premiere. As Brighella addresses the pimp Pontio, the music becomes more chromatic, coloring the words with threateningly somber hues:

Purifizieren,—durch solchen
  Wandel,

durch schnöden Sauf- und
  Liebeshandel?

Auf dir ruht gräßlicher Verdacht,

du schlossest Eh'n für eine Nacht!

PONTIO:

Ach, glaubt das nicht; für eine Stunde
und kaum so lang!

BRIGHELLA:

Nur für 'ne Stunde!

Pontio, du sprichst dich um den
  Hals;

geliefert bist du jedenfalls!

Ich sprech' dich aller Ehren los,

und die Verbannung sei dein Los!

Purify? Through such conduct

By such filthy trade in drink
  and sex?

A ghastly suspicion rests on you,

you agreed marriages for one night!

PONTIO:

Oh don't believe that; for an hour
or hardly so long!

BRIGHELLA:

Only an hour!

Pontio, you're threading a noose
  round your neck;

you're caught in any case!

I declare you stripped of all your
  rights,

banishment shall be your lot!

More than forty years later, Wagner is still thinking of the shock value of "only an hour of love" when Kundry repeats the same line in her final attempt to seduce Parsifal: *"Nur eine Stunde mein!/nur eine Stunde dein."*[8] Even if the effect of music written in 1878 is startlingly different, the preoccupation remains. There is little actual pleasure in lust found in

Wagner's libretto for *Das Liebesverbot*. Instead the libretto wallows in images of debauchery, as in this speech by Friedrich:

Verworfnes Volk!	*Depraved people!*
Seid ihr denn ganz	*Are you then wholly sunk*
versunken im Pfuhl der Lüste,	*in the murky pool of lusts,*
im Schlamme der Begierden?	*in the sludge of desires?*
Nur nach Vergnügen, Freude	*You think of nothing but*
steht eu'r Trachten,	*pleasure and joy;*
in Rausch und Wollust	*you know life only through*
kennt ihr nur das Leben!	*intoxication and debauchery!*
Mich ekelte das sündenvolle	*I've been nauseated by your sinful*
Treiben.	*acts.*

Given this moralizing fervor, Wagner's claim that he intended *Das Liebesverbot* as a social statement seems a little ridiculous. One only has to recall a dramatic work from the very same year by another twenty-three-year-old—*Woyzeck* by Georg Büchner—to put Wagner's "libertinage" in context. *Woyzeck* still shocks us today with its powerful unmasking of social hypocrisy, while Wagner's opera is not only dependent on its Shakespearean model but also traffics in a host of operatic clichés. In the unfinished fragments of 1836, Woyzeck has been force-fed a diet of peas to prove the doctor's absurd "scientific" view about human freedom, and the doctor humiliates Woyzeck for having "pissed against the wall like a dog" instead of controlling his bladder. This kind of stark naturalism and implied moral outrage underlying the scene couldn't be further from Wagner's text and music. Even a modernist such as Alban Berg, some eighty years later, couldn't cope with the franker expression of Büchner's social critique and had to bowdlerize the graphic text to make it acceptable for the opera stage. Instead of urinating, Berg's Wozzeck coughs against the wall. By comparison with Büchner's *Woyzeck*, *Das Liebesverbot* unmasks precious little about societal power relations and is a far cry from social critique.

What Wagner instead achieves in *Das Liebesverbot* is an inchoate depiction of a character's erotic predicament and submission to his sexual yearnings. In Act II, Friedrich confronts his burning desire for Isabella, which will lead him hypocritically to flout his own ban on illicit sex. In what is perhaps the most effective scene in the opera, Wagner composes a striking *scena ed aria* (no. 10) in which he introduces and punctuates the opening recitative with a motivic extension of the chromatic Ban anticipating Ortrud's dark diminished sevenths in Act II of *Lohengrin*, or even more strikingly, Klingsor's anguish in *Parsifal* (symbolized by the Torment of Love).[9] (See Example 2–1.) Unable to control himself, Friedrich sings (with *vibrato*, as the performance direction indicates) the following words to the orchestra's hyperventilated set of crescendos and diminuendos in each bar:

Ja, glühend, wie des Südens Hauch	*Yes, glowing like southern breath*
brennt mir die Flamme in der Brust;	*the flame burns in my breast;*
verzehrt mich auch die wilde Glut,	*even though wild passion consumes me,*
genieß' ich doch die heiße Lust!	*I do enjoy the hot ecstasy!*

So pained is Friedrich at breaking his own ban that he undertakes to sin with Isabella and then face the same death as his victim Claudio. The musical language that ensues prefigures both the frantic tone of the Dutchman and of Tannhäuser in their most desperate states of recklessness. Particularly moving are the aching, dissonant appoggiaturas which summon forth the demons that "convulse" through Friedrich's body and the fever that "flushes through his blood,"[10] music more advanced even than the chromatic vein of Bacchantic raptures in the Venusberg. *Das Liebesverbot* may have betrayed its ideological point, but Wagner's first fanning of erotic flames foreshadows a devotion to a theme that will occupy him forever after.

Salvation from Arousal

Which life experiences emboldened this recognition? Biographical evidence suggests that in his early years, Wagner saw his guilt-ridden sexual desires as a plague to be exorcised. Even much later in his autobiography, *Mein Leben*, he was still taking pleasure in chastising his own dissolute student life, as when he recounts a shameless tale of gambling away his mother's money in Leipzig. So low had he sunk that

> I even bore with complete indifference [*Stumpfsinn*] the contempt of my sister Rosalie, who, with my mother, could scarcely bare to glance at the incomprehensible young libertine [*Wüstling*] who appeared only seldom before them, pale and disturbed. (*ML*, 64)

Libertinage portends disaster and is therefore denounced. In his *Communication to my Friends* of 1851, Wagner recalls his twenties as a time marked by "the fantastic debauchery [*Lüderlichkeit*] of German student-life," which, "after intense over-indulgence [*nach heftiger Ausschweifung*], soon became abhorrent to me: Woman had begun to present herself to my consciousness" (*JA* VI, 224). But this Woman had to be saved from the lusty desires of modern man, as one reads in a curious and obscure passage that illustrates just how low these desires could stoop. (It is significant that Wagner took pains to excise this sentence from a later edition of *A Communication*.) Here he seems to admit to brief sexual encounters with loose women or prostitutes, which are part and parcel of the "vices" of the modern male:

> The timid reserve towards the female sex that is inculcated into all of us—this ground of all the vices of the modern male generation, and no less of the stunting of Woman's nature [*Verkümmerung des Weibes*]—my natural temperament had only been able to break through by fits and starts and in isolated utterances of a cocky hot temper [*kecke Heftigkeit*]: a hasty, conscience-stinging snatch of pleasure must form the unrequiting substitute for instinctively-desired delight.[11]

To counteract this descent into illicit sensuality, Wagner—now strongly under the thumb of Ludwig Feuerbach—searches for a true form of love to cure the ills of the modern world. "In contrast to the directly experienced hedonism [*Genußsinnlichkeit*] which surrounded modern life and art, [my desire was for] a pure, chaste, virginal, unapproachable and intangible form of love," he writes (*JA* VI, 253). In Feuerbach's terms, "Love is the middle term, the substantial bond, the principle of reconciliation between the perfect and the imperfect, the sinless and sinful being, the universal and the individual, the divine and the human."[12] For Wagner, as for Feuerbach, this Love is utterly amorphous. As he puts it in *Das Kunstwerk der Zukunft* [*The Artwork of the Future*] (1849) dedicated to Feuerbach: "[Man] yields himself, not to a love for this or that particular object, but to Love in general" (*JA* VI, 35). In a letter to his young friend and acolyte Karl Ritter, sent in 1849 with the *Artwork* essay, Wagner notes that "Nowhere have I found the natural healthy process so clearly and so consciously expressed as by Feuerbach, and I confess that I am greatly indebted to him."[13] "The natural healthy process" is a euphemism for Feuerbachian views of sex, and, as we shall see in Chapter 5, this pure and chaste version of Love was as much indebted to Goethe and Schiller as it was, at least in part, to tragic homoerotic models from Greek antiquity.

The new Romantic ideal in Wagner's mind specializes in a confused relation between love, sexual urges, and eroticism. It is a love that wants to rise above base desires and that at the same time cannot exclude a sexual element: "Yet what was this longing at base but the yearning for a real love," he writes in the *Communication*, "seeded in the soil of the most complete sensuality—yet only a love that could *not* be satisfied on the loathsome soil of modern sensuality" (*JA* VI, 253). As late as January 1854, some ten months before Wagner began reading Schopenhauer, he is still moaning to Liszt about his two opposing tendencies:

A too hasty marriage at the age of 23 to a worthy woman utterly unsuited to me has made of me an outlaw for life. For a long time I tried to escape the general stress of my living situation with ambitious plans and aspirations, tried to conceal the void of my heart by becoming famous. In fact, I lived until my 36th year [1849] without having noticed this terrible emptiness: until then my being was equalized by two conflicting elements of desire, one of which I sought to still through my art, whereas the other I aired out with a series of lustful, fantastic sexual excesses [*durch brünstige, phantastische, sinnliche Ausschweifungen*]. (You know my Tannhäuser, this idealization of what in reality is so often a trivial form of behavior.)[14]

We confront a man disturbed by his sexual impulses who at the same time yearns to ennoble them into an all-embracing philosophy of world salvation. At least this was the mood Wagner was in, he tells us, when he came to compose *Tannhäuser.* The confession is surprisingly frank:

> It was in a state of all-consuming and lascivious arousal [*verzehrend üppige Erregtheit*] that held my blood and every nerve in a fevered flush as I sketched and worked out the music for *Tannhäuser.* My true nature—which in my loathing of the modern world and my drive to discover something nobler had quite returned to me—now seized the most extreme forms of my being as in a violent and lusty embrace, and both flowed into *one* stream: the highest desiring for Love. (*JA* VI, 253)

Convinced he was a man torn apart by opposing affective tendencies, Wagner looks back at his early operas from the 1830s and 1840s, and sees them veering from one pole to the other, from the idealized spirit of the fairy-opera *Die Feen* to the carnality of *Das Liebesverbot*, and then from the high-minded *Holländer* to the erotically-charged *Tannhäuser* to the first sketch for the lighthearted *Meistersinger:*

> One will see that there was a possibility of my developing along two diametrically opposite lines: on the one hand there was the holy seriousness [*heiligen Ernste*] of my original sentiments—on the other a cocky inclination toward wild sexual recklessness [*zu wildem sinnlichem Ungestüme*] nourished by my lived experience. (*JA* VI, 226)

It was not only the choice of subject matter for his librettos but also the musical treatment that fell prey to his indecision, for it is music, he writes, which "always exercised a decisive influence upon my powers of emotional perception [*Empfindungsvermögen*]." This music is specifically identified with his conflicted view of Love:

> I cannot grasp the spirit of Music as anything other than Love. Filled with its holy might, and with its emergent powers of insight into

human life, I saw set before me . . . the need for Love burdened by loveless formalism. (*JA* VI, 236)

Love is even indistinguishable from friendship:

> Our language is so rich in synonyms that, having lost an intuitive understanding of their meanings, we imagine we may use them arbitrarily and draw distinctions between them. Thus do we use and distinguish between "Love" and "Friendship." As for me, the more my consciousness has matured, the less I'm able to think of friendship without love, to say nothing of experiencing such a distinction. (*JA* VI, 200)

As a result, one is left—at this stage in Wagner's thinking—with a baffling incoherence about the concept of Love. It must avoid being low and trivial, it might or might not—as in friendship—embrace a sexual element, but it must always aim high. Given this kind of woolly thinking, one can see that, for Wagner, music—in the guise of Love—might be called upon to serve several incompatible masters. Little wonder that Newman—as against many contemporary writers—could exclaim in exasperation: "He is no philosopher."

Wilhelmine Schröder-Devrient

Wagner's muddles over the nature of Love extend to his ideas about women, in particular to the female characters who populate his operas, and nowhere is his mystification more pronounced than in his reverence for the soprano Wilhelmine Schröder-Devrient (1804–1860), a woman to whom, he tells us repeatedly, he owed an understanding of the true nature of drama. At the very least, his fascination with her reveals some important aspects about his views of women and erotic love.

It was Schröder-Devrient's Fidelio that prompted the 16-year-old Wagner—so he claimed in his autobiography, *Mein Leben* [*My Life*]—to write an effusive letter to the soprano in which he swore, based on her example, to become a musician. "Whoever recalls this wonderful woman from this period of her life"—Wagner writes—"must have been able to witness in one way or another the almost daemonic warmth which necessarily spread over one from the so humanly ecstatic performance of this incomparable artist" (*ML*, 49). A letter dropped off at her Leipzig hotel—the account in *Mein Leben* continues—declared that from that day forward, his life had taken on a significance: should she ever hear of his fame, she should know of his oath sworn the evening he first encountered her. (During rehearsals for *Rienzi*, Schröder-Devrient surprised Wagner by reciting the contents of the letter to him.)[15] Wagner never tired of singing her praises, and her subsequent creation of three of his early roles—Adriano (in *Rienzi*), Senta (in the *Dutchman*), and Venus (in *Tannhäuser*)—marked a high point in his relation with any of his performers. He was happy to forgive her stage histrionics: She would interpolate spoken words amid passages meant to be sung, a habit that Berlioz, for example, found "grotesque," saying he would "far rather hear tragedy sung than opera spoken."[16] According to many reports, Schröder-Devrient was famous for an improvised *Sprech-stimme* that lent dramatic immediacy to a particular word or phrase, and she resorted to this theatrical gesture ever more as she lost her singing voice. Her performances struck Wagner all the same as entirely engrossing, judging from his frequent mention of them. Nine years his senior, Schröder-Devrient exerted a potent personal influence over Wagner, and decades later, he is repeating anecdotes about her, indeed still dreaming about her, as Cosima reports in July 1871:

> I dreamed . . . of Schröder-Devrient, I had relations [*Beziehungen*] with her." "Of what sort?" I ask. "As always, not at all of the amorous kind [*gar nicht zärtlicher Art*]. No, she could never have aroused my sexual desire [*Liebes-Sehnsucht*]; there was no longer enough modesty there, no mystery to probe.[17]

Wagner even dreamed of Schröder-Devrient two days before he died, when he exclaimed to Cosima, "All my wenches [*Weibsen*] are passing before me" (*CT* IV, 1111).

Modesty was not exactly Schröder-Devrient's middle name. In fact, she was quite the looming female vamp and as early as 1863, Alfred von Wolzogen (1823–1883), her first posthumous biographer, claimed that her two deadliest enemies were "passionateness and sensuality."[18] Even in print, Wagner notes that "one main sorrow went through her life: she didn't find the man completely worth her making happy" (*JA* IX, 263), a delicate way of disparaging the character of her lovers and husbands. There had been, as one author has put it, "three marriages, four children, and a succession of infatuations with thoroughly unsuitable younger men. Her first husband divorced her for adultery and won custody of the children; her second embezzled her money."[19] Hers was an exciting, successful, but far from happy life.

In private, Wagner revealed more about her escapades than in print. There had been some "precarious sides" to their relationship in Dresden, he writes, when she made him her confidant, pouring out to him "the really catastrophic affairs of her heart [*bei wirklich fatalen Vorgängen in ihrem Herzen*]" (*ML*, 282). It is unlikely, though, that he was much put out by her confidences. As Newman remarks, Wagner was "a bit of a connoisseur himself" in this area and therefore probably "not uninterested in her singularly frank confidences."[20]

The real problem was that Wilhelmine continually humiliated him, criticized his precious use of language, and taunted him for having married so young. As Cosima Wagner notes in 1874, "Richard forbids our painter the word 'colossal' which he constantly employs; he tells me that he also used such words in his youth before Schröder-Devrient drew his attention to it, and told him, 'don't be so affected'—'a sign that she took an interest in me, and I was ashamed,' R[ichard] adds" (*CT* II, 856). Obviously playing the *femme fatale* with pleasure, the soprano ridiculed Wagner for his lack of sexual experience, and even years later Wagner admits that he found her attentions both exciting and degrading. He reports to Cosima in 1881, for example, "how Schröder-Devrient once said to him in [a state of] passionate agitation, 'Oh, what do you know, you hen-pecked husband [*Sie Ehe-Krüppel*, lit. you whom marriage has crippled]?' And how strange that made him feel. He was 32 at the time" (*CT* IV, 814). A related anecdote is recalled in 1879: "Then he speaks of men who marry early, who are lost; for this reason Frau Schröder-Devrient had complete contempt for him and called him 'the marriage-cripple'[*den Ehekrüppel*]" (*CT* III, 352). Though quite the emancipated woman, Schröder-Devrient was anything but trivial: "Everything [about her] was life, soul, warmth, and an expression of joy," as Wagner put it to Paul von Joukowsky in 1881 (*CT* IV, 687). His affection and respect for her art never diminished, and had its most public outing in the conclusion to his essay "On Actors and Singers" (1872) dedicated "to the memory of the great Wilhelmine Schröder-Devrient" (*JA* IX, 263).[21] No other woman earned such public accolades in Wagner's writings.

Given this idealization, it is fascinating to observe how this dominant and dominating personality inspired such a wide panoply of soprano roles—Wagner's only trouser role, Adriano in *Rienzi* as well as Senta in the *Dutchman*, the ideal woman loyal to her man unto death, and finally, Venus in *Tannhäuser*, the embodiment of the female seductress. In each case Wilhelmine's sensuality furnished the key to her theatrical credibility as well as Wagner's attraction to her. "Discussing the bust of Schröder-Devrient, which always touches R[ichard]"—Cosima writes in 1869—"he tells me: She was no longer very reputable when I started to associate with her, but for a person possessing such a tremendous talent, there was only one compensation, and that was [her] sexual allure [*Sinnlichkeit*]; without this she could never have coped with the strain [*es nie aushalten können*]" (*CT* I, 177).

The sensuousness that Wagner ascribes to Schröder-Devrient embodied a decidedly masculine element, and it is no coincidence that he singled out her famous roles *en travesti* for their dramatic conviction in portraying an ardent male lover. Not only as Fidelio and as his own Adriano rescuing his lover Irene from the burning Capitol on horseback, it was especially Schröder-Devrient as Romeo in Bellini's *I Capuleti e i Montecchi* (based on Shakespeare) that Wagner found overwhelming in Leipzig (1834) and Magdeburg (1835), despite his scorn for the thinness of the music. Although he came to reject trouser roles for women, he believed that these "succeeded only once, in Schröder-Devrient's Romeo, where she acted in an extraordinarily intimate manner" (*CT* IV, 1068). Her acting was so noteworthy in the love scenes with Juliet, that, astoundingly, Wagner connects it with the composition of the Second Act of *Tristan und Isolde*. Speaking to Cosima in 1878, he declares:

> How ever did I create the rapture [*Überschwenglichkeit*] of the 2nd act? I know! Through seeing Schröder-Devrient as Romeo, and it isn't so

foolish to have a woman in that role, for these little runts of men, mostly tenors, are never any good at those lovely frantic caresses. (*CT* III, 67)

The anecdote is even more astounding when one learns that the Juliet in the Magdeburg performances was Marie Löw (1809–1885), one of Wagner's first adolescent loves—among three such Jewish girls in Leipzig—whom he later befriended again on a visit to Prague where he met her two daughters Lilli (1848–1929) and Marie (1851–1931) Lehmann, both of whom played Rhinemaidens in the 1876 Bayreuth *Ring*, with Lilli going on to establish a major operatic career as a Wagnerian soprano.[22] One can gain further insight into Wagner's memory of Schröder-Devrient's performance from a letter from 1852 written to Hans von Bülow. Recalling the scene for the Finale in Felice Romani's adaptation of *Romeo and Juliet*, Wagner notes that whereas Bellini's treatment was "trivial," the "whole graphic subject matter of the poem is encapsulated in a single moment. . . . Love, tender in its beginnings, growing ardent, reaching its jubilant climax—finally consumed by the element of hatred which, inwardly consumed, fades into a lament. Thus: the triumphs of love!" (*SL*, 254).

For someone whose theoretical writings seem to insist on such a strict division between the male and female principles, Wagner reveals rather a lot in linking Romani and Bellini to his own *Tristan*, which goes some way toward amplifying the repertoire of erotic attractions found in his operas.[23] For who would guess that a spark igniting Tristan and Isolde's ecstasy first flamed in a love scene played by two women? Wagner even divulges that the encompassing female dominance of Kundry harks back to Schröder-Devrient. In the midst of the final rehearsals for the *Parsifal* premiere in 1882, Cosima reports his grumbles:

The big scene between Kundry and Parsifal will surely never be performed in the way he created it. R[ichard] complains about how oblivious [*ahnungslos*] the performers are to all there is in it, and he thinks of Schröder-Devrient, how she would have said "*so war es mein Kuss, der hellsichtig dich machte.*" ["So it was the my kiss that made you clairvoyant."] Now the music has to take charge of everything. (*CT* IV, 977)

The memory of Schröder-Devrient's powerful femininity left an indelible mark if some half-century after Wagner first saw her on stage in trousers, he is writing music to revive what she achieved via dramatic gesture in a variety of roles. I say gesture because even Wagner admitted that her voice "had never been an extraordinary vocal instrument" (*ML*, 270). Prefiguring a kind of nineteenth-century Maria Callas, Schröder-Devrient represented to Wagner far more than what she produced lyrically.

Schröder-Devrient's femininity became notorious after her death in 1860 when a German publisher of erotica, Prinz in Hamburg-Altona, issued two versions of an epistolary novel entitled *Aus den Memoiren einer Sängerin* [*From the Memoirs of a Singer*] or, as in another printing by Prinz, *Galante Abenteuer der Sängerin Wilhelmine* [*Galant Adventures of Wilhelmine the Singer*].[24] Though the book appeared in its first edition without a named author, people naturally assumed that Schröder-Devrient had written it. Even today the text is considered—next to Sacher-Masoch's *Venus im Pelz* [*Venus in Fur*]—one of the classic German pornographic novels of the nineteenth century.[25] The "Memoirs" consist of a series of letters written to a male doctor friend, answering his questions about the author's colorful sexual history. It begins with a graphic description of the future diva at the age of fourteen whose life changes the day she surreptitiously observes her parents engaged in exciting conjugal relations on the occasion of her father's birthday. It then moves on to her first sexual experiences with her adventurous female cousin. The voyage of sexual discovery—at least in the first part of the book—is all the more effective because of its convincingly personal tone. The realism of the discourse is enhanced because the author makes observations about sexual practices she finds disgusting, such as the discovery of a coachman and a milkmaid indulging in "desecrated sensuality" in a cow stall, as well as recording her hilarious failures to seduce her rehearsal pianist, Franzl.

The case for Schröder-Devrient's authorship was always spurious. The publisher, August Prinz, seems to have written the text himself, trading unscrupulously on the singer's recent death and dubious reputation, which, as we saw previously, Wagner could not deny. Although Wagner never referred to the *Memoirs*—certainly Cosima makes no reference to them in the diaries destined, after all, for her children—it is likely that he got wind of the scandal when the book was officially banned in Germany in October 1877.[26] His subsequent scattered published remarks about Schröder-Devrient might even constitute an attempt to restore her posthumous reputation, focusing on her artistry and away from her moral standing. Knowing her as he did, he would have found the notion of her writing pornography absurd.

Schröder-Devrient was, in fact, far closer to the Wagnerian school of high-minded erotic sufferers. A host of biographical evidence supports this view, including an authorized book of reminiscences by the feminist writer and translator Claire von Glümer (1825–1906) that appeared after Wilhelmine's death.[27] The hopes Schröder-Devrient pinned on her third marriage in 1850 show her investment in the Romantic enterprise, as in this letter to close friends, which sounds as if it could have been written by Wagner for Elsa in his *Lohengrin*:

> How shall I make it clear to you how Heinrich's appearance in my life's path transformed my entire being? It was worship, adoration which I felt for him and when he raised me up to his heart from my lowliness, there flashed a love in my soul which I'd never before experienced. (*GE*, 121)

The high-minded approach can also be glimpsed in diary entries in which she speaks, for example, of the spiritual gift of her voice as the only religion in which she believes: "My soul has sung a Hallelujah to the Creator as good as in any church—and this Hallelujah came from deep in my breast" (*GE*, 161). Her devotion to High Art can be seen in a letter written to Clara Schumann in 1850:

> I've loved my art and practiced it with sacred enthusiasm—whether I've achieved something, or whether I've passed on something to those who come after me? That's the question!. . . . What is happening to truth, to nature? Where is the godly spark which ignites weak as well as strong minds? Straw fire, repellent unnaturalness, screaming and howling and instead of being shaken to one's depth with holy ardor, one departs lethargic, restless and angry, having thrown away money on gilt decorations and faked fires which fill the emptiness and only cover up the obvious weaknesses in all these concoctions."[28]

Another letter to Clara from 1853 expresses Wilhelmine's outrage at the superficiality of Halévy's *La Juive:* Having just walked out of the performance in Paris, she cries, "What will happen to the holiness of art?" (*GE,* 129–130). These high-minded rants scarcely depict an author who titillates with naughty tales of Lesbian orgies or of pleasurable gropings in cattle stalls.

The main point about Wagner's appreciation of Schröder-Devrient's "daemonic warmth" is not that she symbolized debased carnal love, but rather that she straddled the fuzzy boundary between Romantic love and tragic Eros. As a result, Wagner's promotion of a chaste higher love in his early works can be unmasked as a sham. That is, given his reverence for Schröder-Devrient and what she represented for him as a woman, Wagner must already have suspected that tragedy—whether for Bellini's Romeo or Beethoven's Leonora—was unthinkable without an erotic component. If anything, his castigation of lower sensuality—much like those "really catastrophic affairs of the heart" that she disclosed to him in the 1840s—betrays nothing other than his fascination with it. When Wagner finally reaches his Venusberg, therefore, he undertakes a musical translation of the erotic that is worthy of the importance the subject held in his own mind, even if, like his character Tannhäuser, the composer remained something of a sexual coward.

The vision of Schröder-Devrient not only inspires Wagner's Venus in *Tannhäuser* but also the *Tristan* love duet and the brazen femininity of Kundry, whose smothering kiss from a dominating position of superiority brings worldly clarity to the men she seduces. So much was Schröder-Devrient a cornerstone of Wagner's art that he lived below a specially commissioned image of her found on the portal of his house at Wahnfried. Etched onto its façade in 1874 on the left was a painting of Schröder-Devrient—a *sgrafitto* or "scratched" layer of colored plaster—representing Classical Tragedy balanced on the right by Cosima Wagner as the muse of Music flanking the Young Siegfried. Whereas Wagner found his ideal helpmate in Cosima, onto Wilhelmine he projected an erotic of his own passivity, of a wish, like Tannhäuser's, to relinquish and submit to sexual control. And who occupied the center between Wilhelmine and Cosima Wagner? That would be the first Tristan, Ludwig Schnorr von Carolsfeld, an emblem of one of Wagner's important Romantic friendships, clothed as Wotan the Wanderer flanked by two fluttering ravens. To Ludwig II, Wagner wrote that a copy of the image would be sent to him, and he explains that the Wotan figure is conversing with both women, "relat[ing] the tidings he has received" (*SL*, 842). Although the idea for an historico-mythic scene was apparently Cosima's, she, not surprisingly, was less than enthusiastic about the *sgrafitto*. "I would rather have left our house unadorned," she notes in her diary, but "keep this a secret from R[ichard], who is delighted with the decoration" (*CT* II, 862). Schröder-Devrient had been dead for sixteen years, but Cosima was forced to accept in public the equal standing she shared with her in Wagner's estimation.

Although Wilhelmine Schröder-Devrient was never Wagner's lover—but rather his "great teacher" or "master craftswoman" [*meine grosse Meisterin*] as he refers to her in *Mein Leben*—the vision of his infatuation with her dominant femininity accompanied him throughout his life. As an older man, Wagner encountered another strong and independent-minded woman, the much younger Judith Gautier. Not only does he identify Gautier with Schröder-Devrient but he also finds a way to indulge his fantasies in an erotic correspondence with her, particularly those connected to his penchant for silk, satin, and rose-scented fragrances to be discussed in Chapter 4. These visions and idealizations form important cornerstones of Wagner's erotic world and help guide us to a host of musical and extra-musical representations.

Arthur Schopenhauer

In 1854, Wagner discovered Arthur Schopenhauer's *World as Will and Representation*, an event justly celebrated in the literature as a decisive moment in the composer's life. Although one reads about the philosopher's seminal influence on Wagner's dramatic thinking and aesthetics, it is really with regard to his erotics that Schopenhauer should take center stage. For sexual desire occupies an especially prominent, even hegemonic, place in his philosophy, which makes its first major cultural impact in the 1850s, due in part to Wagner's efforts to promote him. As Schopenhauer put it: "We should be surprised that a matter that generally plays so important a part in the life of man [that is, sexual love] has hitherto been almost entirely disregarded by philosophers, and lies before us as raw and untreated material."[29] As a result of Wagner's enthusiastic reaction to what he read, the composer felt forced to retract his previous positive assessment of Feuerbach, especially that author's optimistic views on Love as expressed in the *Essence of Christianity* and in *Thoughts on Death and Immortality*. Despite Feuerbach's own dismissal of Judaism as excessively utilitarian, selfish, and narrow-minded, there was an added bonus for Wagner in his adoption of Schopenhauer's philosophy. In 1850, the composer had published his often derivative rant called *Judaism in Music* and now read that the target of Schopenhauer's criticism—optimism in general—was a quintessentially Judaic trait: It was the problematic God of Genesis, Schopenhauer repeatedly cites, who surveyed his creation "and saw that it was good," a God who thereby diminishes the importance of human misery and suffering. Yet despite Schopenhauer's repeated criticisms of Judaism, he is very far from exhibiting Wagner's more choleric response. In treating the myth of the Fall of Man, which he reckons, like the whole of Judaism, is borrowed from the *Zend Avesta* (Bundahish, 15), Schopenhauer admits that "it is the only thing" that "reconciles me to the Old Testament" (*SW* II, 580). His fundamental, if crude, objection to Judaism was philosophical rather than racial. As he describes God congratulating himself on his creation:

> But if we proceed to the *results* of the applauded work, if we consider the *players* who act on the stage so durably constructed, and then see how with sensibility pain makes its appearance, and increases in proportion as that sensibility develops into intelligence, and then how, keeping pace with this, desire and suffering come out ever more strongly, and increase, till at last human life affords no other material than that for tragedies and comedies, then whoever is not a hypocrite will hardly be disposed to break out in hallelujahs. (*SW* II, 581)

Wagner's objections to Judaism were more personal than philosophical, and radiate anything but wit. In 1851, he put it to Liszt: "I nursed a long-standing grudge against the Jewish ménage [*Wirtschaft*] and this grudge is as essential to my nature as bile is to blood. The moment came when their damned scribbling really angered me and eventually I exploded" (*SB* III, 544–545). Wagner's letters praising Schopenhauer to Liszt and

August Röckel from 1855 and 1856 show how pleased he was to discover that, in addition to his own ideas on the insidious influence of Judaism on music and arts, there was an even more fatal flaw he hadn't previously detected.[30]

Wagner's intellectual U-turn after delving into Schopenhauer—he worked his way through the two volumes four times within a year—caused him little embarrassment. Not only did he see all kinds of foreshadowing of the Frankfurt philosopher in his own theories, but Schopenhauer conveniently let composers of music off the hook by suggesting that the source of their insights lies with their inner Will and powers of perception, not with logical or rational accounts of their ideas. "Nothing good is achieved through [concepts] in art," Schopenhauer writes, whereas "all genuine art proceeds from knowledge of perception, never from the concept" (*SW* I, 57). Moreover, "the composer reveals the innermost nature of the world, and expresses the profoundest wisdom in a language that his reasoning faculty does not understand" (*SW* I, 260). By 1856, Wagner is parroting this very position to his friend August Röckel: "That which is most unique to us as individuals we owe not to our conceptualizations but our intuitions. . . . Rarely, I believe, has anyone suffered so remarkable a sense of alienation from himself and so great a contradiction between his intuitions and his conceptions as I have done, for I must confess that only now have I really understood my own works of art . . . and I have done so with the help of another person [Schopenhauer] who has furnished me with conceptions that are perfectly congruent with my intuitions" (*SL*, 356–357). For someone with so prolific a gift of the gab, this was quite an admission, and Wagner was happy, for example, to recommend similar ideas on genius to Liszt, oblivious to Liszt's aversion to atheists.

In one sense, though, Schopenhauer's general pardon issued to composers failed to assuage Wagner's conscience, since his poem for the *Ring of the Nibelung*—if no longer headed for an optimistic ending with the gods restored to Valhalla—was still deeply in tow to Feuerbach's ideas on healthy sensual Love, which promiscuously confused sexual lust with every other kind of love: love for the great hero, empathetic love, sisterly love, parental love, even children's love for their parents. As a result, the uniquely destructive power of erotic passion, one of Schopenhauer's central points, got lost in the muddle. For Feuerbach, Love can cause grief, though it is overshadowed by the all-consuming goodness of the overall experience:

> You only exist when you love. Being is only being when the being is that of Love, but at the same time your entire existence, your separate individuation, bases itself in Love. You exist only in the beloved object, everything apart from it; without it you yourself are nothing to yourself. Love is the source of all joys, but also all sorrows.[31]

Wagner later suggested that he had been "taken in" by Feuerbach's confused ideas, but adopted them in the late 1840s because they seemed to mirror the aesthetic idealism the composer came to preach after the failed Dresden uprising. In a later preface (1872) to *Die Kunst und die Revolution* [*Art and Revolution*] (1849), Wagner writes as follows:

> From my reading of some essays by Ludwig Feuerbach, which at the time vividly inspired me, I borrowed various terms which I applied to artistic ideas to which they didn't always clearly correspond. In so doing, I surrendered myself without critical reflection to the guidance of a clever writer who best reflected my mood at the time in the way that he abandoned philosophy (which he believed to be just a disguised form of theology), and turned instead to a grasp of human existence in which I clearly thought I recognized my own view of an artistic individual. From this arose a certain impassioned confusion, which proved itself as both injudicious and obscure in invoking philosophical models. (*SS* III, 3)

In line with this "impassioned confusion," Alberich's renunciation of Love was the same Love he renounced to forge the Ring, the same cursed Love by which Fafner kills Fasolt, the same Love Sieglinde feels for Siegmund, and the same Love Wotan feels for Brünnhilde. Finding himself in October 1854 in the midst of composing the Second Act of *Die Walküre*, Wagner had to hope, in his continual quest for self-justification, that his music would echo the core Schopenhauerian values beyond that of the words in the libretto. Ultimately, as is well known, he hadn't the heart to carry on with this charade past the Second Act of *Siegfried*, and felt drawn instead to the drafts for *Tristan* into which he could dive headlong with his new-found philosophical stirrings.

Wagner's burning interest in Schopenhauer's every word—particularly in the mid-1850s—is well documented, and one idea that surely enthralled him in particular is the link between music and erotic desire. This coupling is less explicit in the first volume that Schopenhauer had written in 1819 but that no one (save Goethe) seems to have read. That earlier tome contained four undifferentiated large-scale chapters together with the exasperating "advice" that the reader will have "to read the book twice (and do so the first time with much patience)" (*SW* I, xxi). But in the spirited and far more digestible second volume (1844), with its fifty-some helpful headings, only two of the chapter titles, those for Chapters 39 and 44, invoke the imposing word "Metaphysics"—the first is *Zur Metaphysik der Musik* [On the Metaphysics of Music], the second, *Metaphysik der Geschlechtsliebe* [Metaphysics of Sexual Love].[32] The striking feature of this parallelism carries over into the treatment of the two subjects, which occur within a few pages of one another.

Schopenhauer argues that, since music lacks clear references to ideal forms (unlike poetry or painting), it doesn't exhibit Ideas of the unconscious Will-to-live, that animal urge to stay alive at all costs and propagate the species. Rather, music is "the most powerful of all the arts" because it "exhibits the Will itself," which is why it acts directly on our "feelings, passions and emotions, so that it quickly arouses these or even alters them" (*SW* II, 448). As he put it in the first volume, music "expresses the metaphysical to everything physical in the world, the thing-in-itself to every phenomenon. Accordingly, we could just as well call the world embodied music as embodied Will. . . . Music . . . gives the innermost kernel preceding all form, or the heart of things" (*SW* I, 262–263). By the metaphysical aspect of music, Schopenhauer means "the inner significance of its achievements" (*SW* II, 450), which are exceedingly remarkable. Unlike the terrors of "real life," where the "Will itself . . . is roused and tormented," music, concerned with its own sonorities, "never causes us actual suffering, but still remains pleasant even in its most painful chords; and we like to hear in its language the secret history of our Will and of all its stirrings and strivings with their many different delays, postponements, hindrances, and afflictions, even in the most sorrowful melodies" (*SW* II, 451). (Wagner parrots the content and rhythm of this text in his prose program for *Tristan*, distributed for the Paris concerts in 1860.) The constant "discord and reconciliation" that occur in music—Schopenhauer goes on to explain—are a "copy of [the origin of] new desires and then of their satisfaction. Precisely in this way, music penetrates our hearts by flattery, so that it always holds out to us the complete satisfaction of our desires" (*SW* II, 454). A contrapuntal suspension "is clearly an analogue of the satisfaction of the Will which is enhanced through delay," and for this reason "music consists generally in a constant succession of chords more or less disquieting, i.e. of chords exciting desire . . . just as the life of the heart (the Will) is a constant succession of greater or lesser disquietude through desire or fear with composure in degrees just as varied" (*SW* II, 455).

How this gnawing metaphysical desire functions in actual life—he asserts only a few chapters later—is felt most profoundly in the sensation of sexual desire:

The sex-relation in the world of mankind . . . is really the invisible central point of all action and conduct, and peeps up everywhere, in spite of all the veils thrown over it. It is the cause of war and the aim and object of peace, the basis of the serious and the aim of the joke, the inexhaustible source of wit, the key to all hints and allusions, and the meaning of all secret signs and suggestions, all unexpressed proposals, and all stolen glances; it is the daily thought and desire of the young and often of the old as well, the hourly thought of the unchaste, and the constantly recurring reverie of the chaste even against their will, the ever ready material for a joke, only because the most profound seriousness lies at its root. . . . Indeed, we see [sexual desire] take its seat at every moment as the real and hereditary lord of the world, out of the fullness of its own strength, on the ancestral throne, look down from there with its scornful glances, and laugh at the arrangements made to subdue it, to imprison it, or at any rate to restrict it and if possible to keep it concealed, or indeed so to master it that it appears only as an entirely subordinate and secondary concern of life. But all this agrees with the fact that the sexual impulse is the kernel of the Will-to-live, and consequently the concentration of all

willing; in the text, therefore, I have called the genitals the focus of
the Will. Indeed it may be said that man is sexual impulse made concrete. (*SW* II, 513–514)

Schopenhauer is even more explicit in his unpublished notebooks:

If I am asked where the most intimate knowledge of that inner essence of the world, of that thing in itself which I have called the Will-
to-live, is to be found, or where that essence enters most clearly into
our consciousness, or where it achieves the purest revelation of itself,
then I must point to ecstasy in the act of copulation. That is it! That
is the true essence and core of all things, the aim and purpose of all
existence.[33]

Schopenhauer's descriptions of sexual desire are astonishing for their
time, and all the more so for the way that the "stirrings and strivings" of
music are conceived as a parallel form of sexual desire, both of which expose the "secret history of the Will." The difference is that in life the
stakes are more extreme. "The sexual impulse," Schopenhauer writes:

is the most vehement of cravings, the desire of desires. . . . accordingly,
its satisfaction, corresponding to the Will of anyone, is the summit
and crown of anyone's happiness, the ultimate goal of his natural
endeavors, with whose attainment everything seems to him to be at-
tained, and with the missing of which everything seems to be missed.
(*SW* II, 514)

Whereas music offers satisfactory conclusions, prospects for sexual fulfillment are grim:

Indeed, [sexual desire] robs of all conscience those who were previously honorable and upright, and makes traitors of those who have
hitherto been loyal and faithful. Accordingly, it appears on the whole
as a malevolent demon, striving to pervert, to confuse, and to over-
throw everything. (*SW* II, 534)

The self-evident superiority, if also brutality of this philosophy of sex over Feuerbach's visions of Love can't be crystallized more succinctly than in Schopenhauer's brilliantly negative conclusions. Sexual longing, the most profound emblem of the Will-to-live creates a unique delusion in which "even this exalted passion is extinguished in the enjoyment, to the great astonishment of those involved in it" (SW II, 550). And "not only . . . does the unsatisfied passion of being in love sometimes have a tragic outcome, but even the satisfied passion leads more often to unhappiness than to happiness" (SW II, 555). Therefore, "because the passion rested on a delusion . . . the individual falls back into his original narrowness and neediness, and sees with surprise that, after so high, heroic, and infinite an effort, nothing has resulted for his pleasure but what is afforded by any sexual satisfaction. Contrary to expectation, he finds himself no happier than before; he notices that he has been the dupe of the Will of the species. For this reason the ancients represented love as blind" (SW II, 557). One can just imagine the spellbound reaction to these passages by a composer writing a *magnum opus* based on unsatisfied passions and tragic outcomes.

Wagner kept Schopenhauer at his bedside for several years and continued to dip into him for the rest of his life, and it is fair to say that from the moment of first acquaintance, all his thinking on love and sexuality—his erotic intentions—are tinged with Schopenhauerian formulas. He even makes explicit his burning interest in Schopenhauer's views of sex in a tantalizing fragment of an unsent letter he drafted to the philosopher in 1858. Commenting on a passage from the chapter on the "Metaphysics of Sexual Love," in which Schopenhauer asks about the seemingly inexplicable communal suicide of a pair of lovers prevented by outward circumstances from consummating their relationship, Wagner writes as if to clear up Schopenhauer's confusion by offering the philosopher what he—Wagner—takes to be a Schopenhauerian resolution. The problem isn't—Wagner implies—that lovers don't take the rational step of escaping the immediate impediments preventing their union and "living happily ever after," but that, in his own experience, "the design [*Anlage*] of sexual love follows a redemptive path [*Heilsweg*] toward the self-recognition and self-abnegation of the Will—and not only of one's individual Will" (SS XII, 291). This statement suggests a Tristanesque—rather than a Schopenhauerian—solution to the conundrum, in which a mutually willed death appears as a kind of substitute for sexual lovemaking. Schopenhauer's own view of sexual union was even more sinister and offers no path whatever to salvation. (In fact the "question" Schopenhauer raised was rhetorical and is addressed later in his chapter, explaining perhaps why Wagner abandoned the letter once he read further into the text.)

Opera, Not Philosophy

Thereafter, whether it is love's frenzy in *Tristan*, the resignation from sexual love in *Meistersinger*, or the hope for a compassionate love in *Parsifal*, Wagner is tangling in one way or another with Schopenhauer's riveting descriptions. Having said this, Wagner is far from a pure disciple of Schopenhauer: To believe otherwise is to turn a gifted composer into a great thinker, whereas, even according to his own assessment, he is a philosopher *manqué*. To claim that *Tristan*, *Meistersinger*, or *Parsifal* transforms Schopenhauer's thought into music is therefore nonsensical. To put it bluntly, *Tristan* is no more a philosophical treatise than *The World as Will and Representation* is an erotic novel.

It is worth reviewing the fundamental differences between aesthetic and philosophical modes of thought. A piece of music, a poem, a painting, even an opera, strives for coherence on the level of its own aesthetic materials. As a matter of course, these materials, as signs within a public domain, invoke all sorts of meanings that we can furnish with names, sources, and contexts. But it is quite another matter to demand of an artwork a similar kind of coherence on the level of its signified ideas, though it is easy to fall into this trap. The error is a simple one committed by those who study the arts: Coherence is demanded of one's own work; one observes coherence in the art work; one investigates an artist's thinking coherently, and then— surprise of surprises—one imputes coherence to the meanings readable in the art work. This last inference is almost always unjustified because artists, as anyone who knows them can tell you, are far too busy devoting themselves to the arduous job of making art to be worrying about a form of coherence that can exist only in someone else's discourse. Rather like the people who made it, an opera projects a glorious sense of its reason and irrationality, its intentions and frustrations, its blindness and insight—in short, its art and humanity.

I belabor this point because Wagner of all people, someone who devours masses of prose and writes it as prolifically, is most often charged
with a host of "coherent" interpretations of his works on the basis of the
hermeneutic trap that commentators have laid for him. So as one explores
his musical erotics after his confrontation with Schopenhauer, we need to
see how, in the hands of Wagner the musician and dramatist, ideas are
worked out in their own way and in their own time. It is less a case of
holding Wagner to any one standard than of responding to the effects of
these impulses in each opera.

In the case of *Tristan*, Wagner was extraordinarily forthcoming in
showing just how loose the link was between Schopenhauer and the ideas
germinating in the opera. As he put it in *Mein Leben:* "It was in part the
serious mood in which Schopenhauer put me, and which now encouraged
an ecstatic expression of its fundamental traits, which inspired me with
the idea for a *Tristan and Isolde*" (*ML*, 594). Rather than analyze, as did
Schopenhauer, "the ecstatic expression" of that "serious mood," Wagner
gave in to it wholly, functioning therefore as one of the philosopher's objects of study, not one of his pupils. This impression is extended by an
equally anti-philosophical if histrionic statement that Wagner made to
Liszt as he was drafting the poem for *Tristan*. It occurs in the same letter
as he begs Liszt to read Schopenhauer and tell Wagner what he thinks of
him: "But since I have never in my life enjoyed the true happiness of love,
I intend to erect a further monument to this most beautiful of all dreams,
a monument in which *this love will be properly sated* [emphasis added] from
beginning to end: I have planned in my head a *Tristan and Isolde*, the sim-
plest, but most full-blooded musical conception; with the 'black flag' that
flutters at the end, I shall then cover myself over, in order—to die—" (*SL*,
323–324). A monument to "properly sated" love cannot possibly adhere to
Schopenhauer's philosophy of sex. Wagner even admits his "emenda-
tions" of Schopenhauer to Mathilde Wesendonck, and in 1858 notes that
he "reached conclusions which complement and correct my friend Schopenhauer. But I prefer to ruminate on such matters rather than to write
them down" (*SL*, 434).

In fact, while composing the music for *Tristan* in 1858, Wagner's statement of artistic intent turns Schopenhauer on his head by rearing once
again the notion of a "redemptive path" for sexual union:

It is really a matter of proving—something no philosopher has done, not even Schopenhauer—that the recognized redemptive path [*Heilsweg*] to the complete pacification of the Will is through Love, and in fact not an abstract human love but rather by means of sexual love, that is, a love germinating in the attraction between man and woman.[34]

Far from being doomed to failure and eternal disappointment as in Schopenhauer's clear exposition, Wagner's notion of sexual love becomes a means to assuage the gnawing desires of the Will-to-live. Even Schopenhauer admitted in his second volume that there is a difference between understanding renunciation as a philosopher and practicing it as an ascetic mystic, a statement that undercuts the effect of his philosophical conclusions, since he is unable to subscribe in practice to the only remedy he can devise to cope with the pesky Will-to-live. Perhaps Wagner intended to air a legitimate criticism of Schopenhauer's unconvincing pseudo-Buddhist account of renunciation. But as soon as one examines the composer's assertion about sexual love, its logical inconsistency becomes glaring. For if sexual desire (according to Schopenhauer) embodies the essence of the Will-to-live, it is nonsense to allow sexual love to pacify the Will. It is like giving whiskey to cure an alcoholic, or pornography to treat a sexual obsessive.

Here we come to the heart of Wagner's erotic impulse. For what makes for a nonsensical thesis sparks an astonishingly wonderful opera. And why should this inconsistency be so implausible? After all, it expresses a psychological truth accepted even by Schopenhauer, namely that feelings both exciting and delusional descend on human beings the moment they fall in love. "This time," they say, "I shall escape my misery and everything will turn out all right." Rather than having digested the content of Schopenhauer's dismal philosophy, Wagner pilfered it to expunge the last vestiges of puritanical censure that had characterized his earlier erotics. Considering the exhilarating if also unconsummated affair he had embarked upon with Mathilde Wesendonck—not to mention his later scandalous if sexually unadventurous liaison with Cosima—this change of heart turned out to be rather useful. But despite his most strenuous intellectual efforts, Wagner hadn't, after all, escaped his Feuerbachian,

indeed, "Judaic" optimism. Until the end of his days he continued to modu-
late between two musico-erotic themes—the idealistic, Romantic vision
of love the redeemer and the darkly obsessive vision of sex as curse. Both
of these views crystallize in Wagner's musical erotics, as first heard in
Tannhäuser.

CHAPTER THREE

Harmonies

Before *Tannhäuser*, it is fair to say, Wagner never aimed to compose music with erotic harmonies; music, that is, that represents sexual arousal. *Das Liebesverbot* (1836) nodded in this direction when it cast a chromatic pall on a hypocritical villain whose guilty thoughts turned to fornication, but thereafter, Wagner steered clear of sexually charged topics for almost a decade. His *Rienzi* (1842), for example, showed little interest in sexual love. The title character sings a brief ariette on the chaste affection for his sister Irene, and there is an exciting if aborted abduction scene, but Adriano and Irene's declarations of passion ape all the clichés of grand opera, even though the lovers are played by two women. Perhaps Wagner expected Schröder-Devrient's passionate gestures to spark Adriano's erotic ardor.

Der Fliegende Holländer

In the *Flying Dutchman* (1843), too, Wagner missed a perfect opportunity to develop his musical erotics because the drama centers on Senta's infatuation with the "wandering Jew of the ocean."[1] The literary source—a comic pseudo-memoir by Heinrich Heine that Wagner later pretended not to know—even included an amusing if very low-brow erotic interlude in Amsterdam, in which the narrator interrupts his viewing of a theatrical rendition of the fable by making off with a rapacious Dutch blonde for a sexual "quickie" before returning to catch the tragic ending of the play, where "Mrs. Flying Dutchman" throws herself off a high cliff as "a sure way to keep faith" with her husband unto death (*HW* IV, 83). Although Wagner could scarcely have wished to set Schnabelewopski's titillating escapade in a serious Romantic opera, he might well have imbued Senta or the Dutchman with some musico-erotic fervor. Instead, he shrinks from the merest suggestion that his protagonists act on the basis of their "lower" sexual instincts. Whatever dramatic overtones of sexual obsession color one's understanding of Senta's mesmeric trance—or are brought into the rendition of her role—Wagner's music for her ballad ensures her unsullied purity of feeling, a "mixture of prayer and lament," as he describes it in his prose program for the Overture (*SS* V, 176).

Right from the beginning, Senta was to represent the ideal of a woman's fanatic loyalty. Yet Senta, Wagner writes, was also to embody a "powerful madness as is peculiar to those [Nordic girls] of quite naïve natures" (*JA* II, 50). The trance-like yodel of her invocatory first phrase is meant to strike a strange, even mad tone. The more cooing second phrase evokes a prayerful innocence and wistful sadness, but certainly nothing desirous or yearning. And even as her obsession reaches a fevered pitch in the Ballad's final strain—at least this is what Mary and the girls of the Spinning Chorus believe—Wagner serves up the noble heroics of his *Rienzi*, which, like a battle call in the service of a righteous cause, reinforces Senta's high-minded intentions in the sharpened, commanding rhythms of her *cabaletta*. No doubt this modulation of mood recalling Adriano proved congenial in the first production to Schröder-Devrient, who had sung the heroic trouser role before assuming that of the infatuated Norwegian maiden.

The anguish of the tormented Dutchman, by contrast, receives a splendid musical portrait embellished in Wagner's depiction of every subsequent sufferer, from Tannhäuser to Siegmund, Tristan, Kundry, Amfortas, and Parsifal. Yet the Dutchman, too, like Senta, steers clear of Eros in recounting his ordeal that, in keeping with German versions of the legend, results from a vague religious apostasy rather than any carnal sin. As Vanderdecken puts it, his ghostly ship is the "horror of every pious person" [*das Schrecken aller Frommen*]. Having taunted the Devil about the seaworthiness of his vessel, the Dutchman paid the price in tempting fate for his arrogance by his eternal banishment at sea. The vagueness of his condition also mirrors popular legends (circulating in the German *Vormärz*) about characters suffering from a *Weltschmerz*, or world weariness, in which "existence as such becomes our misfortune," as Dieter Borchmeyer has characterized it.[2] The religious, rather than erotic, accent in Wagner's Dutchman means that even as the protagonist is overcome each seventh year with the desire for a woman who might redeem him, he yearns not for a sexual union, but for redemption in death gained through her fidelity. "The old yearning grips him anew," Wagner writes, and Daland's description of his daughter revives in the Dutchman his desire "for redemption through a woman's loyalty" (*JA* II, 47). Nor does Senta's union with the Dutchman promise much fun for either of them: "Oh, if you only suspected what fate you'll have to share with me, you'd be warned against the sacrifice you offer in swearing loyalty to me. Your youthful vigor [*Jugend*] would flee in horror from the lot you wish to choose" (Act II, sc. iii). Once the curse on the Dutchman is lifted as a result of Senta's ecstatic leap into the open sea, the lovers—we need remind ourselves—do not set off for the Venusberg.

Only Erik, Senta's hot-tempered if feeble suitor, dares—briefly and elliptically—to call a spade a spade. Senta's sympathy for the Dutchman is, he says, nothing other than *eine Schwärmerei:* "Will you not call a halt to this infatuation?" Erik demands of her. She has—he claims—"shunned the wound which her behavior has inflicted on *his* 'love-sickness' [*Liebeswahn*]," although the fact that he levels this charge during the course of a comely four-square cavatina makes it difficult to take his erotic anguish seriously. Only in the stirring account of his Dream does Erik hint at the sexual core underlying Senta's infatuation. In this idealized version of Senta's own fantasy—Wagner's stage directions implausibly ask her to "sink into a magnetic sleep so that it seems she too dreams the same dream he recounts" (*SS* I, 276)—Erik sees Senta "collapsed at the foot of a stranger, hugging his knees." After being raised up, she "hung onto him full of ardor and kissed him with hot desire." "And then?"—Senta asks, anxious for the end of the story. Erik looks at her "astonished" because her shameful question surely requires an unmentionable answer, and while two bassoons prolong his moral censure with a musical ellipsis, he jumps to the end of the tale in which he sees her "fleeing out to sea." Senta, however, clearly reads the erotic subtext of Erik's evasion, for she "is quickly aroused to the highest ecstasy," according to Wagner's stage directions. For his part, Erik experiences an equally hysterical reaction in which he "collapses in complete horror" and exits the stage to the blaring of horrified diminished seventh chords in the orchestra. Wagner has composed music that is strong on censure but weak on arousal.

Yet even the manifest sexual content in Erik's Dream fails to inspire Senta's first encounter with the Dutchman in the very next scene. Left alone by Daland, the two protagonists "remain motionless in their places, absorbed in mutual contemplation." No histrionic flinging to the ground, no hugging of the Dutchman's knees, not a single hot kiss. The nearest the Dutchman comes to her is "one or two steps" from where he first stood. Neither does either character traffic in euphemism or erotic allusion in this odd love scene. Instead, Senta proclaims "a woman's sacred duties" to put her beloved out of his suffering and to "dedicate herself to her one gift: loyalty unto death!" Sounding more like a palliative nurse administering a lethal injection than a lover sacrificing herself to the object of her infatuation, Senta ensures that a de-sexualized interpretation of her madness prevails by the end of the opera. Even Erik, at the climax of the opera, calls for Senta to be rescued from taking her own life, not saved from sexual slavery or moral perdition.

Wagner thus insulated the *Dutchman* from Eros, although, given his later view that Kundry incarnated aspects of the Wandering Jew, an allusion to sensuality might well have crossed his mind even in 1840. Such a thought did occur to him in 1860: When writing to Mathilde Wesendonk in the midst of composing the Second Act of *Tristan*, Wagner notes how he, like his Dutchman, yearns for rest and a home, not "the wanton pleasures of love" (*SL*, 397). Given this urge for respite above all else, any overtly sexual overtone would have compromised the nobility of the Dutchman's character. Only in tacking on a Tristanesque harmonic progression to the conclusion of the Overture (and to the conclusion of the opera) in 1860 did Wagner hint at a regret that the *Holländer* failed to share in the erotic insights of the 1850s. But unlike *Tannhäuser*'s Venusberg, the musical vocabulary of *Der fliegende Holländer* was simply too old-fashioned to be updated in any credible way.

Tannhäuser

By contrast, *Tannhäuser* (1845), which succeeded the *Dutchman*, was composed, we are told, in a "state of all-consuming and lascivious arousal." The pendulum had swung back to his "true nature"—Wagner claimed— "as in a violent and lusty embrace" (*JA* VI, 253). His erotically charged mood coincided, moreover, with his ever deepening friendship with the flamboyant Schröder-Devrient, for whom—after Adriano and Senta—he concocted a third leading role: Venus. While one might smile at the idea that a single erotic mood colored the composition of an entire opera, Wagner's admission suggests that erotic stimulation contributes to the opera's themes and their treatment. There is even good evidence of a link between Schröder-Devrient and the impetus for *Tannhäuser*, in that Wagner first drafted a prose sketch (in her honor) for an opera to be called *The Saracen Woman* [*Die Sarazenin*]. Schröder-Devrient rejected the idea because "the artist didn't want to abandon her [own] notion of Woman [*das Weib*]," a "secure instinct," Wagner says, which he later conceded was correct (*JA* VI, 250–252). The idea to compose an arresting portrayal of the character of Venus struck him shortly thereafter.

The symbolic importance of Venus for the opera *Tannhäuser* has been curiously overlooked in the literature. Although eventually called *Tannhäuser and the Singing Competition on the Wartburg* [*Tannhäuser und der Sängerkrieg auf Wartburg*], the original conception bore the far more provocative, even obscene title, *The Mount of Venus* [*Der Venusberg*]. Indeed, every word of the text had been penned before Wagner decided to rename the opera *Tannhäuser*. As he noted in a letter to Samuel Lehrs in Paris,[3] who had supplied him with literary background reading on the Wartburg song competition: "The text to the *Venusberg* is finished: this summer [the music] will be composed" (*SB* II, 235). That was in April 1843. By June he was already referring to the opera as *Tannhäuser* in a letter to Robert Schumann (*SB* II, 275). Interestingly, Wagner later asserted in *Mein Leben* (*ML*, 355) that he changed the title later only after his publisher pointed out to him that people were making "the most disgusting jokes" about his title, especially the teachers and students at the medical clinic in Dresden, where the Latin expression *mons Veneris* was common parlance for the female pubic region. Whatever the exact chronology of his alteration, Wagner shows that he remained sentimentally attached to the original title: *Der Venusberg*. But why call this opera *The Mount of Venus?* Given a scenario in which the minnesinger Heinrich Tannhäuser escapes the court of Venus, pursues the love of Elisabeth in a song competition, and seeks redemption from the Pope for his sexual wanderings, it seems odd that Wagner should ever have alighted on the original title. The Venusberg, after all, names the realm of the pagan goddess of Love who fled to a subterranean cave beneath the Hörselberg, a mountain in Thuringia where the protagonist Tannhäuser has taken only temporary refuge. Not only does the title diminish the importance of the saintly Elisabeth but it also ignores the opera's conclusion when Tannhäuser is redeemed from the Pope's curse.

The *Venusberg* was in one way the key to Wagner's initial poetic conception, which intended to reconcile two contrasting images: the immoral sensuality of the Venusberg and the salvation of religious redemption. Wagner clarifies this intention in an explanatory program for the *Tannhäuser* Overture (written in 1852). Here he claims that the final rendition of the Pilgrim's Chorus in the overture "is the exultation of the Venusberg itself, redeemed from the curse of sinfulness, which we hear amid the holy hymn" (*JA* II, 107). Sounding more like a publicist for *Parsifal* than for *Tannhäuser*, he concludes: "So all the pulses of life well up and spring into a song of redemption; and both segregated elements, spirit and senses, God and Nature, are entangled in the hallowed kiss of uniting Love" (*JA* II, 105–107). Rather than reject sexual desires as unholy, Wagner means to elevate them.

This point is missed by many commentators, who assert that Wagner's conception of love in *Tannhäuser* is firmly rooted in an antipode. Sven

Friedrich, for example, suggests that "Eros and renunciation are *a priori* separated: Tannhäuser's decadent state with Venus represents the erotic principle, while Elisabeth's renunciation offers the exact opposite [*den Gegenpol*] which succeeds vicariously for Tannhäuser."[4] Indeed, it is easy to see how Wagner's libretto obscured his intention. The final chorus of Young Pilgrims (that concludes the earliest textbook version of 1845) speaks of how "redemption newly blossoms for the sinner in hell's fire" but fails to mention love. A later couplet Wagner composed (and sung by the full chorus) which is contained in all later versions (from 1847 onward) tries to improve on this message by asserting that the "penitent receives the salvation of grace as he is now received into a blessed peace" (*JA* II, 98–99), yet these lines stop short of making explicit his desired reconciliation of carnality and spirit.

Whatever the thematic confusion at the end of the opera, Wagner made a point of identifying the reconciliation between spirituality and sensuality as it occurs in the overture to the First Act. It takes place, he says, in the passage depicting a "whirring and rustling" that, once superimposed over the Pilgrims' theme, is transformed into a unified vision of hallowed bliss. (This passage can be heard in the Dresden versions of the Overture at m. 309 just as the triangle, cymbals, and tambourine stop playing.) As Wagner describes the passage:

The storm dies down. Only a lustful, sorrowful whirring livens the air, a forbidding wanton rustling spreads over the place, like the breath of an unholy, sensuous lust upon which the ravished unhallowed magic manifests itself and upon which night now falls. But already the morning is dawning: from the remote distance one again hears strains of the pilgrims' hymn approaching. As this hymn draws ever nearer, and as day gradually extinguishes night, there is also an intensification of that whirring and rustling of the winds, which previously seemed to us like a dreadful lament, but which now appear in the form of more joyous waves, so that, as the sun finally rises in its majesty, and as the pilgrims' hymn declares with powerful enthusiasm to all existence that salvation has been won, the wave swells into the heavenly din of inflamed sublimity. (*JA* II, 106–107)

The idea of overcome and ennobled erotics lies at the heart of this opera. Perhaps one can forgive literary commentators their misapprehension that religion vanquished rather than embraced the carnal realm because Wagner also seems to have had misgivings about how best to represent the reconciliation. At least this may explain his change of heart about the title of the opera. Perhaps to himself he admitted some degree of failure in working out an artistic solution that did justice to the ideas motivating the opera.

Erotics in the Literary Sources

The specific flavor of *Tannhäuser*'s erotics emerges with great clarity when one watches how Wagner tampered with his literary sources. As a boy, he read Ludwig Tieck's *The Loyal Eckart and Tannenhäuser* [*Der getreue Eckart und der Tannenhäuser*] (1799), and he returned to the fairy-tale novella in 1842 as a source for the opera. But Wagner grew critical of what he calls *The Loyal Eckart*'s "Roman Catholic frivolity"— not noticing that the writer was a Lutheran!—and disapproved of its mocking twists and turns (*JA* VI, 242). After Tieck's Tannenhäuser tells of his sexual sojourn in the Venusberg, for example, his friend Friedrich breaks the spell of his tale by showing him that the supposed pretexts for Tannenhäuser's departure—his unrequited love for Friedrich's wife, the pious Elisabeth-like Emma, and his struggles with his Wolfram-like friend—hadn't existed. Tannenhäuser, Friedrich says, has concocted the entire episode in a state of delusion:

> Everything you've told me is only a figment of your imagination. For Emma is still alive, she is my wife, and never have you and I fought or hated one another as you believe; in fact you disappeared from the district before we married, but even back then you never breathed a single word that you were in love with Emma.
>
> Thereupon he took the befuddled Tannenhäuser by the hand and led him into another room to his wife, who had come back to the palace, having been away for several days visiting her sister. Tannenhäuser was silent and pensive. He beheld in calmness the figure and countenance of the lady; then shook his head and said, "By God, this is the strangest of all the incidents that have ever befallen me."[5]

No fan of ironic plot reversals, Wagner saw little to admire in this casual wave of the hand that undid all the work that went into creating the magic of Tieck's literary Venusberg. For what gripped Wagner the librettist were the fantastic descriptions in Tannenhäuser's narration before the author debunked them. First there were the desires for rose scents that fuelled the erotic obsession driving the protagonist to the Venusberg:

> An unutterable yearning for roses seized me, I couldn't hold myself back, I forced my way through the iron rods, and was now in a garden. At once I fell down and embraced the bushes with my arms, kissed the roses on their red mouths, my eyes flooded with tears. (*TW*, 129)

Then there was the image of a secret mine where, in addition to the luxurious precious metals, Tannenhäuser hears a subliminal kind of seductive music:

> My path now descended into an underground mine. The passageway was so narrow that I had to edge my way through. I heard the sound of hidden meandering waters, I heard ghosts formed by the ores and gold and silver, created so as to seduce the human spirit, and I found the deep sounds and tones weird and cryptic, from which terrestrial music arises; the deeper I went, the more it felt as if a veil had been draped over my face. (*TW*, 133)

These evocative images play directly into Wagner's textual and musical imagery. Tieck's erotic images also surface in Wagner's stage directions and in his 1852 prose program for the *Tannhäuser* Overture, as one can see from the following passage from Tieck's novella:

> A bevy of naked girls surrounded me invitingly, perfumes swirled magically around my head, as out of the most intimate heart of nature there resounded a music which cooled with its fresh waves the yearning of wild carnal desire. A terror, which crept so stealthily across the fields of flowers, heightened the ravishing noise. (*TW*, 133)

Another important source for the opera—if famously unacknowledged by Wagner—is Heinrich Heine's essay *Elemental Spirits* (1836), in which the poet enthuses over the erotics of the medieval *Tannhäuser-Lied* before producing his own rendition of the verse in archaic style (*HW* V, 309–374). (Heine explains that he only knew seventeenth-century versions of the medieval ballad.) Apart from the *Song of Songs*, he considered the *Tannhäuser-Lied* "the most flaming song of tenderness" ever penned (*HW* V, 365). Especially important for Wagner is Heine's prose description of the love-goddess Venus, who "when her temple was destroyed, fled into a secret mountain where she leads an adventurous life of joys with the most mirthful airy band, with beautiful forest and water nymphs, also some famous heroes who have suddenly disappeared from the world" (*HW* V, 360). These are characters who are missing from the medieval sources but who populate Wagner's ballet. (Later, the Grail Knights seduced by Klingsor's Flower-Maidens in Wagner's *Parsifal* will likewise "fail to come back from their journey," having been lured to a "wonderful forest of flowering trees" of "never before-seen splendor," out of which "pour all around magically sweet birdsong and intoxicating perfumes.")[6] For Heine, the overt eroticism associated with the pagan gods promotes "Hellenic mirth, love of beauty, and a flourishing lust for life" as opposed to "an over-intellectual Judaism afraid of sensuality or a Christianity crippled by a disembodied asceticism" (*HW* V, 354). It is Heine's idea of Classical hedonism that underlies Wagner's Naiads or water nymphs and his Bacchants, the Maenads or wood-nymphs, along with the male partners in the "loving pairs" who figure in the *Tannhäuser* ballet, all of whom engage in wild ritual dancing as part of Venus's entourage.

Wagner also drew on the erotic imagery in E. T. A. Hoffmann's *Der Kampf der Sänger* (1819), which serves as the source for *Tannhäuser*'s song competition itself. In Hoffmann's account of the competition, Heinrich began to sing songs that "attacked the ladies at court with shameful and contemptuous words, and that continued to praise the beauty and purity of Dame Mathilde alone in a heathen and heinous manner."[7] One also reads of Nasias, who is in the service of the "spirit of lies": Master Klingsohr. (*Klingsaere* means "itinerant musician" in Middle High German.) Nasias has just lost a contest with Wolfframb von Eschinbach and "now began a song about the beautiful Helena and about the surging pleasures of the Mount of Venus. In fact, the song sounded downright seductive, as if the flames that Nasias sprayed on himself had turned into lascivious longings and fragrances smelling of sexual lust, in which the sweet tones rocked up and down, like flittering gods of Love" (*HW*, 306). The sound of seductive melodies (and scent of erotic fragrances) that cause such an uproar at court play directly into the *Tannhäuser* libretto, despite Wagner's claim that Hoffmann "had a distorted view of this old material."[8] It was actually the literary scholar named C. T. L. Lucas who supposed that the Tannhäuser who sojourned in the Venusberg and the minnesinger Heinrich von Ofterdingen who sang in the singing competition were one and the same person: Wagner read Lucas approvingly, most likely because there is an erotic subtext in both stories.

The literary background sheds light on what Wagner was up to in crafting his arresting *musical* imagery for the Venusberg in 1843, for musical ideas, he insists, preceded the opera libretto. (There are also even surviving sketches for musical leitmotives.)[9] A year later, he described his compositional process in a letter to a Berlin journalist:

> It is not that I choose some arbitrary subject matter, put it in verse, and then consider how I want to compose appropriate music for it. . . . My manner of production is . . . different: first a subject attracts me only when it displays—not merely its poetic but also *simultaneously*—its musical significance. Before I even begin to script a line of verse, or sketch out a scene, I am already intoxicated with the musical fragrance of my creation: I have all the notes, all the characteristic motives in my head so that, when then the poetry is complete and the scenes are ordered, the *actual* opera is also already finished and the detailed musical treatment is more a tranquil and careful reworking [*Nacharbeit*]. (*SB* II, 358)

Wagner goes on to claim that music joined to poetry gets at the heart of the aesthetic experience: "If the contemporary task of the dramatic poet is to clarify and spiritualize the material interests of our time from a moral standpoint," he writes, "then it is left to the opera poet and composer to conjure up the most sacred poetry in a fragrance wholly its own [*in dem ganzen ihr eigenen Dufte*] which wafts [*anweht*] toward us from the legends and history of the past, for here music provides the means to a combination forbidden to the poet alone, mostly dependent as he is on our actors." As for *Tannhäuser*, he continues: "With this subject matter, I believe it will become entirely clear how only a musician can treat it" (*SB* II, 359).

A Tour of the Venusberg

The characteristic motives that comprise the musical fragrance of the Venusberg are easy to identify because Wagner makes no secret of the links between the music and the central images underlying his depiction. By consulting his stage directions, libretto and subsequent prose program for the Overture, one can reconstruct Wagner's first musico-erotic tableau for this opening scene of the opera. Given the composer's famous economy of means by which motives recur throughout an opera, the sense of what the musical signs are meant to convey is easy to decipher. In fact, one can readily assemble a musical guide to Wagner's Venusberg to tour its main attractions. (See Example 3–1.)

First there is the Venusberg itself, the magic mine dedicated to the pleasures of love. (The motive is twice named by Tannhäuser, in Act II, sc. iv and Act III, sc. iv, by the Chorus in Act II, and in Wagner's prose program of 1852.) With its shimmering high orchestration of repeated notes in the strings, its asymmetrical syncopations, and two dotted figures with their contrasting stresses, the Venusberg evokes an airy realm of erotic myth and magic. The music's unpredictability is ingenious, considering how its harmonic idiom makes do with nothing more complicated than diminished seventh chords. Sustained throughout by a pedal tone, the progression features two chromatic lines—one rising, one falling—converging in an irregular pattern as if being squeezed together within a musical palindrome. It is a delicious effect, and the Venusberg can still send shivers up the spine. One sees how effective this motive is when Wagner embeds it, as he often does, in a harrowing sequence that rises by minor thirds.

One can search in vain for a similar musical *frisson* in the contemporary works of Mendelssohn, Schumann or Liszt, but there is really nothing else quite like the Venusberg snippet. In 1845, Robert Schumann wrote Felix Mendelssohn a letter, shaking his head over the recent publication of the

Tannhäuser score, chock full, he grumbles, of forbidden parallel fifths and octaves. But after hearing the opera in performance (November 22, 1845), he admitted to Mendelssohn that he had to "take back some of what he'd written after . . . reading the score: everything seems rather different when presented onstage [*von der Bühne stellt sich alles ganz anders dar*]. I was deeply moved [*ganz ergriffen*] by a lot of it."[10] As for Clara Schumann, she notes in her diary: "I can't agree with Robert—for me, this just isn't music—though I wouldn't exclude the possibility of Wagner making a great career as a dramatist. At best I keep quiet about Wagner, because I can't really speak against my conviction and feel not even the slightest scintilla of sympathy for this composer" (*LK* II, 109). Given her later reactions to *Tristan*, one wonders whether her antipathy to Wagner's self-aggrandizing manner as well as to his brazenly erotic themes didn't blind her to *Tannhäuser*'s musical achievements.

The Venusberg theme often appears in tandem with another simple two-bar phrase that Tannhäuser refers to as the Balmy Breezes. "Don't you feel the *milden Lüfte?*," he asks Wolfram. The Balmy Breezes include both a visual and an olfactory dimension, as in "the rosy mist" (Act I), and "the pleasing scents" (Act III), and boast pairs of thirds that waft in wave-like patterns that cannot easily be sung: They signify Nature rather than the human voice.

On the other hand, the motive's close cousin, the Call of the Sirens, takes one of the Breezes' internal shapes and sets it to the words of the Sirens who entice men with their seductive invocation to "approach the shore where your desires will be fulfilled in the arms of torrid Love." They manage this, despite calling from deep within the Hörselberg and no longer from the Aegean islands or, even like the Loreley, positioned on high cliffs overlooking the Rhine. The Sirens seduce via a lush accented chord that falls on their strongest beat, producing what is surely meant to evoke a voluptuous dissonance. The tonal and melodic closure of the phrase suggests that satisfaction will be obtained in the most pleasant possible manner.

Then there is Venus herself, who sings a sixteen-bar melody of seduction to Tannhäuser. When the theme appears in the Overture, Wagner describes it as signaling "Venus herself," "an inexpressibly alluring female form" who "promises the adventurer the satisfaction of his wildest desires." Tannhäuser himself names her melody in Act III, iii, as he sings, "To you Lady Venus I return, in the magic of your holy night, to your court I climb down."

Venus also makes use of her own disembodied Call, nearly a melodic inversion of the Sirens' invocation. The texts linked to this motive are all tied to the goddess's seductive powers, the "divine elixir" (Act I, sc. ii) that Tannhäuser sipped from her lips or his recollection of the "bliss and delight" (Act III, sc. iii) she bestowed on him. There is also an eight-measure cadential phrase proper to Venus depicting "the blissful fervor [*wonnige Gluth*]" enjoyed by Tannhäuser, named as such by Venus in Act I, sc. ii. This phrase harmonizes a falling chromatic fourth, binding its imagery to the lascivious chromaticism of the Venusberg. In one particularly inspired passage, Venus sings her song and her cadential phrase of bliss while the solo violin intones her siren call.

Next come the erotic creatures who inhabit the Venusberg, the water and wood nymphs, and those figures Wagner calls "the loving pairs," mythic duos of lovers danced by couples from the *corps de ballet*. (The Grail Knights as lovers of the Flower-Maidens in *Parsifal*, as mentioned, manifest the same idea much later.) Wagner crafts three distinct images for the Venusberg inhabitants: the Voluptuous Dance, Jubilant Shouts, and Bacchantic Rapture.

In the Voluptuous Dance, Wagner depicts the "frenzied," "drunken" and "raging" gestures of the assembled nymphs whose "whirlings of a fearfully voluptuous dance" are heard in a macabre theme built on the resolution of a diminished seventh chord to a major triad. (For the Paris production, Wagner characterized this music as a "mythological can-can.")[11]

Next there are the militant dotted figures emitted by those engaged in the wild orgy of the Bacchanal, which he names as Jubilant Shouts in the prose program. In fact, Wagner makes it easier to identify this theme in his original version of 1845, as Tannhäuser names them in his rhetorical question to Wolfram in Act III, sc. iii—"Don't you hear the jubilant sounds?"– just as the orchestra sounds the theme.[12] In the 1847 revisions, in which the character Venus (and not merely her ghostly presence) reappears, Wagner sacrificed this clear link he had earlier established, sensing perhaps that it was less necessary now that he had crafted a more vivid dramatic scene.

Finally, there is the music for the drunken Bacchantic Rapture that revels in a repeated motivic cell, a swooning octave fall, and a wild upward leap of a diminished seventh. Its rapture is projected within a rising spiral of sequences. As Wagner describes this music in the prose program: "Heart and senses burn within him; a torrid, blistering passion fires the blood in all his veins; with irresistible force it thrusts him nearer" (*JA* II, 106). And as Tannhäuser puts it (beginning with the 1847 version) in Act III, sc. iii: "Rapture courses through my senses [*Entzücken dringt durch meine Sinne*]." The thrusting passion is depicted in consecutive diminished seventh chords (at *un poco accelerando*), and it is fascinating to see how a traditional trope of Romantic opera that expressed the increasing danger of an ominous presence now represents the intensification of an equally dangerous erotic passion. The sequence, however, not only rises by step, but then stays fixated on a melodic motive suspended over a pedal as a gesture of obsession—the dominant-seventh chord with the added ninth functioning as an appoggiatura. And if that weren't enough, the fall of the leaning note down a whole-step coincides with quick syncopations of excited hyperventilation. (So no rest here, either for the weary or the erotically stimulated!) Together with a notated *accelerando* marked in the Overture, the Bacchantic Rapture is a simulacrum of frenzied desire.

Safely excluded from the erotic landscape is Tannhäuser's pleading and profoundly un-arousing Hymn to Venus, composed in a grand heroic mode. As the stage directions state, "Tannhäuser, emboldened to a sudden resolve, takes up his harp and presents himself ceremonially before Venus." And despite the fact that Venus has invited Heinrich to sing it so as to recall how he won over the goddess in the first place, Wagner intended each strophe of the *Venuslied* in the end "to challenge the wanton magic of the Venusberg" (*JA* II, 106), as he put it in the prose program.[13]

Scanning the geographical expanse of Wagner's Venusberg, one discovers a region never before surveyed in music. On the one hand are the stock, "lower" characters from Classical mythology who, exempt from the restrictions of Christianity, engage in raucous sexual activity. Their playful shouts and animal-like gestures evoke depraved devotees of free love, but they do not represent characters who hawk their wares erotically. To do this, the frenzied Naiads would have to offer something more enticing than shrill clarinets and oboes blaring their crass appoggiaturas in the Voluptuous Dance. In a sense, the music of these Classical revelers represents the most old-fashioned form of eroticism, which depicts the activities of those succumbing to their basest instincts. Like the nymphs and satyrs in canvasses by Titian or Poussin, Wagner uses them to paint a lascivious backcloth for the Venusberg, hence the later reference (for the Ballet Master in Paris) to a *Can-can mythologique,* an invented notion that plays on the breathless footwork introduced into Paris in 1830 that allowed young couples great improvisatory freedom. The can-can's most characteristic step was a kick of the legs as high as possible, thereby exposing the women's laced petticoats in what was seen as indecorous and shocking behavior.[14]

Wagner crafts especially novel markers of the erotic for the music connected with Venus, the Sirens, and the Bacchantic Rapture. In contrast to the themes associated with the nymphs and revelers, these motives explore the interior feel of sexual stimulation: the shivers that accompany erotic attraction, the cooing sounds of seduction, the symptoms of rising passion, the compulsive fixations, even the languishing sighs of fulfillment. By embodying gestures in legible musical signs, Wagner provokes explicit erotic thoughts, even in the opera's earliest incarnations in versions from 1845–1847. So successful is the creation of his erotic universe that the overall drama of the opera, one can argue, suffers as a result. For after all the excitement toward the end of Act III as Tannhäuser announces his intention to make his way back to the Venusberg, and Wolfram shudders in horror, Wagner's listeners are scarcely likely to hope that Tannhäuser will rebuff the love-goddess so as to ensure his religious redemption. Next to Wolfram's prudery, the musical Venusberg is well-nigh irresistible. However much Wagner's libretto moralizes against "wanton sensuality," the dramatic inclinations in his music recommend it without qualification. While the conclusion to *Tannhäuser* falls prey to a fatal *dramatic* flaw, what occurs just before the end marks the inauguration of an erotic high style never before heard in European music.

With hindsight, having completed *Tristan und Isolde* and contemplating the revisions of the ballet for the Paris *Tannhäuser* in 1860, Wagner disparaged his accomplishment of the mid-1840s. Writing to Mathilde Wesendonck, he notes:

> This court of Frau Venus was the palpable weak spot in my work: without a good ballet in its day, I had to manage with a few coarse brush-strokes, and thereby ruined much; for I left this Venusberg with an altogether tame and ill-defined impression, consequently depriving myself of the momentous background against which the ensuing tragedy is to build up its harrowing tale. All later reminiscences and warnings, whose grave significance should send a shudder through us (the only explanation of the plot), lost almost all effect and meaning: dread and instant trepidation kept aloof from our minds. But I also recognize that, when I wrote my *Tannhäuser*, I could not have made anything like what is needed here; it required a greater mastery, by far, which I only now have attained: having written Isolde's last transfiguration, at last I could find the right close for the *Flying Dutchman* Overture and also—for the horrors [*das Grauen*] of this Venusberg. (*MWE*, 220)[15]

Having forgotten his original intention to redeem sensuality from the curse of sinfulness, Wagner now emphasizes to Mathilde—and perhaps exaggerates—the shudders of horror the Venusberg was supposed to evoke. Whatever the intended effect of the Dresden Venusberg, it is true that its themes are neither extensively elaborated nor intermingled with much sophistication, a technical lapse overcome by the late 1850s. Yet what he underestimates is the vivid distillation of concrete images conveyed by his earlier score—which is far from "tame and ill-defined"— confirming a truism that artists inevitably measure their technical development with a yardstick of presumed progress. Only with this retrospective thinking did Wagner find it necessary (if useful) to denigrate his original Venusberg, underestimating what he achieved in light of later accomplishments.

What the composer never acknowledged is that even the 1845 *Tannhäuser* conveyed a very particular erotic message. As soon as one writes off the imagery of the explosive public orgy staged by the minor characters, what remains are some rather unusual sexual inclinations. Tannhäuser himself, for example, is completely detached from the bacchanal. His pleasures are rather more prim and sedentary, but above all, passive. What he initiates isn't sex, but a song asking permission to go home. It is Venus who promises him the fulfillment of "his wildest desires." But what exactly are these desires? While the Maenads rage in drunken gestures, Tannhäuser wishes only to lay his head on Venus's "warm breast" surrounded by "rosy mists." All very touching, but it's best to call a spade a spade: Tannhäuser, more than anything else, engages in a fantasy of female superiority and domination. Whereas the Sirens lure men into the Venusberg harem, once Tannhäuser is there, he wishes only to lie back and allow Venus to stimulate him into a blissful stupor. As Wagner puts it: "The Maenads wrench Tannhäuser away into the hot loving arms of the goddess herself, who embraces with raving passion him who is drunken with bliss and bears him away to the far distant realm of nothingness." It is true that, later in the Singing Hall, Tannhäuser boasts of having been the dominant male: "Only he who has enclosed you passionately in his arms knows what love is. You pathetic one who has never enjoyed her love, move up to the mount of Venus." On the other hand, he could scarcely have admitted in public to being a mere plaything manipulated by Venus. Even when Tannhäuser is desperately seeking Venus in the Third Act, he yearns to submit to her regal sexual authority: "To you, Lady Venus, I return, in the magic of your holy night, to your court I climb down [*zu deinem Hof steig ich darnieder*]." Tannhäuser's attraction to the goddess requires him to relinquish rather than maintain control, and indeed, he must gain her consent to leave the blissful realm.

It is Wagner who invents Tannhäuser's passivity, as none of his literary sources suggest anything similar. In the seventeenth-century version of the *Tannhäuser-Lied*, the singer wished to sample a promiscuous assortment of beautiful women among the marvels of the Venusberg:

Der Tannhäuser war ein Ritter gut,   *Tannhäuser was a gallant knight,*
Er wollt' gross Wunder schauen;   *He longed to see great wonders;*
Da zog er in Frau Venus Berg,   *So he to Venus's mount drew nigh,*
Zu andern schönen Frauen.   *To beautiful women in numbers.*

In Heine's version, moreover, Tannhäuser and Venus even indulge in some playful sadomasochism:

Tannhäuser, edler Ritter mein,   *Tannhäuser, my noble cavalier,*

Das sollst du mir nicht sagen,   *That you must not tell me,*

Ich wollte lieber, du schlügest   *I'd much prefer you struck me*

    mich,   *hard,*

Wie du mich oft geschlagen.   *You've done it oft to fell me.*

Ich wollte lieber, du schlügest   *I'd much prefer you struck*

    mich,   *me hard*

Als daß du Beleidigung sprächest,   *Than utter such offense,*

Und mir, undankbar kalter Christ,   *Ungrateful, cold and Christian*

                                     man,

Den Stolz im Herzen brächest.   *Who'd break my pride immense.*

(*HW* V, 368)

From a Wagnerian vantage point, the idea of a Venus who asks for a beating is a tasteless gaffe. Nothing could be further from Wagner's own soft and gentle erotics which shun the slightest suggestion of discomfort. The worst that can be said for his fantasy of female domination is that, after a while, it becomes a bit stifling, and one needs to come up for fresh air. "Enough of rosy perfumes," Tannhäuser exclaims, "I yearn for forest breezes—[*Doch ich, aus diesen ros'gen Düften/Verlange nach des Waldes Lüften*]"—an outburst he conveniently forgets in Act III when temporarily inhaling the "ravishingly beloved fragrances" emanating from the "sweet Venusberg."

In Chapter 1, it was suggested that the *absence* of erotic objects in music accounts for its uniquely seductive power over that of literature or the visual arts. But given Wagner's *Tannhäuser*, one can propose that even in the *presence* of erotic objects—words, images, even voluptuous bodies—music drowns them out when it takes command of the erotic experience. For on its own, no music, not even Wagner's, can depict the smell of roses, the taste of a lover's divine elixir, the feel of a warm breast or the image of a perfectly formed object of desire. Yet this failure is music's great advantage because it allows listeners to surmount the limitations of Wagner's erotic repertoire. Instead, they may make it their very own, for everyone understands the aura and mechanics of sexual desire which, in *Tannhäuser*, Wagner begins to lay bare in a few slender phrases.

While Wagner makes erotics his explicit concern in *Tannhäuser*, it took more than a decade for him to address the subject again, head on. The 1845 prose draft for the *Meistersinger* sidesteps the erotic and proposes a comic riposte to Tannhäuser's *serious* song competition. And in *Lohengrin*, Wagner romanticizes a Love likewise devoid of erotic allure. The chromatic idiom of the Venusberg, based on collections of diminished seventh chords, now descends to the lower depths of the orchestra to depict Ortrud's malicious sorcery. Even where there are sexual overtones in the musical treatment, as when Ortrud taunts the weakness of her husband Telramund, or when she plants seeds of doubt over Lohengrin's identity in Elsa, it is difficult to tell erotic signs from the evil ones. It is as if, shocked by his own display of "lascivious arousal" in *Tannhäuser*, Wagner retreats to a safely conservative position and again demonizes the erotic.

Love in the *Ring* Poem

Considering the overriding role played by Love in the final versions of the four dramas of *Der Ring des Nibelungen*, it is striking how in Wagner's original conception outlined in "The Nibelungen-Myth as Sketch for a Drama" (1848), the composer avoids even the slightest interest in the erotic. Wagner drafts this self-consciously archaic text in a pseudo-mythic style within which any intrusion of a modern Romantic love would seem anachronistic. Instead, characters merely wed one another, males force themselves on females, and women decide to submit to superior males. Or there is rape, as when Alberich "overpowers" Grimhild, mother of Gunther. Hagen, it is true, convinces Gunther that Brünnhilde is desirable, but, for his part, Gunther wishes to "take possession" of her. Only in one passage in the early sketch does Wagner link ardor to an attraction when "Gudrun, inflamed to love by the praises [Hagen] has showered on Siegfried . . . welcomes Siegfried with a drink prepared by Hagen's art." Yet even in the 1848 prose draft for *Siegfrieds Tod* [*Siegfried's Death*], Gudrun never gives vent to her attraction, exclaiming only *Siegfried mein!* in response to Hagen's promise that he will become her husband.[16]

Instead of sex, Wagner's early narrative highlights primeval cunning and raw power; freedom and bondage; curses; oaths and vows; and, of course, revenge: Alberich does not foreswear love to seize the Rheingold, but merely "abducted it from the waters' depth, and forged from it with cunning art a ring that gained him the dominion over all his race, the Nibelungs." Neither do the giants vie for the goddess Freia, nor do the wish-maidens provide sexual favors to the fallen heroes: the Valkyries rather shelter the heroes, who "resume a glorious life of jousts in Wodan's [sic] company." Siegmund and Sieglinde, both suffering in unhappy and childless marriages, merely "mate one another [*begatten sich*] so as to beget a pure Volsung," and even Brünnhilde, when awakened by Siegfried, "joyfully recognizes him as the most glorious hero of the Volsung tribe, and surrenders herself to him [*ergibt sich ihm*]" without further ado. Before her immolation when she again dresses in full Valkyrie garb, Brünnhilde leads Siegfried by the hand to restore Wodan's domination: "One only shall rule, All-father, you glorious one! As sign of your eternal might, I lead this man to you" (*JA* II, 274–285). All a very far cry from a redemption through Love, a theme conspicuous by its absence from the vivid plot outlines that remain remarkably intact during the next quarter century of the *Ring*'s gestation.

Only when Wagner begins to extend his conception of *Siegfried's Death* in the autumn of 1851 under the influence of Ludwig Feuerbach, first devising a preliminary heroic comedy [*ein heroisches Lustspiel*] called *The Young Siegfried*—and working further into the narrative past, conceiving *Der Raub des Rheingoldes* [*The Rape of the Rheingold*] and *Die Walküre* [*The Valkyrie*] (in that order)—does he once again become obsessed with sexual love. Echoing Feuerbach's *Thoughts on Death and Immortality*, Wagner now sees the world's chief problem as a lack of Love. Only with the upsurge of more love, especially the sexual union between man and woman, but also every other kind of derivative love, can the world hope to redeem itself from its misery. As late as January 1854 in an important letter to August Röckel—a year after the completion of the *Ring* poem—Wagner is speaking privately even of his *Lohengrin* in Feuerbachian terms: That opera, he writes, "symbolizes the tragic situation of the present day" in which the desire for Love remains unachievable. So when the Swan Knight "descended from the most intellectual heights to the depths of love, the longing to be understood instinctively," this wish was "a longing which modern reality cannot satisfy." As for selfless sexual love, it is an idealized place for "perfect happiness" and gives insight into an eternal reality, "the most perfect reality" [that] "comes to us only in the enjoyment of love [and] is thus the most eternal of all sentiments" (*SL*, 304–307).

From the perspective of Wagner's developing erotics, what is striking is not the composer's naïveté about love—this is something his reading of Schopenhauer will famously sort out—but rather that Wagner's *Ring* poem, an uneasy mixture of raw myth tempered by Feuerbach's optimism, displays an ambivalent and often dismissive view of erotic arousal. Emblematic is Brünnhilde's love for Siegfried. Though she ultimately consummates a bodily union with him, her initial declarations of love for him are utterly lacking in erotic stimulus. "Oh if you only knew how I've always loved you," she tells the hero. "I nourished you, tender one, even before you were conceived: my shield sheltered you when you were still in the womb." Ever the fan of nourishing and redeeming female figures, Wagner could scarcely have written these verses in a less alluring way, yet he insisted to Röckel that Brünnhilde's reactions are utterly amorous: "From the moment Siegfried awakens her, she has no longer any other knowledge save that of love." (Setting these verses to music after having composed *Tristan* therefore posed a special challenge.) Love, he continues, is really just the "'eternal feminine' itself," and within this model, Siegfried becomes "a complete 'human being'" only by uniting his masculinity with the femininity of this "suffering, self-immolating woman [who] finally becomes the true, conscious redeemer" (*SL*, 307). These ideas conspired, therefore, to obscure the exploration of erotic desire and sexual desire in Wagner's initial conceptions for the *Ring* poem.

Even after the explicit infusion of Feuerbachian themes of Love in 1851, Wagner was still ambivalent about the role of erotics in the love scene that follows Brünnhilde's awakening. In the poem for *Der junge Siegfried*, for example, he drafted and then crossed out the following text for his young hero: "If I enfold you, hold you tight, press my chest to your bosom, suck your breath from your mouth [*saug' ich deinen Athem dir vom Munde*], then you are, were, and will be mine; faded is the worry that you're now mine!" (*WS*, 95). The same image of a kiss is repeated in the final erotic stage direction of the Third Act, also later deleted: "Brünnhilde falls into Siegfried's arms: they remain intertwined with one another, mouth to mouth [*sie weilen verschlungen, Mund an Mund*]. In the final version of the poem, the only kiss in the opera is the "long and passionate" one Siegfried plants on the sleeping Valkyrie: in the Finale, despite all the ecstatic declarations of Love, the curtain falls as soon as a rather prim Brünnhilde "falls into Siegfried's arms."

Wagner believed his new theories on ideal love represented a great step forward, and he discourses about the subject at length in the same letter to Röckel. No longer was sexual love to be demonized as wanton and sinful, but if given an unselfish form, it can save the world. As a result, Wagner carved up Eros in a new way. For elemental creatures such as Alberich, the Rhinemaidens, or the giants, sexual desire figures as a base if universal instinct whose significance is commonly destructive. For the Rhinemaidens, it is a serious matter to renounce love—as Alberich will have to do—and its universality is recognized by Wellgunde when she notes that "whoever lives wants to love/no one wants to shun Amor" [*denn was nur lebt, will lieben;/meiden will keiner die Minne*]. While Alberich's desires are therefore natural—Alberich "behaves like a man in love" (*SL*, 238–239)— it was also "natural," Wagner writes to Röckel, "for [the Rhinemaidens] to repulse Alberich" (*SL*, 307). For this reason, the music with which the three Rhinemaidens feign their seduction of the dwarf flirts only for brief moments with luxuriant and pulsating ninth chords to signal some inchoate but suppressed erotic intent. For "higher" beings such as Wotan, Brünnhilde, and Siegfried, on the other hand, all-embracing Love in the *Ring* poem smothers erotic impulses so decidedly that they become all but invisible.

Die Walküre

The irony is that sacrificing erotics on the high altar of Feuerbachian Love, as Wagner does in the *Ring*, almost removes them from serious consideration and hence musical treatment. I say "almost removes them" because when Wagner comes to write both the text and later the music for *Die Walküre*, even before his acquaintance with Schopenhauer, he relies on his gifts as a talented if undeclared eroticist. In fact, the only intentionally erotic scene in the entire *Ring* occurs in the first act of the *Walküre*, when the twins Siegmund and Sieglinde fall in love and find themselves incapable of resisting their impulses. Wagner was in no doubt that he was composing in a heightened, arousing style, for at the time of the composition

sketches he inserts sixteen cryptic annotations that parallel his own infatuation with Mathilde Wesendonck (*NL* II, 526–527). The annotations,
all in first initials of the words in upper- and lowercase, were given a plausible reading by Otto Strobel and gloss specific moments in the text: To
take just one example, after Siegmund sings to Sieglinde, *Die Sonne lacht
mir nun neu* [Sunshine laughs on me anew], the composer notes: *I.l.d.gr.*,
deciphered as *Ich liebe dich grenzenlos* [I love you boundlessly]. The sexual
union between Siegmund and Sieglinde, it is true, occurs after the curtain
"quickly" falls on the First Act, but all the ingredients of the most passionate ardor are already well in place.

Even the earliest prose sketches for *Die Walküre* (from November 1851)
show how Wagner—for the first time since *Tannhäuser*—intended to create
a love scene of extraordinary, even voyeuristic intensity. Sieglinde, having
seen the ravaged stranger draw the sword planted in the ash tree by Wodan
(as Wagner still calls him at the time), suspects that Siegmund must be a
Volsung:

> During the night she slips back in to learn more of his fate: he erupts in
> ever more rampant sexual yearnings [*er entbrennt in immer wilderem
> Liebessehnen*]; her concern for his lot is transformed against her will
> into likewise ever more burning sexual desires [*Liebesverlangen*]. As he
> forcefully embraces her, he calls out at the same time: "I'm a Volsung,
> and Siegmund is your lover." Horrified but at the same time entranced,
> she cries: "You're embracing Sieglinde, your sister!" Siegmund: "Wife
> and sister, may the blood of the Volsungs ever glow [*glühen*]!" He em-
> braces her with furious desire. The curtain falls. (*WS*, 204)

In a slightly later conception, Wodan even remains in the room where he
witnesses the incest of his children! (*WS*, 212 and *WWV*, 364). As the poem
took shape in Wagner's mind, it became clear that the "rampant sexual
yearnings" and "burning sexual desires" could not be directly reflected in
the text which, for the sake of theatrical decency, would pursue a more
muted strategy. So even though the final stage direction in the opera before
the First Act curtain reflects the steamily expressed outburst of the original
conception—"that she sinks with a scream on his breast"—it was in the
music that Wagner realized his erotic intentions.

The musical strategy Wagner devises to depict this *risqué* subject matter of incest is both daring and clever, especially when one thinks of the
moral censure he was courting. Rather than revealing too soon any musical signs of erotic attraction, Wagner begins by painting the siblings'
dawning awareness of each other in archly lyrical and Romantic tones.
Their first sounding of the Love motives—emerging out of three plaintive statements of Siegmund[17]—recalls, more than anyone else, Robert
Schumann, and stakes few erotic claims. (See Example 3–2.1.) Love motive
(a) derives from the end of Freia's music in *Rheingold*, linked not only to
her flight away from the giants, but also to her identity as the goddess of
Youth and Love.

When Sieglinde first looks yearningly at Siegmund in a theatrical pan-
tomime, one hears a melody at the top of a cello octet that actually com-
prises material Wagner will treat as two discrete motives. By gradually
eroticizing each of them throughout the course of the First Act, Wagner
is able to embody the course of Siegmund and Sieglinde's love as it becomes more passionate, tragic, and uncontrolled. The motives, for example, adorn that moonlit realm in Example 3–2.2 where, as in the Venusberg, the aura of the "dazzling spring night" and the heightened awareness
of the lovers become indistinguishable. What Wagner called a "wanton
whirring and rustling" in 1845, he now (in 1854) shapes into a vertiginous
array of arpeggios shimmering with ardent passion.

Unlike in *Tannhäuser*, Wagner transforms characteristic motives across
the course of an entire opera. What is more, the transformations are so
skilful that he projects them in ways not easily audible on first hearing. As
a result, he is able to save his most impressive trick for the *dénouement* of
Act I, sc. iii, in which he sharpens the rhythmic values of both motives,
whips them up in a final *accelerando*, and transforms Love into frenzied
lust. Like the Bacchantic rapture in *Tannhäuser*, but evincing a more advanced harmonic technique, the Love motives in the *Valkyrie* (shown in
Example 3–2.3) give vent to the uninhibited obsession of the lovers. At the
conclusion of the scene, the twins recognize one another with the "raging
passion" mentioned in the stage directions, while the audience is only dimly
aware of manipulations of music heard less than an hour before. While the
same music had originally intimated no more than the first inklings of
friendly sympathy, it is now the eroticized, hysterical versions of both Love

motives with which Wagner launches the exciting conclusion for the First Act finale, the very same "alluringly tempting" music which, it will be re-called from Chapter 1, caused Gustave Stoeckel's "whole soul" to be "be-witched by an irresistible power."

The motivic transformations and elaborations seen in Example 3–2.3 are composed with such deftness that many listeners may no longer relate the climax consciously to the lyrical first encounter between Siegmund and Sieglinde: Perhaps Wagner actually banked on his successful masking of the source of his music for the Finale. On the other hand, he has taken great care to shape musical processes that depict the rising pitch of erotic excitement. Not only is the racing pulse of Love sped up under rhythmic diminution, but there is also the obsessive refusal (at the passage marked *Immer schneller*) of Love (b) to surrender its final melodic tone down a semitone: Instead of "coming through with the goods" and setting up a downward sequential progression, the music stays riveted on one pitch. (The half-diminished chord in m. 1488 supports the frustrated desire for closure by preparing a cadential resolution that never appears.) Following the dramatic combination of the Love (b) snippet with that of the still ominous Sword (beginning in m. 1498), the obsessive behavior further compresses the rhythmic figure into four equal eighth notes at the passage marked *furioso*, and the fury continues as a distressed Love motive (a) lands on a dissonant diminished seventh (in m. 1507), inaugurating an anarchic sequence—first downward by step and then upward aiming toward the fi-nal cadence. The cadential activity is itself "beyond the law" in the blaring of the upper appoggiatura in m. 1519, which flaunts its presence in two boastful and grammatically inappropriate ways: first in triumph and then in horror (in m. 1521). The final tonic chord resolves on an unpredicted beat, and is literally "the last straw," its shock value lasting long beyond its final echo. In all these ways, Wagner embodies erotic frenzy by making the musical processes—lyrical utterance, rhythmic articulation, harmonic function, and hypermetrical organization—behave as if they are observ-ably out of control, as if the music both mimetically acts out carnal de-sires, even imagines precise emotional reactions in a heightened state of erotic fervor. The musical experience reflects the obsessive, erratic behav-ior of Wagner's characters as much as it does the desires and knowing ex-perience of his audience, thereby depicting in musical terms the "eruption" of "passionate sexual yearning" from his prose sketch without needing to utter a direct word about it, nor even to portray a single "point of view". (Wagner will achieve something similar at the end of the Annunciation of Death scene in *Die Walküre* (Act II, sc. iv), in which Brünnhilde's grasp of the erotic bond between Siegmund and Sieglinde is likewise captured in the orchestral postlude that evokes a similar erotic crescendo.)

Tristan und Isolde

By the end of 1856, having delved deeply into Schopenhauer, Wagner is already drafting an opera called *Tristan und Isolde* about the torment of love. As was seen in Chapter 2, no matter how deep the imprint on Wagner's thinking of Schopenhauer's dark ruminations on sexual love, the artistic result was far from a consistent application of philosophical thought. Even Wagner admitted that his obsession to compose *Tristan* demanded an "ecstatic expression" of the "essential traits" found in Schopenhauer's writings, a very different idea from a poetic and musical recasting of a coherent philosophical vision. Brooding about his *Ring* poem in a letter to August Röckel in 1856, Wagner reveals that Brünnhilde's final address in *Götterdämmerung* asserting that "love alone brings happiness . . . required a complete revolution in my rational outlook, such as was finally brought about by Schopenhauer . . . who provided me with a truly fitting keystone for my poem, which consists in an honest recognition of the true and profound nature of things" (*SL*, 358). Yet intuitions, Wagner writes, are in any case more important than concepts, "especially if one feels as little a philosopher as I do." Rather than "expose oneself as a dialectician," his métier is "to speak only in works of art." Only two paragraphs later, he speaks of completing all the plans of which he is still full and mentions: "I have in my head a *Tristan and Isolde* (love as fearful torment) and my latest subject, *The Victors* (supreme redemption, Buddhist legend), both of which are clamoring for my attention." From this formulation, one can see how—at this stage of Wagner's thinking—two aspects of Schopenhauer's thought had been split into distinct poetic projects: the diagnosis of erotic suffering as against its remedy, renunciation.

As a musico-poetic exercise, Wagner's task in working through the "fearful torment" in *Tristan* was on a far grander scale than anything he

had ever undertaken. For even if *Tannhäuser* had required a detailed musical tableau to capture the aura of the Venusberg, the musical bits and pieces
were static musical objects and in no way capable of sustaining more than
a few scenes of an opera. The transformations of the Love motives in
Die Walküre advanced a dramatic technique of musical characterization,
but these themes shared the spotlight with many other motives, and on
their own could scarcely have prolonged a full act of the drama. With
Tristan, Wagner thought of his "characteristic motives" in a new way.
Rather than tying them to the scenic design or to the plot, the music was
allied from the start to experiential ideas on erotic love to which he
wished to give "ecstatic expression." Already in 1854, in the same letter to
Franz Liszt in which he first brings Schopenhauer to Liszt's attention, he
notes that the *Tristan and Isolde* he has drafted in his head is "a most full-
blooded musical conception." From what we know of Wagner's reading
and thinking, it would be nonsense to suggest that by "musical" he means
something formally abstract, non-representational or detached from
words. Rather, a musical conception signifies one in which—according to
Schopenhauer—music behaves analogously to the dictates of one's innermost desires. It is in this sense that one should understand Wagner's
statement—reported in Cosima's diary in 1873—that "in [my] other works
the motives serve the plot, [whereas] here [in *Tristan*] one might say that
the plot arises out of the motives [*entspringt die Handlung aus den Motiven*]"
(*CT* II, 728).

To appreciate the density of the eroticism in *Tristan*, one has only to
seek out passages unconnected to some inner view of sexual love. There
are exceedingly few of them. The sailor's innocent love song—at the start
of the opera—about the Irish maid he has left behind immediately provokes Isolde, who in her pent-up erotic fury, reacts irrationally, as if the
song were mocking her. Kurwenal's brief narrative and choral refrain on
Tristan the Hero at the end of Act I, sc. ii functions in a similar way: The
story of Morold's and Tristan's heroism seems outfitted to provide respite
from the dark gloom, but Isolde expresses her outrage precisely because
she knows the erotic underbelly of Tristan's heroism. Likewise, there is
the hair-raising conclusion to the First Act, in which the approach of King
Marke's vessel to the ship (set in the unsullied key of C major) serves as an
ironic foil until both contrasting theme and key areas—those of Desire

and the Hail to Cornwall—become intertwined at the curtain's fall. Not one moment in the Second Act is divorced from the main erotic plot, and if the poem for Act III seems to deal with subsidiary issues—Tristan's desperate illness or memories of his youth—Wagner's music attaches Tristan's precarious state to his enduring passion for Isolde. Even the secondary characters, Brangäne, Kurwenal, and Marke, each make a point of proclaiming not only their loyalty but also their own one-sided ecstatic love for either Isolde or Tristan, homoerotic bonds to be discussed in Chapter 5. Clara Schumann was right to see the opera as obsessed by sexual infatuation [Liebeswahnsinn].

The Tristan Chord

The chief marker of the Tristan erotic is of course the rising four-note chromatic motive (often called Desire) that occurs at the beginning of the opera. Embedded in the famous half-diminished chord and given a slinky bit of voice-leading with an irregular resolution, the progression mystified someone even as sophisticated as Berlioz. Or did it? Although, as quoted in Chapter 1, he pretended not to have "the least idea" of what Wagner was up to, Berlioz described the opening passage of Tristan with rather a great deal of insight when he called it "a kind of chromatic moan . . . whose cruel effect is reinforced by long suspensions which appear in place of proper harmonic resolutions."[18] Even in his disapproval, Berlioz, like many others, grasped what came to be recognized as a quintessential emblem of mimetic sexual desire.

The identification of the "erotic" first chord of the Tristan Prelude or Einleitung [Introduction], as it is marked in the score, makes more sense if one consults the pre-history of the "half-diminished" ($^{\o}7$) chord in Wagner's own works, a narrative that sheds light on its subsequent erotic significance. The collection of pitches, stacked up from the bottom with two minor thirds and a major third on top, and inverted in every which way, functions in a wholly innocuous and conventional way as a colorful antepenultimate chord in an 1840s cadence, as seen in several passages from Lohengrin. Significantly, it is absent from the Tannhäuser Venusberg motives. As far as I can detect, Wagner first takes the chord seriously—that is, not merely as a chord of dominant preparation—in the opening music of the Second Act of *Lohengrin*, where it is interpolated between diminished seventh collections harmonizing Ortrud's Temptation motive as an accented upper neighbor upbeat in the bass line: the momentary harmonic ambiguity serves well to indicate evil and plotting. (See Example 3–3.)

The extraordinary flexibility of the half-diminished (°7) chord, with its evil associations, carries over into *Das Rheingold*, where it shows up in the First Scene at the moment Alberich has foresworn Love and announces he will forge an all-powerful Ring. Wotan's descent into Alberich's realm of Nibelheim—no surprise here—is likewise marked by the chord, but Wagner still uses it in a formulaic way as a heightened, more menacing form of a diminished seventh. It is in the Second Act of *Die Walküre*, though, in the Annunciation of Death scene, where both Fate and Death exploit the half-diminished chord in a new way. By moving through a French sixth to an unresolved dominant seventh, Wagner crafts a fine piece of voice-leading in which (at m. 1471) he embeds Fate (with the half-diminished chord) into the end of Death. With each change of vertical sonority, there is only a single note held over in common. (See Example 3–4.) This may be the first time that Wagner foregoes the evil connotation of the half-diminished chord, here to express the noble tragedy of Siegmund's fate as he is commanded by Brünnhilde to foreswear Love and retreat to Valhalla.

This reconfiguration of the motive's harmonic context and the subsequent shift in significance away from evil to that of a noble death based on the renunciation of Siegmund's erotic love for Sieglinde occurs to Wagner, perhaps not uncoincidentally, in the very months when he is first devouring Schopenhauer. And at the very least, then, it seems plausible that in the same period when he is first drafting musical ideas for a drama about an erotic love-death, complaining at the same time that he has "never in [his] life enjoyed the true happiness of love," the idea of an unusual chord tied to an unusual chromatic resolution should seem to him so compelling.

Musical Paradigms in the *Tristan* Prelude

Whatever the source of the Desire motive, Wagner's use of the *Tristan* chord within the opera itself proliferates in ways not seen before in his music, and from the beginning, the Introduction signals a manifestly erotic intent. This Wagner clarifies in his prose program already mentioned in Chapter 1 (written for the Paris concerts in 1860) where he announces the theme of his tale as "yearning unappeasable, desire forever born anew, thirsting, languishing" (*JA* IV, 104). And it is this theme that his orchestral Prelude takes as "its introduction to his love-drama." Within a few lines, Wagner maps out a course of erotic feelings that adheres rather closely to the music:

> [The musician] therefore caused insatiable yearning [*das unersättliche Verlangen*] to swell upwards in a long articulated breath [*im lang gegliederten Zuge*], from the most timid confession [*dem schüchternsten Bekenntnis*] and the most tender attraction [*der zartesten Hingezogenheit*], through anxious sighs, hopes and fears, moans and wishes, joys and torments, until the mightiest blast [*Andrang*], the most violent effort [*zur gewaltsamsten Mühe*] to find the rupture which unlocks for the boundlessly craving heart the path into the sea of unending sexual bliss [*Liebeswonne*]. In vain! Swooning [*Ohnmächtig*] the heart sinks back so as to languish in yearning, in yearning without success [*Erreichen*], since every success is only again a renewed yearning, until, in the final wilting [*bis im letzten Ermatten*], an inkling dawns on the interrupted glance of achieving the highest bliss: the bliss of dying, of being no more, of the final release [*Erlösung*] into that wondrous realm, from which we strayed the furthest, where we strive to penetrate [*einzudringen*] with the most vehement force. Do we call it Death? Or is it the nocturnal world of miracles, from which, as the legend informs us, a (strand of) ivy and a vine once grew upwards on the grave of Tristan and Isolde in the most ardent embrace. (*JA* IV, 104–105)

Compared with Wagner's text from 1852, which describes the content of the *Tannhäuser* Overture, or with the programs that accompany the *Lohengrin* Prelude or the *Flying Dutchman* Overture, his gloss on the *Tristan* Prelude is a distinctly odd text. Instead of characterizing disjunct musical passages or motives that reflect aspects of a coherent literary narrative, Wagner does the opposite and maps a disjointed text onto a coherent passage of music. Far more ambiguous than Wagner's text for the *Tannhäuser* overture, the *Tristan* program does not "interpret" the Prelude so much as "perform" its musical content in words. For if Wagner had intended a serious "explanation" of the music, he frustrates his readers by confusing the poetic point of view. Is it Wagner the composer, or is it the craving heart which undergoes the torments described therein? Who is it that experiences or creates "the mightiest blast" seeking "the rupture which unlocks . . . the path . . . to bliss?" Wagner, Tristan or yearning desire itself? And who or what finally wilts while gaining an inkling of that bliss? Toward the end a new grammatical subject appears: it is "we" who have strayed from the wondrous realm. It is we who strive vehemently to enter the realm of bliss, though we don't know if this entails our actual death, or whether death is merely a metaphor for sexual bliss. Or is the realm one in which we symbolically recall the searing love of Tristan and Isolde? We can ponder these verbal puzzles until the cows come home, but they pose no problem for music, which has no need of grammatical subjects, and yet evokes a wholly communicable set of sensations and erotic markers.

For this reason, it is worth seeing how the composer's poetic allegory on the Prelude relates to the specific musical content of the work. Indeed, Wagner made a point of stressing how the treatment of his theme occurs within the "most intrinsic and unrestrained elements of music," as if, in this instance, he allows music to ignore a more legible narrative trajectory. It takes little imagination, for example, to locate "the mightiest blast" or "rush" [*Andrang*] at the *fortissimo* in m. 83, this "violent effort to find the rupture unlocking the path to love's bliss." (See Example 3–5.) Having announced the Prelude's subject matter as "insatiable yearning," Wagner must have expected listeners to recognize the euphemism of a sexual climax. Certainly the music encourages that view. Yet Wagner assures us that this climax, this "violent effort to find the rupture" was "in vain," that it did not succeed. The rupture wasn't found because the lovers weren't united: Presumably the male failed to find the female because their love was forbidden by social convention. Wagner is true to his announced theme, especially "desire forever born anew, thirsting, languishing," because after the climax, "the heart sinks back . . . into a renewed yearning" until he notes a "final wilting," "drooping," or "sagging" of desire followed by the thought of a transcendent death.

Reading this text alongside the music, it is difficult to avoid the impression that Wagner has devised a musical depiction of a male sexual fantasy moving in waves of arousal toward an explosive climax. Whether the great moment is meant to have occurred through self-stimulation or purely as an erotic fantasy in the mind is naturally left unsaid. Yet if the composer wished to ensure that no one understood the climax as sexual, he surely could have found words other than "until a final wilting" [*bis im letztem Ermatten*] of desire to describe what happened after the "mightiest blast." It is true that the word can equally be translated as "wearing down," "exhaustion," or "languishing," but given the context, the association to a physical "drooping" is hard to avoid.

So far the climax and aftermath of the erotic episode are clear. Working backward, one can pinpoint in the music several discrete elements of Wagner's prose, deficient as words are to capture the economy of means concentrated in the *Tristan* Prelude. In fact, only a handful of harmonic progressions—repeated in sequential cycles—contribute to what appears as a protracted, arched structure. (See Example 3–5, which analyzes the three key musical paradigms in the Prelude according to Wagner's prose program.) The "long articulated breath" of the opening that "swells upwards" via a chromatic ascent through the octave embraces the three statements of insatiable yearning leading to the deceptive cadence characterizing unquenchable desire (mm. 1–17). Wagner repeats and develops this substantial musical paradigm in three subsequent passages—in mm. 66–75, 81–90, and 100–111—accounting, in sum, for nearly half the Prelude.

The reconfiguration and re-orchestration of later restatements is key to understanding this particular version of the Wagnerian erotic *crescendo* and (for the first time) the necessary *descrescendo* that marks the crucial inability to achieve the highest bliss. For example, in the second iteration, rather than rely merely on an intensified and elaborated orchestration, Wagner presents only the core ascending progression composed of the three statements of Desire, but without the plaintive introductory Grief. In this denuded form, the opening representation of Desire sounds urgent and bald. In the third climactic statement, Desire is literally overcome with Grief, for one discovers in m. 81 that—with a slight chromatic alteration to Desire—they combine simultaneously in a breathtaking bit of counterpoint over a rocking fifth-based pendulum: The erotic excitement proceeds from an unexpected "squeeze" of musical materials compressed into their own ecstatic embrace. Wagner's orchestration also plays a key role: It is once again the cellos who declaim Grief, but they are now doubled by violas (playing tremolo) along with French horns and bass clarinet in such a way that Grief both shivers and is blared out over and against the wailing of Desire in the first Trumpet. The obsessive repetition of the new contrapuntal combination on the same scale degree (in m. 82) before the climax betokens, moreover, a greedy refusal to disengage, a musical moment of undeniable and overwhelming power. The shattering disappointment in m. 84 that follows the *Andrang* is all the more heartrending because the musical path of rising Desire, now marked *piano*, is well trodden and leads one only in circles. (The climax was "in vain," as Wagner puts it.) At the final statement of Insatiable Yearning in m. 101, the paradigm merely peters out exhaustedly, dropping in successive octaves, the location, perhaps, of its "final wilting." In place of the paradigmatic third statement of Desire at mm. 107–109, Wagner even strings out his *Tristan* chord as part of a scarcely audible and no longer harmonically meaningful horizontal bass line. (He seems to characterize this in the program as the "bliss of dying.") The pitches growl in a seeming evocation of primeval chaos. Desire, at least for the moment, has been dismantled and is emptied of expressive content, and the musical line substituting for it is strangely insensate and inert, a moment "of being no more," as Wagner terms it.

The second key element in the musical construction of the Prelude is what Wagner calls "the most timid confession." This melody—later associated with the story of the Glance in Act I—first occurs in mm. 17–22 and paints a rosier picture sketched from a rising linear progression, diatonic this time rather than chromatic, a kindlier *alter ego* of Insatiable Yearning. Intoned by the cellos in their most lyrical register, the music recalls the very similar and equally timid first intimations of Love in *Die Walküre*—likewise played by the cellos—with the crucial difference that the hopes of its opening strain remaining in the realm of major mode are dashed by the dynamic "swoon" in mm. 20–21 when the harmony retreats to the more somber D minor area via diminished and Neapolitan chords. The nuanced experience of continually renounced expectation in the Timid Confession can also be heard in its melodic profile, the encouraging diatonic rise in the major mode foiled by the gradually chromaticized fall in minor. The paradigm is replayed in four later restatements—in mm. 32–36, 55–63 (where it doubles back on itself at m. 58), 74–81, and 94–100—and accounts, all told, for another third of the Prelude. A chromatically altered version of Timid Confession's head motive also allows Wagner to create an erotic crescendo in miniature throughout the Prelude to signal the "renewed yearning" in the prose program. See, for example, the reference played by the cellos in m. 23, and more strikingly the passage at mm. 77–80 and mm. 84–88 where, in the third statement of Insatiable Yearning, the head motive of Timid Confession contributes to "the heart sinking back so as to languish in yearning." By this point, the confession is no longer timid, but brazen and demanding.

Yet another musical element is what Wagner calls "the most tender attraction" in the prose program: it first occurs in mm. 25–28 and then again in mm. 45–48. In the orchestral score, Wagner labels this passage as "tender" [*zart*] at its two appearances.[19] Patterned by two sweet sighs of a falling seventh (in m. 25 and m. 27), this feminine gesture is supported by warm major harmonies and secondary seventh chords: It sheds a consolatory light on the ravages of desire by setting the four-note chromatic rise—G♯–A♮–A♯–B♮—in a comforting reharmonized cradle where the *Tristan* chord is notable by its absence. No wonder that words impart the sense of these refined experiential nuances only in a lengthy and verbose discourse, whereas the music itself projects a clarity of expression with relative ease.

One can also decode other bits of the program, expressed as dichotomies, by observing the shifting juxtapositions among the core elements. So, for example, Wagner's phrase, "joys and torments," captures the passage at mm. 63–73 where the joyous rush upward in a diatonic sequence by whole step alternates with tormented yearnings that restate the opening of the Prelude. The surging power of the passage and its shattering effect result from Wagner's brilliant dovetailing of two compositional paradigms: the positive rising passion of the diatonic sequence that is interrupted, indeed thwarted by the repeated statements of Desire with their ominously ascending chromatic melody linked to the unsatisfying harmonic resolution of the *Tristan* chord. The erotic sensations of the *Tristan* Prelude—about which a great deal more could be written—stem directly from the concentration of musical materials, which, as Wagner says, swell upward with a desire for sexual bliss that can never be sated, yet which never abandons the vain hope of trying. But perhaps the most crucial point about Wagner's prose program is that no one has ever needed it: once one recognizes the erotic genre, the representations in the Prelude project an unequivocal set of feelings and experiences.

Tristan, Act II

Given this pronounced, if also exasperating, aesthetic, the love music in the Second Act must be heard, at least on the most literal level, as a lengthier depiction of unfulfilled desire, furnished with a range of new musical motives tied to the dramatic situation, many of them strewn with the yearning *Tristan* chord: First there is the obsessive frenzy of Tristan's arrival, then the cursing of the Day that keeps the lovers apart, and then the Hymn to the Night. It is at this point that "Tristan draws Isolde gently down on a flowery bank, sinks on his knee before her and rests his head on her arm." With this imagery of flowers, of nocturnal bliss, and of a hero lying recumbent before his beloved, Wagner beckons far more toward the balmy breezes of the Venusberg than to the erotic crescendo of *Die Walküre* or even to the mighty "blast" of the *Tristan* Prelude. In fact, the music for *O sink hernieder, Nacht der Liebe* [Descend, O night of love] projects more than anything else the tranquil bliss that follows, not precedes, the exertions of lovemaking. The lovers' serenity appears *after* the agitated fury of their greeting and the grandiose heroics mocking the cursed Day. They sing of their wish "never again to awake" and pass into a dreamlike state: "Their heads sunk down, both [remain] in a long silent embrace."

Yet Wagner is no dramatic naturalist, and his prose draft makes clear that both the opening of Act II and the scene just before the lovers are discovered were intended to represent varieties of the frenzy of sexual desire. When they are first united, for example, "Tristan rushes in. Long fiery embrace. Overflowing of long repressed feeling(s) . . . Highest exultation of bliss" (*SS* XI, 334). Nor need one exclude the possibility that even the somnolent embrace during which Brangäne sings her watchman's song at the advent of dawn stands as a polite stage metaphor for the lovers' sexual intimacy. Even though she refers to them as sleepers, she is offstage and is no witness one way or the other. It is the orchestra, above all, who suggest lovemaking. As the music abandons the irregular pulsations of *O sink hernieder*, the orchestra settles into a musical nocturne with its lilting bars of three beats, redolent of Chopin and Donizetti, yet infiltrated by the yearning overtones of *Tristan*'s harmonic language. At the same time, contrasting pairs of obbligato melodies suggest two bodies who copy each other's ardent gestures.

The prose draft assumed that there would be some physical touching and intimacy: The lovers first "sink on a bank of flowers. Gradual mollification of the storm toward more gentle caresses [*zur sanfteren Zärtlichkeit*]." Subsequently, the music moves at the end of the section toward a climax that fails, significantly, to cadence. It posts yet another sign of lovemaking as rising passion stopping short of fulfilled desire, the unobtainable *Erreichen* of the prose program. Rather than expressed by the stage characters directly, Wagner's erotic intention is displaced onto the orchestra when he comes to write the music:

> Fear of awaking! . . . Isolde's increasing worry about Tristan; placated by him through new rapture [*Verzückung*] . . . —Let us entwine [*Laß uns umschlingen*] so as never more to part! Increasing ecstasy [*Ekstase*]. New, highest intoxication—the most fervent [*brünstig*] embrace—Brangäne's scream. (*SS* XI, 336)

This final erotic episode between the lovers was to be understood—at least on some level—as a sexual consummation (though lacking a climax) for the simple reason that Wagner has Melot boast to King Marke in the final libretto: "I've shown him to you in the blatant act [*in off'ner Tat*]." At the same time, it is vital to *Tristan*'s theme of unfulfilled desire that the act never be dramatized onstage, even if music's ambivalent powers of suggestion remain fully in charge.

What is truly remarkable (if enervating!) is how each of the large-scale erotic crescendos of the Second Act paints a distinct variant of an erotic sensibility through its peculiar musical material and motivic development. For example, the first episode—which begins as Isolde "throws the torch to the ground"—celebrates her "passionate impatience" in waves of erotic excitement as she awaits Tristan's approach. One can follow the musical sense of the motive's treatment with great clarity in the stage directions: First, "she listens and peers [*späht*] down an avenue of trees, at first timidly." Then "stirred by mounting yearning, she goes . . . and peers out more boldly, and finally with "passionate impatience" she "waves her kerchief . . . faster and faster." The second episode marks her "sudden rapture [*plötzliche Entzückung*]" as she beckons to her lover. This material extends into Tristan's entrance at the opening of Scene ii, moving from an obsessively repeated cell with a dotted figure to a syncopated variant, the lovers at that point "embracing wildly," to the frenzied orchestra playing *fortissimo*. A parenthetical note to the succeeding tempo designation states that the passage "must be executed dependent on whether the expression is impassioned [*feurig*] or affectionate [*zärtlich*]," and it is through musically unprepared moves into tender expression that the composer both replicates the quicksilver vagaries of sexual experience and operates on the sensibilities of the listeners by unmotivated changes in the texture, dynamics, and tempo. For this reason as well, the Second Act of *Tristan* modulates so effortlessly into the somnolent mode of gentle caresses, if only because of the extreme exhaustion that results from the thwarting of so much unfulfilled desire.

Renunciations of Love

The lavish retouching of the most traditional Romantic trope for discreet lovemaking is a step toward which Wagner had been moving since he first depicted the goddess Venus. He had painted her—not as a frenzied nymph or as one of the rapturous Bacchae, but—as a woman enveloped in "balmy breezes" and "blissful scents." Through her song—like Brangäne's Alba, also in the tonality of F sharp—she exudes the quintessence of "rosy fragrances" and "blissful fervor," a maternal siren. Wagner himself reveals the tie binding the *Tristan* nocturne to Venus when, in 1860, he comes to revise *Tannhäuser* for Paris. In addition to injecting the Tristan chord into the "horrors of the Venusberg," he also fleshes out the soft and caressing erotic which, even in the 1845 version, had marked Venus's allure for Tannhäuser. It is an erotic "calmed on the softest cushions" [*besänftigt auf weichstem Pfühle*], as Venus puts it to Tannhäuser. "Come, my sweet, friend,

follow me," she adds in Paris, as the orchestra sinks into the nocturnal delight of the *Tristan* chord. Exalting the erotics of a soft caress over other
forms of lovemaking has a personal meaning for Wagner and seems connected to his dream for an end to all sexual desire, a hope dressed up with
the grandiose word "renunciation." Writing to Mathilde Wesendonck
while submerged in the composition of *Tristan* Act II, Wagner writes:

> There is a voice in me which calls yearningly for rest—for a rest
> which years ago I had my flying Dutchman crave. It was the yearning
> for—home [*Heimat*]—not the voluptuous pleasures of love [*nach üp-
> pigem Liebesgenuss*]! Let us dedicate ourselves to this beautiful death,
> which salvages and stills all our yearning and desires" (*MW*, 30).

Even more telling, and equally plausible, is what Wagner later revealed to
Cosima in 1882 about the composition of *Tristan*. Speaking of "the part
played by life in art," Wagner notes that the subject

> reminds me of the King of Prussia, who in connection with *Tristan
> und Isolde* said how much in love Wagner must have been at the time.
> Now anyone who knows something of my life knows how bland and
> trivial [*fade und nichtig*] it was, and how impossible it is to write a
> work like that in a state of infatuation. No doubt it was my desire to
> lose myself in an ocean of love to escape my pitiful existence. And it
> is this unfulfilled yearning which motivates such a work, not [life]
> experience. (*CT* IV, 952)

The obsession with—yet also the recoiling from—"voluptuous pleasures"
is deeply embedded in Wagner's character, and his life entailed a significant degree of forfeit. It seems amply clear, for example, that the great
love affair with Mathilde Wesendonk, was never "consummated," a fact
about which Wagner even boasted. Mathilde's husband "has nothing for
which he can ever reproach me," he wrote to an intimate, Carolyne von
Sayn-Wittgenstein. "With what sacrifices this has had to be achieved, not
only on my part, but more especially, on the part of his wife, you can well
enough imagine. . . . Yet . . . there [is] no one else with whom we would
wish to exchange places" (*SL*, 386). Even a few months earlier, he admits

that he is "not fated to enjoy any pure and refreshing happiness." Art, and especially the composition of music, provides not only solace but also a hidden form of compensation. What attracts Wagner to great poets, he writes "is what they conceal by their silence." As for himself: "What makes me love music with such inexpressible joy is that it conceals everything, while expressing what is least imaginable: it is thus, strictly speaking, the only true art, the other arts being merely adjunct" (*SL*, 384–385). This pleasure in the pain of abstinence has a long history in European culture, but only in Wagner's world is it transformed into such a powerful musical erotic.

Die Meistersinger and Götterdämmerung

Each of the later works builds on the techniques developed in *Tristan*, every one of which makes the representation of sexual longing so believable. In *Die Meistersinger*, in which the concept of *Wahn* or delusion both embraces but also overwhelms sexual desire, Wagner asks whether bittersweet resignation can mitigate the most harrowing excesses of erotic misery, whether the artist, Sachs, can control unruly desire to recompense the madness and rage [*Tollheit und Wut*] where music is in charge, as in *Tristan*. The answer in the Third Act seems to come in several metaphorical propositions that soften *Tristan*'s gloomy assertions: Desire causes damage, true, but perhaps not always eternal suffering or the torment of sin (as *Parsifal* will suggest). The erotic impulse underlying *Die Meistersinger* suggests instead that the mere dream of art actually dispels delusion [*Wahn*]. This precious fantasy, so close to Wagner's preferred setting in his own silken boudoirs, and so far removed from the hellish "horrors of the Venusberg," signifies a positive tinge to the erotic celebrated by this opera, if only in fantasy. Yet dreams speak true, as Sachs indeed replies to Walther's song [*Freund! eu'r Traumbild wies euch wahr*], even as Walther admits, words don't suffice [*Genug der Wort'!*]. For it is music that is better suited to the dream, to the stilling of harsh delusions, and in the *musical* apotheosis of the opera—in the Quintet that transcendentally overturns the over-theorized dualities of poetry vs. music in *Opera and Drama*—Wagner reworks the Desire of the *Tristan* chord to embrace the enchantment of passion. For intertwined into the musical language of the Quintet is not the "mild and soft" [*mild und leise*] transfiguration of impossible love as in *Tristan and Isolde*, but rather, as Eva and Walther envisage it, the dream of "a mild and holy tune" [*einer Weise mild und hehr*] that "conquers my heart's sweet complaint [*meines Herzens süß' Beschwer*]."

The subtle admixture of newly juxtaposed *Tristan* chords now reveals an erotic "conquered" by a beautiful dream. In the Quintet, Eva both names and quotes Walther's dream song, but at the end of her second phrase, as if to hypnotize the five characters who sing together for the first time, Wagner initiates a unique progression—some of the most ravishing music he ever composed—that infuses the text setting with a new bittersweet adaptation of adjacent *Tristan* chords. "I hardly dare say what it means," Sachs says [*d'ran zu deuten wag ich kaum*], though he surely suspects its significance. What is true, though, is that words fail to capture its experience. One needs to listen rather to the musical metaphors of ravaged Tristanesque Desire [*Verlangen*] now tempered by sweetest suffering [*süss'te Not*] within the dream of a mild and holy melody. On the one hand, the *Meistersinger* poem proposes an erotic goal counter to that of *Tristan:* Eva and Walther eagerly await the pleasures of the day while Tristan and Isolde fear the light of dawn. Eva's words—"Let me be blessedly wakened to the morning of bliss" [*Morgen voller Wonne . . . selig mir erwacht!*]—can be set apart from Isolde's "Never waken . . . let the day yield to death" [*Nie erwachen! . . . Laß den Tag dem Tode weichen*]. Wagner's music, however, intimates something more complex by embodying a transformation of *Tristan*'s erotic within the very heart of *Die Meistersinger*'s poetic intentions. Connected by common-tone voice-leading, the adjoining *Tristan* chords marked in Example 3–6 (from Act III, sc. iv, mm. 1707–1716) lead to a disruption of the hypermeter after the $D\flat^7$ dominant chord, giving way to a cadential climax that dies away in a blissful diminuendo. Wagner's magic results from harmonic trickery: He briefly resolves his *Tristan* chord to the remote comforts of A major before anticipating a close in $D\flat$ that itself reveals itself as a dominant to $G\flat$, thereby requiring the "extra" fifth beat to reach the tonic. The onstage characters, beholden to and transfixed by this transformed erotic, "scarcely dare interpret it," as they say, for its beauty captures what is ordinarily so unattainable.

In *Götterdämmerung*, too, Wagner depicts the beautiful but destructive power of every erotic encounter by writing music in a Tristanesque idiom.

This new psychological tool invigorates his now creaking *Ring* poem and deepens the musical characterizations of Gutrune, Gunther, Brünnhilde, Siegfried—even the Rhinemaidens—all of whom express thoughts colored by an erotic undertone. If one recalls that the poem preceded the composition of the music by almost twenty years, what is fascinating is how Wagner exploits the erotic potential of scenes that would have turned out rather differently had the score to the *Ring* been completed in the mid-1850s. The blatant promiscuity of the *Tristan* chord imposed on the harmonic grammar of leitmotives that didn't contain it before is especially striking in *Götterdämmerung*: it is as if all the symbols of evil and temptation (from *Lohengrin*), immoral power *(Das Rheingold)*, Death and Fate *(Die Walküre)*, and erotic passion and frenzy *(Tristan* and *Siegfried*, Act III) are merged within one perverse chord that now embraces them all. Not only does he revise and Tristanize leitmotives like Magic Sleep and the so-called enslavement or *Frohn*-motive (creating a frightening ninth collection by placing a major third below the *Tristan* chord) but also the entire Norn scene, for example, which recounts the *Ring* narrative from its primeval origins is inflected with *Tristan* harmonies. The stately music opening Brünnhilde's immolation meant to evoke the "towering heap of logs from the world ash tree piling up around Valhalla" (first explained by Waltraute in Act I) is likewise built on an harmonic sequence consisting of alternating *Tristan* chords. To inform Siegfried of his fated Death, the Rhinemaidens taunt him with a three-fold apodictic rendition of the *Tristan* chord. Of course, this is a notionally messy way of treating erotics on the one hand, but on the other, demonstrates a firm belief in the seepage of Desire into every area of human life. Only on the very last pages of the Immolation Scene (Act III, sc. iii) does Wagner offer an imagined solution by his near avoidance of the *Tristan* chord. Copying its identical *coup de grace* at the end of Isolde's *Verklärung* and the Tristanized conclusion to the *Dutchman*, he now pacifies the love-sick symbology: Instead of endlessly resolving to nowhere in particular, the *Tristan* chord is now demoted with some great relief to a functional half-diminished chord that merely—but blissfully—anticipates a punctuating cadence at final rest.

Parsifal

It is in *Parsifal*, though, that Wagner has his final say on matters erotic. Here he not only reframes the central issues of *Tristan*—far more than as a clever mnemonic device as he briefly does in *Meistersinger*—but also composes music for Kundry's Kiss, an unseen rendition of her seduction of Amfortas, as a palimpsest overlaying the *Tristan* chord. In fact, Wagner situates the Kiss on the very same pitches, which, over and over again in *Tristan*, have proclaimed his theme of insatiable yearning. Wagner's revisiting of erotic desire takes on even deeper metaphysical associations when, later in the Second Act, Kundry recounts the origins of her curse, thereby linking Eros with the sin and the agony of the Crucifixion. (The crucial identification of the music's referents occurs twice in Act III, when the Crucifixion sounds after Gurnemanz announces its meaning for the magic of Good Friday.) Again, one hears the *Tristan* chord on the very same pitches, this time harmonizing the Communion motive, an association recapitulated twice by Gurnemanz in the final act during the Good Friday Spell, *Karfreitags-Zauber*. (See Example 3–7.) It is as if Wagner takes *Tristan*'s Desire so as to propose a new elaborative allegory that captures another of its implicit corollaries. In his early plans for the opera *Tristan*, the character Parzifal [*sic*] was to pay a visit to the forlorn knight's sickbed in Cornwall (in Act III) while finding his way back to the Grail. There is even a musical sketch for Parzifal's song that Wagner discarded. In compensation for the loss of Parzifal from *Tristan*, Wagner supplies the opera *Parsifal* with a shadowy Tristanesque *alter ego* that ensures that one hears audible connections between the sufferings of a sex-obsessed Wandering Jewess, her erotic conquest of a Grail King and failed seduction of a Fool, as well as the Passion of the Christian Savior on the Cross.

Wagner, it is important to grasp, never repudiated *Tristan*, and his development of erotic themes in *Parsifal*—including the characterizations of the Flower-Maidens, Amfortas and Klingsor—serve to enlarge his vision rather than to offer a new and improved alternative, a point which, as we shall see in the next chapter, a philosopher like Nietzsche was bound to misunderstand. This vision, moreover, is colored by means of an ample palette of feelings whose identities are rooted in the music. As Kundry sings *Lass mich dich Göttlichen lieben/Erlösung gabst du dann auch mir* (Let me

love you, immortal one/then you shall redeem me as well), Wagner sets the
plangent supplication of the Flower-Maiden's theme, which, he tells
Cosima, "allows us to perceive the sweet omnipotence of wistful love beyond the savage words" (*CT* III, 178). Cosima's diaries show as well how,
while composing the love duet in Act II of *Parsifal* in 1878, Wagner continually tangled with his earlier treatment of erotic themes:

> Richard goes to the piano and plays a theme for *die Labung, die dein
> Leiden endet* [the refreshing draft which ends your torment]. . . .
> He . . . shows me the piece of paper on which he wrote down the
> theme yesterday. Then he complains about this task, says the duet in
> *Die Walküre* was pure joy by comparison, and in *Tristan* there had
> been at least the bliss of the suffering of desire, but here there is only
> the savage pain of love. (*CT* III, 172)

The range and subtlety of these musico-erotic nuances was a lifelong
project, and what is remarkable—given all the self-quotations and her-
metic allusions—is Wagner's uncanny ability never to repeat himself.

However one judges the strange menagerie of literary themes that inhabit *Parsifal*, it is undeniable that Wagner is still portraying the intoxicating allure of sexual desire, still seeking a solution to the syndrome of
erotic suffering. By wrapping up his thoughts in references that extend as
far back as the *Dutchman* and *Tannhäuser*, he also underscores the central-
ity of the erotic impulse in his music, which exposes much that is express-
ible in language along with quite a lot that is not.

CHAPTER FOUR

Pathologies

By the last few decades of the nineteenth century, Wagner's erotics had become enmeshed with diagnoses of a "diseased" culture and politics, although from an historical distance it is easy to lose sight of how such a link was forged. Wagner himself had famously pronounced on cultural and political matters, and both his scurrilous attacks in *Judaism in Music* and recipes for German cultural regeneration have received widespread attention in our own day. What is significant—and surprising—about critical responses to Wagner in the nineteenth century is that the most pronounced and violent reactions were provoked by his erotics, not his politics. To investigate the nature of the threat he posed, I consider the writings of several influential critics—Friedrich Nietzsche chief among them—who stress that his musical eroticism was not only socially unacceptable but amounted to a sickness that required a pseudo-clinical diagnosis and moral castigation. In all these cases, we can glean insights into Wagner's erotics via negative reactions recorded by critics of his music. At the same time, alongside his erotics, the noxious side of Wagner's politics—in particular his anti-Semitism—was also seen as pathological, indeed, was ridiculed or even forgiven by some German-speaking Jews who might be thought to have had a vested interest in combating it.

Wagner himself was extremely alert to the question of somatic disease, his own above all, but also those of male friends about whom he expressed concern. Naturally enough, he never saw his own erotic desires or the suffering of his operatic protagonists as pathological. For him, Senta, Tannhäuser, Ortrud, Alberich, Siegmund and Sieglinde, Tristan, Isolde, Eva, Sachs, Hagen, Amfortas, Parsifal—even Klingsor and Kundry—are emblems of universal moral and erotic dilemmas, not psychiatric patients requiring medical attention. Nor, as we shall see, did he view his own peculiar sexual leanings as anything but a specially refined form of artistic sensitivity, albeit one to be kept secret. In Wagner's world, in other words, the line separating health from sickness is drawn in an unusual place, and this willful challenge to conventional thinking reveals key components of the composer's moral sensibilities and cultural prejudices as well as his unusual musical erotics.

Certain critics had early on reacted to the moral dangers Wagner posed, as was seen in Chapter 1. His chromaticism seemed to advocate a "profligate libertinage," and his sensualism flouted all the "established rules and customs." From the 1860s and 1870s, moreover, antagonists also began to describe Wagner's works as pathological, in keeping with the rapid spread of medical discourse into critiques of cultural life all across Europe.[1] Clara Schumann, as mentioned, heard the music of Tristan in 1875 as a "sickness" and viewed her friend Levi's Wagnerism in 1880 as "an illness to which he had succumbed in body and soul," but even these expressions are signs of the times and wouldn't have been uttered by Clara thirty-five years before, when she first reacted against *Tannhäuser*. As medicine gained in scientific prestige and advertisements for medical cures based on up-to-date methods became widespread, therefore, it was natural that other areas of life became invested with a medical point of view. Disease lurked everywhere, according to the latest science, even in inanimate objects such as pieces of music. New theories of disease, along with more precise diagnoses, meant that people paid greater attention to their symptoms, so as better to report them to the experts and effect a quicker cure. If music gave rise to sexual thoughts that led susceptible subjects to indulge their weaknesses in excessive behaviors that debilitated them or otherwise made them ill, both cultural critics and physicians felt justified in speaking out, lambasting such music as diseased and dangerous. The legacy of this nineteenth-century obsession with cultural pathology even exerts some tacit influence today, although, given its anachronistic baggage, one would be well advised to take it with a large grain of salt: The silliness of branding some music as sick can be unmasked as soon as one tries to specify why any other music is healthy.

Theodor Puschmann

The story of Wagner's pathology begins with a widely read psychiatric denunciation in 1873 by Theodor Puschmann called *Richard Wagner: eine psychiatrische Studie*. In it, the author, a Munich psychiatrist, proposes to bring scientific objectivity to the diagnosis of a widespread condition spread by a genius who Puschmann concedes "has achieved significance in our cultural history," yet is also the "leader of a pathological movement [*krankhafte Bewegung*] threatening to conquer ever more terrain." It is this movement targeted by Puschmann's study, "not Wagner's person," though the author charitably hopes to offer "a cure and recovery" to the artist himself.[2] Not only is Wagner's "moral degeneration" visible in his use of verbal language and in his personal behavior—the scandalous affair with Cosima von Bülow was still fresh in the public mind—but also in his obviously pathological ideas of persecution by the Jews, a mania reinforced by the recent reissue of *Judaism in Music* (1869), a pamphlet that "offers the psychiatrist a deep diagnostic insight into the most private workings of [the composer's] inner life [*Seelenleben*]" (*PS*, 31). The pathology afflicts Wagner's work since the 1850s in which the composer has

> recklessly scorned the laws of humanity and morality. In the most in-
> considerate manner he has trampled on the holiest feelings of friend-
> ship and love. Ever more he has besmirched the glory of his name. . . .
> Is this our great artist? Is this our beloved and admired Master, who

aroused the most tender, noble and holy feelings, who evoked the
most beautiful dreams, who revived the sweetest hopes which we
greeted with tears and laughter, with whom we suffered and rejoiced?
No! This isn't, this can't be the same one. The Wagner we loved is
dead, and died with the Swan song in *Lohengrin*. (*PS*, 19)

Suffering from a host of maladies, especially "delusions of grandeur," Wagner's "moral insanity" creates dramas that no longer idealize and mirror the
highest values of life, but "descend into the slime and mud of daily life"
(*PS*, 31). The diseased tendency is naturally connected with heightened
erotic obsessions:

It is well known that in the beginning of mental illnesses there often
appears an unnatural increase in sexual desire which stands in the
most stark contrast to physical and psychological impotence which
establishes itself ever more pronouncedly. From the beginning of his
career Wagner allowed sexual impulses to exercise a great influence
on his inner life. . . . His first great opus, *Das Liebesverbot*, exalted
"the victory of free and open sensuality" though it did remain within
the boundaries of respectful decency. But in his latest works the
erotic element [*das erotische Element*] is emphasized so explicitly that
in *Tristan und Isolde* he glorifies adultery and in *Die Walküre* even incest. (*PS*, 59–60)

Wagner's obsession with sex even extends to a surprisingly positive assessment of male homosexuality. Puschmann quotes a passage from Wagner's collected writings that "praises the masculine love [*Männerliebe*] of
the Greeks which, 'in sinking oneself completely in the beloved, is more
noble and pure than the love of man to woman'" (*PS*, 61).

This moral insanity observed by Puschmann isn't just confined to
Wagner's words but "the same obscenity and immorality . . . is also found
in his tone-painting, which may perhaps be the most eminently suitable
stimulus [prompting audiences] to attend his operas." All this diagnosis
leads to the scientific conclusion that Wagner is "no longer psychically
normal but suffers today from definite symptoms of mental illness" (*PS*,
61). His followers, likewise "live in the delusion that they are supporting

the life-altering plans of a sublime genius and are helping prepare the way for a new age, whereas in reality they seek to realize ideas infected by madness" (*PS*, 67). Within a few years, Puschmann's booklet had been reprinted several times and the terms of its critique, as James Kennaway shows, became common currency for long afterward in the anti-Wagnerian literature. On the one hand, Puschmann's onslaught initiated an influential discourse on Wagnerian pathology. On the other, Puschmann provides indirect evidence that it was indeed Wagner's erotics that attracted audiences—depraved or not—to the later operas, buttressing the view that certainly by the 1870s Wagner's erotic intentions were both understood and appreciated.

Nietzsche the Pathologist

The diagnosis of Wagner's sickness was first challenged and then taken up with a vengeance by Friedrich Nietzsche, an intimate of the Wagner circle, who in his late works came to see in Wagner the antipode to his entire philosophy. Nietzsche's early enthusiasm for the score of *Tristan*, with its "lasting sense of ecstasy" and its "spasmodic release of the wings of the soul" perceived by all "genuine musicians" had led to his *Birth of Tragedy* (1872) dedicated to Wagner, as mentioned in Chapter 1. By the time of the first Bayreuth Festival in 1876, however, Nietzsche was having serious qualms about the Wagner project, and in succeeding years he gradually severed his ties with Bayreuth, launching a succession of essays that became increasingly vitriolic in their criticism of Wagner. Yet the mature Nietzsche was still deeply attached to Wagner's music: "The last thing I want to do is start a celebration for any other musician," he writes in 1888. "Other musicians don't count compared to Wagner."[3] What had changed was Nietzsche's critical assessment. Wagner represented the quintessence of decadence, and to be become healthy, one must break with Wagner. "Here my seriousness begins," Nietzsche writes in *The Wagner Case* (1888), "while this decadent corrupts our health— and music as well. Is Wagner a human being at all? Isn't he rather a sickness? He makes sick whatever he touches—he has made music sick" (*NW*, 620). Despite the witty and often humorous tone of the pamphlet, Nietzsche's intent is deadly serious, as he indicates in an aphorism mangled from Horace: *"ridendo dicere severum"* [Through what is laughable say what is somber] (*NW*, 609).

Of the many charges laid at Wagner's feet, the most emotive target the erotic in some way or the other. Whereas the "harmful" Wagnerian orchestra—with its "infinite melody" and "lie of the great style"—causes the philosopher to "break out in a disagreeable sweat," Nietzsche feels "happy," "patient," and "settled" with Bizet's *Carmen*, which represents musical health over Wagner's sickness. *Carmen* makes Nietzsche a better philosopher. Its music "approaches [him] lightly, supplely and politely. It is pleasant. It does not sweat." Bizet "treats him as intelligent, as if he himself were a musician," unlike Wagner, "the most impolite genius in the world," who "treats us as if—he says something so often—till one despairs—till one believes it" (*NW*, 613): Wagner's obsessive strewing of leitmotives drives Nietzsche to distraction. Bizet, on the other hand, he says, "builds, organizes, finishes," which, Nietzsche asserts, again invoking medical terminology, "thus . . . constitutes the opposite of the polyp in music, the 'infinite melody'" (*NW*, 613).

Wagner reeks of too much "steam of the North," a metaphor for his tortured views of love. Nietzsche, by contrast, prefers music that allows him the clarity "to think philosophically," "music which liberates his spirit." In fact, he prefers music—so he claims—that doesn't draw attention to itself, composed by a musician disinterested in philosophy: "I am delighted by strokes of good fortune of which Bizet is innocent—And, oddly, deep down, I don't think of [the music], or don't know how much I think about it. For entirely different thoughts are meanwhile running through my head" (*NW*, 614). As a critique of decadence, this is an odd admission that makes little sense until Nietzsche specifies which thoughts he wishes to avoid: It is Wagner's inveterate attempt to find redemption, but above all, his misunderstanding of love. Wagner, like many artists, Nietzsche says, believed "one becomes selfless in love because one desires the advantage of another human being, often against one's own advantage." In fact, this is far too effeminate a psychology. Bizet possessed a more "southern, brown, burnt sensibility," in which "happiness is brief, sudden, without pardon." It is a love "translated back into nature." "And what is this nature?," he asks. "The deadly hatred of the sexes!" Indeed, the very "essence of love" is found in Don José's final cry: "Yes, I have killed

her, I—my adored Carmen." Love isn't selfless, but about crude possession, and once this fact is recognized, the act of murdering the gypsy constitutes the only "conception of love . . . worthy of a philosopher" (*NW*,
614–615). Nietzsche surely noticed that in not one of Wagner's operas is a
woman killed, not for any reason, never mind out of jealous love. Indeed,
even Wagner's most heinous villains are unfailingly polite in their villainy.
None of his characters perpetrates violence on female characters: The most
they do is express "lovelessness" through some verbal abuse, such as that
visited on Ortrud (by Telramund), Sieglinde (by Hunding), and Kundry
(by Klingsor). Fafner and Fasolt hold Freia hostage and Siegfried—
drugged and assuming the guise of Gunther—abducts Brünnhilde, but
all of them do so in the name of a misguided Love. Cruel, selfish, and
possessive love doesn't figure in Wagner's operatic vocabulary, a pathological fault, according to Nietzsche.

Wagner's quest for redemption in love—in Nietzsche's account—is not
only weak and womanish, but leads countless people into a labyrinth of
decadence where Wagner saps their strength and devours them. "Man is a
coward" who too often succumbs to Wagnerian messages about a woman's love. In fact, "in many cases of feminine love, perhaps including the
most famous ones . . . , love is merely a more refined form of parasitism, a
form of nestling down in another soul, sometimes even in the flesh of
another—alas, always decidedly at the expense of 'the host'" (*NW*, 617).
The charge of pathology in *The Wagner Case: A Problem for Musicians*
(1888)—borrowed in part from Puschmann—makes sense chiefly because
Nietzsche is able to "diagnose" what he takes to be the enfeebling message
embodied in Wagner's erotics. Nietzsche's attack on Wagner latches onto
his rejection of Schopenhauer (another former idol), whom he now views
as an embittered ascetic avoiding, like all idealist philosophers, the swirl
of life.

This is why it is crucial that Nietzsche identifies Wagner's putative
message in his final opera *Parsifal* as "a praise to chastity" (*NW*, 616). In
Nietzsche contra Wagner, he goes so far as to call it "a work of perfidy, of
vindictiveness, of a secret mix to poison the presuppositions of life—a
bad work. The preaching of chastity remains an incitement to perversity
[*Widernatur*]: I despise everyone who does not experience *Parsifal* as an
attempted assassination of basic ethics" (*KSA* VI, 431). Wagner must be

seen to have propounded a philosophical message to be combated at all costs. Wagner is the "protagonist, the greatest name . . . in the whole of European decadence" (*NW*, 621). What is more, his music "increases exhaustion: that is why he attracts the weak and exhausted" (*NW*, 622). In place of decadent views of love, and having asserted that "there is no necessary opposition between sensuality and chastity" (*KSA* VI, 429), Nietzsche presupposes a healthy sexuality, an uninhibited romp through the human jungle, where man virtuously confronts the object of his desire both as enemy, possession, and finally as vanquished beast of prey. I say "presupposes" because you can scour Nietzsche's published works in vain to discover a coherent view of erotic desire. It wasn't a subject he worked out, for it appears nowhere in his major works, not in *Zarathustra*, his most positive piece of writing, not in the *Genealogy of Morals*, nor in his autobiographical *Ecce Homo*. *Zarathustra*, in fact, includes a chapter on chastity in which he suggests that it is "better to fall into the hands of a murderer than into the dreams of a lustful woman," yet stops short of recommending chastity because "for some, chastity is a virtue, but for others it is almost a vice," and in any case, "the bitch Carnality [*die Hündin Sinnlichkeit*] knows to beg for a piece of your mind when she is denied a piece of your flesh" (*KSA* VI, 65). It remains unclear how the erotic might be integrated into the positive values of the Superman [*Übermensch*].

Rejecting an aesthetic that translates aspects of lived (as opposed to ideal) sexual experience into music, Nietzsche insists on treating Wagner as an agent of disease, who, by virtue of his aesthetic powers, leads to a corruption of healthy values:

> I place this perspective at the outset: Wagner's art is sick. The problems he presents on the stage—all of them problems of hysterics, the convulsive nature of his affects, his overexcited sensibility, his taste that required ever stronger spices, his instability which he dressed up as principles, not least of all the choice of his heroes and heroines—consider them as physiological types (a pathological gallery)! All of this taken together represents a profile of sickness that permits no further doubt. *Wagner est une névrose.* [Wagner is a neurosis.] Perhaps nothing is better known today, at least nothing

has been better studied, than the Protean character of degeneration that here conceals itself in the chrysalis of art and artist. Our physicians and physiologists confront their most interesting case in Wagner, at least a very complete case. Precisely because nothing is more modern than this total sickness, this lateness and overexcitement of the nervous mechanism, Wagner is *the modern artist par excellence.* (*NW,* 622)

Who *are* these hysterics on Wagner's stage? Not Siegfried, Elisabeth, Lohengrin, Wotan, Hans Sachs, or Gurnemanz. Rather, they are Venus, Tannhäuser, Tristan, Isolde, Amfortas, Parsifal, and Kundry, whose problems all center on their erotic dilemmas. Nietzsche distances himself from Wagner's neurosis because it makes him too alert to every erotic tremor. One must shun these kinds of feelings to preserve one's health. Indeed, in a deeply wounded and wounding letter to Malwida von Meysenbug of October 20, 1888, who thought he shouldn't have treated an "old, even extinguished love" the way he behaved toward Wagner in print, Nietzsche explodes: "Did you understand nothing of the disgust [*Ekel*] with which I turned my back on Wagner ten years ago, together with all decent people, when the swindle became clear in the first *Bayreuther Blätter?* . . . Did it escape your notice that in the last ten years I have become Father Confessor [*Gewissensrat*] for German musicians, that I have re-instilled artistic righteousness, good taste and the deepest hatred against the nauseating sexuality [*gegen die ekelhafte Sexualität*] of Wagnerian music in every possible place? . . . The *Wagner Case* is a godsend for me."[4]

A further sign of Wagner's erotic decadence lies in his music's denial of enjoyment, an art that constantly withholds satisfaction by "dauntlessly rolling in the mud of the most contrary harmonies," or passing off as passion "what is ugly on the rope of enharmonicism" (*NW,* 624). Parodying Wagner, Nietzsche writes: "Let us never admit that music 'serves recreation'; that it 'exhilarates'; that it gives 'pleasure.' Let us never give pleasure! We are lost as soon as art is again thought of hedonistically. That's the bad eighteenth century" (*NW,* 625). Nietzsche raises a legitimate debating point, but he creates a telling opposition between the erotic as against recreation and pleasure.

Nietzsche's objections presuppose that Wagner's music articulates a coherent philosophy, a logically constructed recommendation for life. Even Wagner, in all the hubris of his essays, never even went so far. Misled by Wagner's belief that his writing represented his artistic intentions, Nietzsche falls into a typical trap of "deep interpretations." On the basis of his perceptions of the music and (mostly) the opera texts, along with his intimate knowledge of Wagner's character, he dreams up a logic of ideas accommodating a grand thesis deserving of censure. Wagner—we are told—is responsible for the cultural malaise Nietzsche diagnoses as decadence. Yet Nietzsche is disingenuous in interpreting the meaning of Wagner's oeuvre, for he mocks Wagner precisely for having "required a literature," for asserting "that his music did not mean mere music. But more. But infinitely more—'not mere music'—no musician would say that" (*NW*, 633). So Nietzsche wishes to have it both ways. If music signifies no more than just itself, he can hardly assert that Wagner's music, devoid of meaning, is sick. This is why his music criticism flirts with bits and pieces gathered from almost anywhere. Perhaps he was aware of problematic underpinnings of his argument, for in an unpublished fragment from 1888, he asserted music's fundamental semi-autonomy from discursive thought: "that music itself ignores words, concepts, imagines, oh, how well it knows how to draw its advantage from this, the cunning 'eternal feminine!'" (*KSA* XIII, 41). Only artists, not philosophers—it turns out—can have it both ways and assert (at different times) music's autonomy as well as it dependence on concepts.

It is no coincidence that Nietzsche's cultural diagnosis of Wagner saddles the composer himself with erotic metaphors. Wagner, Nietzsche writes:

> is a seducer on a large scale, [and] there is nothing weary, nothing decrepit, nothing fatal and hostile to life in matters of the spirit that his art does not secretly safeguard—"this Klingsor of Klingsors"— Here the cunning alliance of beauty and sickness goes so far that . . . it casts a shadow over Wagner's earlier art—which now seems too bright, too healthy. . . . Never was there a greater master in dim, priestly aromas—Open your ears: everything that ever grew on the

soil of impoverished life, all of the counterfeiting of transcendence
and beyond, has found its most sublime advocate in Wagner's art, not
by means of formulas, by the means of a persuasion of sensuousness,
which in turn makes the spirit weary and worn-out. Music as Circe.
(*NW*, 639)

In the art of seduction, *Parsifal* will always retain its rank—as the
stroke of genius in seduction. I admire this work; I wish I had written
it myself; failing that, I understand it. (*NW*, 639–640)

At the same time that he claims Wagner's music is feminized, Nietzsche
now turns the tables and suggests that he has been a willing participant in
an act of buggery; that Wagner himself, having supplied his music as an
intoxicating potion, was the invasive pederast:

> Never was there a man equally expert in . . . all that quivers and
> gushes, all the feminisms from the *idioticon* of happiness! Drink, o my
> friends, the philters of this art! Nowhere will you find a more agree-
> able way of enervating your spirit, of forgetting your manhood under
> a rose-bush. (*NW*, 640)

The characterization of Wagner as a man of questionable masculinity
who drains the lifeblood from his victim and then compromises him under a rose bush plays on two distinct if contradictory stereotypes: the
gushing, effeminate sodomite and the preying pederast who un-mans innocent youths. The passage results in an extraordinary conflation of the
two images, and one wonders whether Nietzsche noticed its odd, if revealing, incoherence.

Like all vituperative reactions to great art, Nietzsche's repudiation of
Wagner unwittingly identifies central features of his unusually powerful
erotics. Stripped of pathological metaphors, Nietzsche's condemnations
even amount to a stunning endorsement: the fact that Wagner makes one
sweat, that he persuades by hammering home his repeated leitmotives,
that he captures the guilt-ridden steam of the North, that his erotics are
often highly feminized, that he dispenses with the "deadly hatred" between the sexes, that his intense erotic attractions feel like a form of

parasitism, that the notion of sexual chastity offers respite despite its anti-natural status, that submitting to his musical experience is blissfully exhausting, that problems of sexual hysterics mirror and magnify those of people in real life, that neurotic music engages the senses and is fundamentally modern in its occasional ugliness, that Wagner is a seducer, even a pederast *par excellence*—recalling Baudelaire's pleasure in "feeling penetrated"—and that the marriage of high musical values and the erotic marks what is so special about the Wagnerian aesthetic. In short, what Nietzsche rejects in Wagner is precisely what make his erotics so significant. As a philosophy of life, such an aesthetic may be noxious or overindulgent, even diseased, but as a set of insights about life captured within music, it is surely unparalleled.

In his sympathetic "erotic biography" of 1912, Julius Kapp had already treated Wagner's "unheroic effeminate nature," and at the heart of Nietzsche's critique is a vivid awareness of an erotic sensibility allied to such a nature. For Nietzsche, Wagner's sexuality is dangerous because it falls short of a masculine domination of its desires. What is debilitating in Wagner is that he expresses both vulnerability and unsatisfied sexual needs, something easy to hear in *Tannhäuser*, *Tristan*, and *Parsifal*. An apostle of strength over weakness, Nietzsche perceives a threatening frailty in musical longings not immediately gratified, which is why he bears down hard in a rain of verbal blows. However one decides to evaluate Nietzsche's dichotomous world "beyond good and evil," what is clear is that there is no room in it for Wagner's soft erotics except as a scourge with which the philosopher whips himself to expunge the memory of his Wagnerian years when he "forgot his manhood."

Interestingly, Nietzsche finds any music infused with late-Romantic yearning [*Sehnsucht*] equally suspect, as in his diagnosis of Johannes Brahms:

> He has the melancholy of impotence; he does not create out of an abundance, he thirsts for abundance. If we discount what he imitates, what he borrows from great old or exotic-modern styles—he is a master of imitation—what remains as specifically his is yearning.— This is felt by all who are full of yearning and dissatisfaction of any kind. (*KSA* VI, 47)

"The sympathy which Brahms inspires," he writes, "long seemed enigmatic to me—until finally I discovered, almost by accident, that he affects a certain type of person," namely the feeble melancholic. For the same reason, he continues, Brahms "is the musician for a certain type of dissatisfied woman. Fifty steps more, and you have got the female Wagnerian—just as fifty steps beyond Brahms you encounter Wagner" (*NW*, 643):

> Brahms is touching as long as he is secretly enraptured or mourns for himself—in this he is "modern"; he becomes cold and of no further concern to us as soon as he becomes the heir of the classical composers. (*NW*, 644)

Sweeping away a composer's entire oeuvre in the flourish of a paint brush, Nietzsche dismisses Brahms by diagnosing a weak erotic nature only steps distant from Wagner's own. Any aesthetic displaying such a feminized trait as yearning is equally suspect and unhealthy.

Nietzsche's case against Wagner turns out to be more an issue of morals than aesthetics, underscoring the great "contrast between a master morality and a morality of Christian value concepts" (*NW*, 646). "Master morality," Nietzsche writes in the Epilogue to *The Wagner Case*, "is rooted in a triumphant Yes said to oneself—it is self-affirmation, self-glorification of life; it also requires sublime symbols and practices, but only because 'its heart is too full.' All of beautiful and great art is found here" (*NW*, 647–648). This morality "transfigures, it beautifies the world and makes it more rational, whereas Christian morality, associated with Wagner's decadence impoverishes, pales and makes uglier the value of things, it *negates* the world" (*NW*, 646). For this reason, he concludes, "one cannot dissociate from [master morality] an instinctive aversion against decadents, scorn for their symbolism, even horror: such feelings almost prove it. . . . One looks in vain for more valuable, more necessary opposites" (*NW*, 648).

Although until the last days preceding his mental illness Nietzsche pines away for his happy times at Wagner's side in his retreat at Tribschen, he insists that, in rejecting Wagner as "imperial German" [*reichsdeutsch*], he was expressing a purely philosophical position, far removed from any personal animus. As he puts it in his autobiographical work, *Ecce*

Homo: "I only attack things where every personal difference is excluded, where every background of bad experiences is lacking." "To the contrary," he says, "my attacks are proof of my goodwill, sometimes even of my gratitude" (*KSA* VI, 275). Yet not much gratitude is expressed in *The Wagner Case*, which—with some exceptions—traffics in insinuations and sexual innuendo. One innuendo is an aside made in the context of discussing the effeminacy of the opera *Parsifal*, which Nietzsche pillories in the Epilogue as a form of "Christianity cleaned up for female Wagnerians, perhaps *by* female Wagnerians—for Wagner in the old days [*in alten Tagen*] was certainly quite of the feminine gender" (*KSA* VI, 51), making a pun on *feminini generis*, Latin for grammatical feminine gender. Although Nietzsche might have written "in his later days" [*auf seine alten Tagen*] to refer to Wagner's later years in the context of the composition of *Parsifal*, this was the period during which contact between the two men had been entirely broken off. By "the old days" Nietzsche means when he was often in Wagner's proximity, and by female Wagnerians, Nietzsche alludes to "unhealthy" women whom he suspects of Lesbianism. In his notebooks for *The Wagner Case* (*LN*, 266) he writes: "As regards the true 'Maenads' who worship Wagner, we can without hesitation conclude hysteria and sickness: something is not right about their sexuality; or there is a lack of children or, in the most tolerable case, a lack of men" (*KSA* XI, 674). Whereas some might see all this as part of a philosophical project, a personal angle is also undeniable.

Worries about Masturbation

The slur on Wagner's manhood might suit the general drift of Nietzsche's critique, but it also responds to a painful incident about a decade before when Wagner expressed doubts about Nietzsche's own masculinity. In a meddlesome letter of 1877, after Nietzsche had begun to withdraw from the Wahnfried retinue complaining of severe headaches, fainting spells, and nausea, Wagner had the temerity to write to Nietzsche's physician, Otto Eiser, to whom he suggested that Nietzsche's impaired eyesight resulted from the practice of chronic self-abuse, a vice thought by most everyone to cause serious organic illness. "In my attempts to assess N.'s condition," Wagner writes:

I have been thinking for some time of identical and very similar experiences which I recall having had with certain young men of great intellectual ability. I saw them being destroyed by similar symptoms,
and discovered only too clearly that these symptoms were the result of
masturbation. Guided by these experiences, I observed N. more closely
and, on the strength of his traits and characteristic habits, this fear of
mine became a conviction. I believe it would be wrong of me to express myself more circumstantially on this point, the more so since
my only concern is to draw a friendly doctor's attention to the opinion
which I have conveyed to you here. It is merely to confirm the great
likelihood that I am right that I mention the striking experience I had
whereby one of the young friends whom I mentioned, a poet [The-
odor Apel] who died in Leipzig many years ago, became totally blind
when he was N.'s age, while the other, equally talented, friend [Karl
Ritter], who now ekes out a pitiful existence in Italy, with his nerves
completely shattered, began to suffer the most painful eye disease at
exactly the same age as N. One thing that struck me as being of great
importance was the news I recently received to the effect that the
doctor whom N. had consulted in Naples some time ago advised him
first and foremost—to get married. (*SL*, 873)

How Wagner managed to "discover" that his young friends' medical
symptoms were "a result of masturbation" isn't revealed, but the next year,
Nietzsche managed to extract the admission from the doctor, an ardent
Wagnerian, that his sudden enquiries about onanism were a result of
Wagner's intervention. In fact, Eiser seems to have shown him the letter,
or at least revealed its contents. It was the doctor's reasonable view that
Nietzsche's enraged reaction sparked and solidified the personal rift that
followed. Eugen Kretzer, a friend of Nietzsche's who interviewed Eiser in
1884, reports the doctor's own account of what happened:

I alone know why Nietzsche fell out with Wagner, for this falling out
occurred in my house, in my examining room when I—with the most
well-meaning of intentions—acquainted Nietzsche with this letter
[*als ich Nietzsche jenen Brief in wohlmeinendster Absicht mitteilte*]. Nietzsche thereupon flew into a rage [*Ein Ausbruch von Raserei war die*

Folge] and was quite beside himself—the words he found for Wagner aren't repeatable—from then on the breach was sealed."[5]

Worries about adverse effects of chronic masturbation were widespread throughout the nineteenth century—a continuous tradition can be traced to Tissot's *Onanism* (1760)—and a popular medical literature on the subject perpetrated the most common fears and misconceptions. An example of one widely disseminated work in Germany was by Samuel La'Mert, and was translated in 1855 from the English "in a greatly expanded and improved edition" by a pseudonymous author in Leipzig calling himself Laurentius. Called *Personal Protection or Self-Preservation*, the subtitle advertizes the book as a *Medical advisor for all diseases of the sexual organs which arise as a result of secret sins of youth, excessive enjoyment of sexual love and through infection.*[6] Appearing in a French translation in 1847—having already reached its thirtieth edition by 1860—the work features frightening and vivid illustrations of medical drawings showing diseased sexual organs and skin ravaged by syphilis. Self-pollution, it is repeatedly claimed, leads to mental insanity, physical debilitation, premature aging, and infertility, among other grave maladies. The 1855 edition was strongly recommended, for example, by the 22-year old Johannes Brahms to Joseph Joachim.[7] Another popular work by a physician Dr. Retau called *Self-Preservation* [*Selbstbewahrung*] from around 1850, also explaining the dire medical consequences of onanism, went through eighty editions, and saw sales of more than 300,000 copies.[8] Only with the second volume of Havelock Ellis's pathbreaking *Studies in the Psychology of Sex* (1897) treating "auto-eroticism" was it first mooted that "in the case of moderate masturbation in healthy, well-born individuals, no seriously pernicious results necessarily follow."[9] (Even this work had to be published in Philadelphia after the first volume was banned as obscene in England.) But it seems to be the case that after about 1877 medical opinion in Germany began to shift somewhat to a less draconian assessment, to the effect that masturbation was a symptom of disease rather than a cause. In *Meyers Conversations-Lexikon*, the third edition (1877) repeated all the harsh effects of onanism, which only disappear in the fourth edition (1896).[10] Wagner's worries in 1877 about Nietzsche and Karl Ritter were therefore no more than common, garden-variety anxieties, even if his letter to Otto Eiser was, even at the time, an outrageous personal intrusion.[11]

Nietzsche, however, clearly understood Wagner's letter as accusing him also of homosexuality (*NB* III.1, 365). As he put it in 1883 to his friend Heinrich Köselitz (whom he called Peter Gast): "Wagner is rich in spiteful tricks [*bösen Einfällen*], but what would you say if I told you that he had exchanged letters . . . (even with my doctors) to express his conviction that my altered way of thinking resulted from unnatural perversions, with allusions to pederasty?" Nietzsche was not exaggerating Wagner's concern, for there was a commonly supposed link between masturbation and same-sexuality: Both occurred in secret, so that engaging in self-stimulation could easily lead, it was thought, to an equally secretive sexuality.[12] Given Nietzsche's reaction, it is likely that some settling of the score—some retribution—underlies Nietzsche's philosophical critique of Wagner's erotics in a posthumous smear that answers one sexual humiliation with another.[13]

It was also a critique about which Nietzsche had qualms. At the same time as *The Wagner Case*, in October 1888, he could write in his personal notebooks with less rancor and rather more insight about the intimate relation between Wagner's music and his sexuality. Theorizing about artists and Eros, he notes:

> The artist is perhaps of necessity a sexual being [*ein sinnlicher Mensch*] according to his type, which is generally excitable, open to every sense and stimulus, even to the suggestion of stimulus approaching from afar. Yet on average in exercising his task, in his desire for mastery, [the artist] is in fact a moderate, often even a chaste person. His dominating instinct wants it to be so of himself: he doesn't permit himself to waste himself on this or that fashion. It is one and the same force which is spent in artistic conception and in the sexual act. There is only one kind of force. To succumb, to waste oneself is traitorous to an artist: it betrays a lack of instinct, of will in general, it can be a sign of decadence—it devalues in any case his art to an incalculable degree. I cite the most unpleasant case, the case of Wagner.— Wagner, under the spell of that most unbelievably perverse sexuality

[*im Banne jener unglaubwürdig krankhaften Sexualität*] which was the
curse of his life knew only too well what an artist forfeits therewith,
namely his freedom and self-respect. He is condemned to be an actor.
His art itself becomes for him a constant attempt to flee, a means of
forgetting oneself, a self-numbing—it alters, and finally determines
the character of his art. Such an unfree being [*"Unfreier"*] requires a
hashish-world of strange, obscure, hazy fumes, and every kind of ex-
oticism and symbolism of ideals to rid himself of *his* reality—he needs
Wagnerian music. . . . A certain catholicity of ideals is above all for
an artist almost the proof of self-reproach, of "the swamp": the case
of Baudelaire in France, the case of Edgar Allan Poe in America, the
case of Wagner in Germany.—Need I add that Wagner also owes his
success to his sensuality? (*KSA* XIII, 601)

The admission that Wagner's baleful sexuality was key to his achievement
is a powerful antidote to the censure in Nietzsche's late published works,
but what doesn't seem to occur to the philosopher, because of his obsession with health, is that sharing the fruits of that success with a public
might provide pleasure and edification without the torments attached to
the composer's agitated personal life. The reason Nietzsche cannot take
this step is that he is still stunned by the dangerous erotic immediacy
Wagner evokes and concludes:

Who dares say the word, the *actual* word for the ardors of the *Tristan*
music?—I put on gloves when I read the score of *Tristan*. . . . [To
guard] against Wagnerian music I consider it imperative to exercise
every caution. (*KSA* XIII, 601)

And yet in *Ecce Homo* (1888): "To this day I am still looking for a work that
equals the dangerous fascination and the gruesome and sweet infinity of
Tristan—and look in all the arts in vain. . . . The world is poor for anyone
who has never been sick enough for this 'voluptuousness of hell'" (*LN*,
152).

Pink Satin and Rose Perfumes

In what becomes a recurrent trope in the *Wagner Case*, Nietzsche made a point of naming in oblique fashion the "most unbelievably perverse sexuality" of which he had personal knowledge: that Wagner, though married with children, and thought to act in a conventionally masculine manner, a man not known to have had male lovers, nevertheless had a unconventional relationship to femininity. In his intimate contact with the family, Nietzsche cannot fail to have noticed that Wagner indulged in a longstanding fetish for wearing and surrounding himself with soft fabrics, especially satin and silk, without which he found it difficult to compose music. Wagner even imposed on Nietzsche to procure some of his needs. A student of Nietzsche's reports encountering him:

> one day just as he had returned from his usual Sunday visit to Wagner, [and] Nietzsche asked me in the most concerned manner [*angelegentlichst*] where he might find a good silk shop in Basel. Eventually he admitted he had undertaken to shop for a pair of silk underpants for Wagner, and this important matter filled him with anxiety; for— added the smiling iconoclast—"once you've chosen a God, you've got to adorn him!"[14]

The incident, which took place sometime between 1869 and 1872, is all the more believable because Nietzsche's former student is only trying to establish a characteristic picture of the philosopher's intimate friendship with Wagner at the time, as is clear from the context. Nietzsche surely knew about Wagner's special preferences: Although partial to yellow, light blue, or white satin, Wagner had one overriding color preference for textiles of any sort, on which he spent a fortune even when penniless—namely pale pink [*rosa*]. An obsession with rose-scented fragrances, though sometimes lilac, rounds out the picture: Nietzsche's reference to a rose-bush in *The Wagner Case* is less than accidental.

Wagner's fixation was given a public airing in June 1877, almost a year after the first *Ring* performances, when a Viennese journalist published in the *Neue Freie Presse* a cache of letters Wagner had written to his Viennese milliner over a period of years. The letters spell out in sensational detail

Wagner's lavish requirements (even sketched drawings) for a succession of pink satin dressing gowns with lengthy trains and flounces, along with voluminous orders for satin undergarments, silk slippers, pillows, quilts, curtains, upholstery, and other embroidered accessories too numerous to name.[15] A certain number of the letters published by this journalist and satirist, Daniel Spitzer (1835–1893), were later acquired by Brahms and found their way into the collection at the Library of Congress, with the remaining letters ultimately transferred to a collection in Eisenach.[16] From the days when Wagner had any money at all, he always surrounded himself with extravagant luxuries, but luxury doesn't begin to explain the hundreds of yards of costly fabric ordered year in and year out. There was the complete refurbishing of his wardrobe and his residence in Penzing outside Vienna, then the outfitting of the house in Munich (where Ludwig II footed the bill), and later regular packages sent to Tribschen where Nietzsche was a frequent visitor. In the Briennerstraße in Munich, for example, Bertha Goldwag, Wagner's milliner, outfitted what was called the Grail or Satin Room, about 22 square meters with 3.5 meter ceilings (11.5 × 14.5 feet with 11.5 foot high ceilings) crammed with a dizzying supply of satin furnishings, draperies, curtains, mostly pink. Even the walls were covered in yellow satin with valances, with artificial recesses in the corners covered with pink satin in folds (*NM*, 130–135).

Wagner and His Milliners

The publication of the letters to Wagner's milliner (the *Putzmacherin-Briefe*) caused a stir not only because of their revelations that Wagner liked to wear and be surrounded by pink satin but also because his style in specifying his requirements was so exacting, as were his detailed listings of fabric, costings, and accumulating financial accounts. Spitzer, revealing the existence of the letters just a year after the 1876 *Ring* premiere (which he attended), was also able to capitalize on the stark contrast between the severe Teutonic heroes from the mythic past who populated the stage of the *Festspielhaus* clad in bearskins and rough cloth, and the softer and rather more feminine and sensuous attire of their author down from the Green Hill in luxurious Wahnfried.[17] Not only do we learn, Spitzer writes, "that the maestro also wears satin waistcoats and pink satin knee-breeches lined with pale pink satin." There is also

> the sixth letter [which] is unique, in fact, since it contains two pen drawings from the maestro's hand. There is a drawing of the eiderdown-padded house robe of pink satin—a magnificent specimen, on any lady at court it would create a sensation—as well as a smaller drawing of the 5-yard sash. This sash worries us a little, considering that its wearer, with his short stature, is likely to stumble over it constantly. The drawing of the house robe betrays remarkable [artistic] training, after the best models of the fashion journals. The "quilted squares" are executed in gentle strokes and reveal a great delicacy of feeling. The "shirred ruffles and bows" demonstrate a sweeping stroke and an energetic hand. The ruffled insertion in front is done with a touch of fantasy, in the manner of Callot. And what spirit there is in the whole![18]

While Spitzer's tirade pokes fun at Wagner's effeminacy, there is—significantly—no pathologizing of the composer's condition, no sense that this attraction was a malady, the result of a diseased mind. The style is that of the seasoned newspaper columnist, a journalist and writer used to the cultural essays and features in the bourgeois weeklies.

Shortly after Spitzer published his revelations, perhaps the most striking caricature of Wagner ever to appear was seen in the humorous Leipzig weekly called *Puck* under the title "'Atlas' in Music." Though exaggerated (and inaccurate as far as the high heels are concerned!), the image encapsulates what contemporaries must have thought when confronting the Milliner letters, linking the composer's high political opinion of himself with the absurdity of the attire in which he is clothed. (See Figure 4–1.) *Atlas* was the common word in nineteenth-century German for a refined variety of satin,[19] and as Ludwig Kusche describes it, Wagner appears as "an effeminate bugbear with his head wrapped in a rose garland and attired in everything that a Madame Pompadour would ever have wanted. The most refined footwear seems to be a particular specialty of his. Above rose garlands drawn atop Wagner's head, one reads on the left

FIGURE 4-1. "Atlas" in Music—from *Puck: humoristisch-satyrische Wochenschrift*, ed. Constantin von Grimm (Leipzig), July 1, 1877, 205 (Klassik Stiftung, Herzogin-Anna-Amalia-Bibliothek, Weimar)

side: 'Invoice 3100 Gulden for satin, roses and shoes,' and on the right: 'Fräulein Bertha—milliner—Vienna.'" Beneath the caricature, Wagner says:

> Hmm, Hmm, but I'll just admit it *sub rosa:* after me the most out-standing man in Germany is the Reichs-Chancellor concerned with matters of state! Truly, truly, if I weren't already the leader [*Träger*] of the musical world and the one who wears the most elegant satin skirts and shoes, I'd quite like to be Bismarck!"[20]

The sixteen published letters—mostly from the year 1867—were less than two-fifths of the total number of letters Wagner wrote to Bertha Goldwag in Vienna. The entire cache runs to some forty-three items and covers the period from Christmas, 1863—that is, before Wagner received the royal summons from Ludwig II—until August, 1871. In addition to drawings, accounts, and precise instructions, there are samples of satin fabric attached to letters: The detail makes for heady reading, and any explanation that Wagner's sensitive skin condition prompted his interest in silk is quickly laid to rest. Wagner's preoccupation with shades of color is especially striking, with pink very much in the ascendency. Writing to Bertha from Starnberg in June, 1864, for example, Wagner requests information concerning the following fabrics:

> Can you obtain from Szontag a fine heavy satin, *light brown* in color, to match the enclosed sample?
>
> The same in *dark pink?*
>
> Is there a good quality fabric obtainable at 4 to 5 florins to match the enclosed *light pink?*
>
> —ditto—the *blue,* but preferably *somewhat lighter,* certainly not darker.
>
> Has Szontag enough of the *new red* or *crimson*-colored heavy satin in stock that you used to line my white dressing-gown (with the floral pattern)?
>
> Do you still have any of the *dark yellow* which we used to make the curtains for the little tables?. . . .
>
> I hope you still have the patterns for my house-clothes?. . . .

P.S. Do not confuse No. 2, the dark pink, with the earlier violet pink, which is not what I mean here, but genuine pink, only very dark and fiery (*SL*, 620).

Forced to leave Munich on December 10, 1865, after causing a political crisis that reached the highest echelons of government, Wagner still found the time to write to Bertha on December 17th, again on January 7th, once again on the 23rd, and regularly again thereafter. Satin was a serious matter for the composer.

Bertha Goldwag Maretschek was herself interviewed for the first time in 1906 and describes in great detail her early work for Wagner in Penzing (outside Vienna), where she executed the interior décor of the entire villa, including one special room, a Venusberg-like grotto luxuriously lined with silk walls, with lavishly hung satin rose garlands strewn all around, costly covers and pillows, soft carpets, and all lighted with a hanging lamp that emitted "muted light." In this "boudoir" as Bertha calls it, Wagner liked to be alone and rarely permitted anyone else to enter.[21] It was where he said he "felt particularly well, because its colorful magnificence stimulated him to work." The composer told his milliner he always needed to feel exceptionally warm, so all his satin garments, even his soft house slippers, had to be stuffed with cotton, and his boots additionally filled with masses of fur and cotton. "Wagner" she notes, "loved everything soft," though she defends him against the charge that his undergarments were satin: "It is wholly untrue that I ever made satin briefs [*"Atlashöschen"*] for Wagner. He wore satin breeches [*Atlasbeinkleider*] but regular trousers [*Pantalons*] with an appropriate jacket."[22] It may be that a few years later Wagner even started wearing satin underwear as well if Nietzsche's student is to be believed.[23]

As for Cosima, there are hints of her adverse reaction to Wagner's fetish: Near the beginning of her diaries in 1869 she notes: "Unfortunately R[ichard]'s passion for silk fabric sparks an observation from me which I should preferably have refrained from making, because it caused a slight malaise" (*CT* I, 42). By 1878, when Cosima puts an end to the private correspondence between her husband and Judith Gautier, she even briefly takes over dealing with the "errands" with which Judith had been charged by the composer to buy silk and perfumes: "Don't make fun of us," Cosima writes to Judith, "for always staging fairy tales to indulge ourselves.— This is our life."[24] And in 1881, Cosima mentions Wagner's silk obsession casually as a kind of an in-joke among the family (*CT* IV, 766–767), as we shall see in Chapter 5.

Wagner's penchant for silk dates from long before the 1860s. One can surmise that its origins lay in his childhood when his heart used to "beat wildly" while touching his sisters' theatrical wardrobe, as he reveals in *Mein Leben* (*ML*, 21). At his wedding to Minna Planer in 1836—he was twenty-three years old—each guest received in commemoration a pink satin handkerchief, one of which found its way into the Burrell Collection. The accompanying anonymous poem suggests that the marriage joins the laurel wreath of a composer with the fragrant flower of a wife, but in retrospect, the blended image suits Wagner himself far better:

Darf erst zum Lorbeer sich die Rose neigen,	*But if the laurel with the rose be blended,*
Dann nennst Du wahres Glück mit Recht Dein eigen!	*You by true happiness will be rightfully attended!*[25]

On the run from Dresden in 1849, Wagner was a wanted fugitive, and the police description of him named "clothing—above all of dark green buckskin with trousers of black cloth and velvet waistcoat, and the usual felt hat and boots" along with "a silk neckerchief."[26] Further police reports from 1853 report on his ostentatious luxury, including his silk curtains (*NL* II, 409). During his 1855 stay in London—if Ferdinand Praeger may be believed in this instance—Wagner suffered from "occasional attacks of erysipelas" and

> wore silk next to the body, and that at a time when he was not the most favored of fortune. In London he bought the silk and had shirts made for him; so, too, it was with his other garments. We went together to a fashionable tailor in Regent Street where he ordered that his pockets and the back of his vest [i.e. waistcoat] should be of silk, as also the lining of his frock-coat sleeves; for Wagner could not endure the touch of cotton, as it produced a shuddering sensation throughout his body which distressed him. I remember well the tailor's

surprise and explanation that silk . . . was not at all necessary, and that the richest people never had silk linings; besides, it was not seen. The last observation brought Wagner up to one of his indignant outbursts, "never seen! Yes: that's the tendency of this century: sham, sham in everything; that which is not seen may be paltry and mean, provided only that the exterior be richly gilded."[27]

On Easter Sunday in 1859, when composing Act III of *Tristan*, Wagner asks Mathilde Wesendonck to obtain some new silk bedding for him in Zurich, of which he "needs quite a lot." What he currently uses is "terribly dirty" and he is ashamed when he thinks of the housemaid making the bed. The color was "green, but if need be, could be red as in autumn herbage." But "for heaven's sake" Mathilde should keep this a secret from her husband (*MW*, 130–131). Thoughts of the purchase made Wagner think of a leitmotive he had just composed, which he attaches as a musical snippet marked Vivace [*Lebhaft*] at the end of the letter—"something new and silken [*etwas neues, seidenes*]," he writes. (See Example 4–1.) The additional note *da capo* shows that the motive was intended to work as a repeating musical loop. In its later form, Wagner uses the leitmotive beginning directly on the second bar of his sketch with an accented *Tristan* chord. It is first heard in Act III, sc. i as Tristan, "beside himself" [*ausser sich*], greets the welcome news that Isolde is en route from Cornwall to Kareol. So ecstatic is Tristan's reaction that "he struggles . . . for words" and "draws Kurwenal towards him and embraces him," thanking his "loyal friend." It is the anticipated ecstasy in this instance connected to a descending chromatic outburst which Wagner experienced as "silken."

Evidence for Wagner's silk and satin fetish is ubiquitous. Between 1869 and 1874, Wagner wrote some twelve letters to a Milanese tailor named Gaetano Ghezzi who worked with his wife, a couturière, Charlotte (or Carlotta) Chaillon, from whom Wagner ordered women's clothing, insisting, for example, on January 1, 1874 that the tailor "send the pink satin dress first."[28] The composer resorted to understandable subterfuges, claiming a garment was for Cosima when it was in reality for himself: The giveaway is the color, for there is no evidence that Cosima ever dressed in pink. Interesting as well is Wagner's apparent slip when he writes in French to the seamstress that "we [*sic*] need two underdresses [to go with] the jacket, one in pink satin, the other in white satin" [*il nous faut deux robes de dessous, pour la jaquette, en satin rose et satin blanc*]. It seems more than likely that the pink satin underdress was for him.[29]

Judith Gautier

Wagner was embarrassed enough about the revelations in June 1877 to think of emigrating to America, and Cosima, the day she discovered the press coverage, was too disheartened to dissuade him from considering the idea of another exile (*CD* I, 969). The storm blew over, and only a few months later, as an indispensable crutch to help him compose *Parsifal*, Wagner was placing regular orders with Judith Gautier in Paris for pink satin, rose-water, amber-grey [scented] bath oils, lilac satin, silk undergarments, and aromatic powders. The letters to Gautier, with their precise details and demanding tone, are a good indication of how very important these garments, oils, and scents were to Wagner's compositional process. Writing to Judith in December 1877, he begins by dismissing out of hand her Jewish composer friend, Louis Benedictus, who "has fallen substantially in my affection." Wagner then turns "to more *serious* matters" such as the identification of his very own personal shade of pink, "very pale and delicate":

> First of all, the two chests which have not arrived. Well! They will arrive and I shall immerse myself in your generous soul. Cancel the pink satin entirely: there would be too much of it and it would be good for nothing. Can I expect the two remnants which I mentioned in my last letter?—The brocade can be reserved: I'm inclined to order 30 meters, but perhaps the colors can be changed to flatter my taste even better; in other words: the fawn striped material would be silver-grey, and blue, *my* pink, very pale and delicate. . . . You frighten me with all your "oils." I shall make mistakes with them: in general I prefer powders, since they cling more gently to fabrics, etc. But, once again, be prodigal, above all in the quantity of oils to put in the bath, such as the "ambergris" etc. I have my bathtub below my "studio," as I like to smell the perfumes rising.
>
> For the rest, do not think ill of me! I am old enough to indulge in childish pursuits!—I have three years of *Parsifal* ahead of me, and

nothing must tear me away from the peaceful tranquility of creative
seclusion. (*SL*, 879)

Two weeks later, Wagner had Judith make some substitutions since the
merchant hadn't been able entirely to comply with the sizable request:

> To be serious!—Since you are obliged to accept other fabrics by way
> of exchange at a certain shop, I suggest—in the circumstances—that,
> to make your choice easier (almost impossible), you take a beautiful
> *white* satin, since in that way we shall avoid any difficulties over shades
> of color, and a white satin will always be useful. Well then! After the
> perfumes, etc. count up what remains of the fortune I deposited with
> you, and spend it on this white satin. Let us reserve the order of bro-
> cade until some other time. The question is always whether you have
> any money left in your account. (*SL*, 880)

The next month, February 1878, having already sent Judith the substantial sum of 2,062 francs, Wagner reports on a little accident that required
immediate action:

> The little bottle of rose-water was completely ruined by cold water,
> and in my clumsiness I dropped the larger bottle as I was trying to
> arrange it with the alcohol: it broke, and its contents went all over the
> carpet; what really surprised me, however, was how little effect the
> smell had, since I would have expected it to have given me 1000
> headaches!—Send me more of it. (*SL*, 881)

Concerned to prevent any further scandal, Wagner had Judith's parcels
sent to him secretly in care of his local barber Bernhard Schnappauf in
Bayreuth (*NL* IV, 607). Perhaps Judith did not realize the enormous
quantity of rose oil which the composer required, or else Cosima's dis-
mayed discovery of the flirtatious dalliance found in their correspondence
meant that Wagner had to look elsewhere for his satin and perfume
procurement.

Julius Cyriax

A few months earlier Wagner was already scouting around for another reliable supplier and found it in Julius Cyriax, a leading figure in the English Wagner Society. Though Cyriax was alarmed by the potential effect of so many strong scents on Wagner's health, he complied with regular requests for silk nightshirts and an unending quantity of oil called *Otto de Rose*. Over the next few years—from September 1878 until January 1881—Wagner wrote twelve letters to Cyriax in London and he specifically requests rose oil in eleven of them. It isn't an exaggeration to say that the supply line formed the basis for the friendship.[30] For Wagner's birthday on May 22, 1879, Cosima arranged for Cyriax to have a pink carpet made from flamingo feathers with a border of peacock feathers. Cyriax was well aware of the link to Wagner's compositional imagination, remarking on his hope that "this charming artwork, worthy to lie in the Master's composing studio, might help him orchestrate Klingsor's magic garden" (*EC*, 29). It is certainly correct to state, as does Barbara Eichner, that unlike in the Gautier letters, there was certainly no erotic subtext in the correspondence with Cyriax. Given the extent of Wagner's harmless if pronounced desires, it would be more accurate to say that in both cases the erotic allure for Wagner lay in the touch of soft pink fabrics surrounded by their olfactory equivalent. Wagner's requests to Cyriax soon betray an impatient and insistent tone. Even Wagner's jokes are serious: "You think I feel flattered when you mention seeing *Rheingold* in Cologne! Yet you don't think to ask whether I still have some rose oil left! Don't you think one has presents to make? Even experiments? Later my requests will be reduced but for the time being you should send me the entire 100 marks' worth of *Otto de Rose*, the money for which I enclose" (*EC*, 43–44). That was on March 2, 1879.

If Cyriax hoped the latest substantial parcel would satisfy Wagner's cravings, he was mistaken, for the consumption of *Otto de Rose* continued unabated. On March 18, 1879, Wagner responds to the news that Cyriax's little infant daughter named after Wagner was rapidly growing:

> Richardis = 15 pounds?!! I intend to live until I have used this weight in rose oil. According to your estimate that would be more than

1000 years; however, you don't know rose oil; at least it seems to be familiar to you only from the purchase orders of the perfumers; that they use so terribly little of the substance only proves that their products are made from feces and putrefaction; admittedly they would have to be more expensive if it were otherwise. *My* experiments, from which you unfortunately seem to fear competition, only extend to the *application* of the rose oil, for which of course nobody can give an instruction because nobody applies it. *Now* I know that the incomparably gentle scent of this aroma is not achieved by violent application: i.e. I have stopped mixing the oil with Eau de Cologne etc. and using it like incense, because all this destroys the effect. Therefore less will be wasted in future. But it is pure fiction that *one* drop only has God knows what overpowering effects. Do believe me. (*EC*, 44–45)

Pale pink satin remained the leading motif of Wagner's intimate attire until the day he died. On February 13, 1883, the last day of his life, an obituary syndicated in the Italian press noted that

Wagner was feeling a little unwell, though he had worked for several hours in the morning exactly as was his habit. Toward three in the afternoon he felt somewhat worse, yet had lunch served to him, but then wasn't able to manage more than some broth. He then ordered a gondola, believing perhaps he might find a little refreshment in the open air and in the poetic calm of our Grand Canal; but before going down into the gondola, he was struck ill. He was in his bedroom and had donned *a dressing gown the color of pink* [emphasis added]; he rang the bell and asked for his wife. His Cosima understood at once, and seeing her husband's condition much worsened, sent for the doctor and gave whatever succor she could to the dying man. But it was all in vain, for when the family physician Dr. Keppler arrived, he could do nothing but verify Wagner's death. Already used to Wagner's attacks as a kind of syncope to which he had often been subjected (in which one seems to be dead from a cardiac abnormality)—his wife refused to be convinced he was dead, and latched onto his neck for hours at a time, with no one able to induce her to leave the body. Everyone can imagine such a scene, including the assembled daughters and the son, so attached as they were to their father.[31]

In the midst of this tragic assembly—the inconsolable widow, grieving children, and helpless doctor—lay the corpse of Richard Wagner, clad in the last article of clothing he ever donned, announced to the entire world as a pink (and no doubt, satin) dressing gown.

Fetishism and Cross-dressing

The erotic side of Wagner's obsession emerges most clearly when one reads his letters to Judith Gautier, in which each successive paragraph alternates between the evocation of soft caresses and an uncompromising list of fabrics and scents Gautier was to supply. It is clear from the plentiful evidence that Wagner took pleasure in enveloping his own body in soft fabrics and feminine perfumes, especially when composing. His intimate spaces approximated Orientalist interiors disdaining any hint of rough edges or hard contours, the kind of boudoirs one glimpses in canvasses such as Ingres's series of *Bathers* or Delacroix's *Women of Algiers in their Apartment* (1834). Although the lady's pink satin dressing gown with flounces and sash, and pair of laced satin knee breeches can in no way be considered luxurious male attire, Wagner did not cross-dress with any wish to parade himself publicly. For his own masculine outerwear, for example, Wagner hid the pink satin in the linings, as the singer Lilli Lehmann noted about his black velvet coat when she met him in Prague in 1863.[32] And even when he made his escape from Vienna in March 1864—as his friend Peter Cornelius (1824–1874) notes—and apparently did so "wearing women's clothes," they were clothes "which Porges had procured," that is, not Wagner's own.[33] Stopping short of donning articles of actual women's outerwear, the composer seems to have experienced a sensuous harmony, erotic arousal, and a creative surge when both wearing and touching women's satin garments in the privacy of his personal grottos, always enhanced by the pronounced scent of roses. Nor did Wagner's inclinations threaten the sense of his own masculinity: He placed his orders with Gautier at the very time (October–December 1877) he was suggesting to Otto Eiser that it was

Nietzsche who suffered from a sexual malady by overindulging in masturbation!

Wagner's passion for satin and rose perfume has never been a secret since the journalistic revelations in 1877, but when referred to at all, has been understood either as an incongruous curiosity relating to the eccentricities of a "great artist" or—more apologetically—as a medical necessity to cope with the skin condition from which Wagner occasionally suffered. In fact, the letter to Eiser makes plain that Wagner's silk fetish was no longer necessarily linked to his troublesome skin problem. As Wagner put it to Eiser, "Years ago a brilliant hydropathist near Geneva completely healed me of a recurrent *erysipelas* [*Gesichtsrose*] of which I had suffered numerous relapses until this plague never again returned to vex me [*bis zur Nie-Wiederkehr dieser Plage*]."[34] If anything—given the important role of the color *rosa* in his life—it is not farfetched to see Wagner's skin problem, his *Gesichtsrose* (literally "facial rose") as a psychosomatic condition related to, if not actually induced by, his color, fabric, and perfume fetish. (It is also true that, at the end of Wagner's life, the skin condition worsened again.)

In Wagner's day, there wasn't yet a special term that encapsulated the composer's particular attachment to pink satin and roses, whether in manufactured silk garlands, real flowers, or rose scents, powders, and oils. And although there is no need to "diagnose" the "condition" from which he suffered, as in some twentieth-century studies,[35] it is the case that Wagner's set of preoccupations—unusual but not unknown—began to be studied by psychiatrists in the period just after his death. In 1886, Richard von Krafft-Ebing, for example, reported some cases of pathological erotic fetishism connected with silk, noting in the first that "what gratified [the subject] more than being with the prettiest woman was to put on a silk petticoat when going to bed." The fashion historian Valerie Steele observes that the prevalence of silk and satin fetishism in fact waned in the twentieth century, but was still witnessed in Emile Zola's *Nana* (1879), and in Stéphane Mallarmé's brief stint as a fashion journalist in which the poet signed himself as *Mlle. Satin*. Unlike today, Steele notes, satin in the nineteenth century was always made of silk, was reserved exclusively for women's garments, and was "woven in such a way as to produce a glossy surface, and a soft, slippery texture."[36]

The term "sexual fetishism" gained currency when the French psychologist Alfred Binet, founder of psychometrics and the Intelligence Quotient (and colleague of Charcot), published a short study entitled *Le Fétichisme dans l'amour* (1888). Binet saw the erotic attachment to particular body parts, or material objects, fabrics, or scents merely as an exaggerated form of normal sexual tastes. Although he devotes a section to olfactory fetishists or lovers of scents, he doesn't name silk as a particular fetish, nor does he connect fetishism with a man's desire to dress in feminine clothing. By the late nineteenth century, however, fetishism became linked to the syndrome of cross-dressing, and both were seen as part of larger "disorder," homosexuality, which uniformly received the most theoretical attention. (Krafft-Ebing, for example, entitled his work, *Psychopathologia sexualis: with especial reference to Contrary Sexual Instinct*.) As for the various degrees of "pathological" cross-dressing, it took quite some time before theorists such as Magnus Hirschfeld (1868–1935) distinguished between the intensity of someone's desire to cross-dress, its constant or periodic nature, and what later would be called "sexual object choice." Psychoanalysts (such as Wilhelm Stekel) were still intent on subsuming cross-dressing under "homosexual tendencies," even though a wide range of case studies showed that the majority of cross-dressers were "heterosexual."

It was Hirschfeld who first treated the question of cross-dressing and fetishism in his pioneering work of 1910 which, significantly, discusses the case of Richard Wagner. Hirschfeld, who coined the term "transvestites" in a book of the same title, *Die Transvestiten*, includes an entire chapter called "Transvestism and Fetishism (Explanation of Richard Wagner's Letters to a Milliner)," in which he sees Wagner's sexual "tendencies" as merging aspects of both cross-dressing and clothing fetishism.[37] Noting that "from the outside, the intensive tendency to cross-dress strongly reminds one of clothing fetishism" and that "representatives of both these tendencies . . . seek to put themselves in possession of pieces of clothing that belong to that sex to which they physically do not belong," (male) transvestites identify "top to toe" with a woman, with the female's clothing "mainly loved as part of themselves." With male clothing fetishists, sexual interests are focused on specific pieces of women's garments, and mostly "lack the expressed urge to put on the form of the beloved object, to identify with it, as it were, to change themselves into it. . . . At times, though, the fetishist takes the woman's slip to bed for the purpose of sexual stimulation. To bring himself as close to 'the beloved' as possible, he in fact also wears the woman's underwear . . . while transvestites like to wear new underwear" (*HT,* 158–159).

The diagnostic problem for Hirschfeld is that Wagner both fetishized the particular fabric satin—along with the color pink and related rose oils and perfumes as a "part attraction" detachable from a particular female love object—at the same time that he had the urge to wear the clothing to spur his creativity and satisfy erotic cravings. For this reason, Hirschfeld says, in Wagner's case the "differential diagnosis between fetishistic tendencies and transvestism is not always so simple" (*HT,* 165). Though he doesn't cite all the voluminous evidence, Hirschfeld sees Wagner's fetishistic side in "the very detailed manner of ordering, the depth, the value that is placed on the coordination of the colors, [and] the exact description of how the articles are to be made" (*HT,* 165), while concluding that "Wagner's particular inclination justifies assuming that there is a feminine characteristic in his psyche" (*HT,* 169). Resisting the temptation to call Wagner's inclination pathological, Hirschfeld adds that this inclination "in no way deserves mockery and scorn," but "to the contrary . . . gives evidence of the unusually rich and subtle complexity of [Wagner's] inner life, the continued study of which would be a difficult as well as a rewarding task" (*HT,* 169–170). While Wagner over his lifetime certainly spent a great deal of time—not to mention a king's ransom—indulging in what one might call his fetishistic transvestism (or transvestic fetishism), there is no evidence that he suffered from or for it—especially after he gained financial security to support his "habit"—or that it in any way hampered his creativity. On the contrary, he took obvious pleasure in indulging his fantasies and allowed them to find their way into his words and music. Rather than diagnosing his desires as diseased, one can see how his departure from conventional norms inspired the plethora of artistic forms assumed by his "erotic impulse."

Fabric and Perfumes in the Operas

Although the niceties of anyone's intimate life are bound to remain imper-
vious to outsiders, it is striking how writings that document Wagner's satin
dressing gowns, embroidered rose garlands, and floral perfumes reiterate
themes spelled out in his opera texts and in their musical representations.
The rosy mists, pleasing scents, and pink lights of the *Tannhäuser* Venusberg (detailed in Chapter 3) are reproduced in the Penzing *boudoir*, but
there is also *Lohengrin*'s bridal chamber, which the chorus describes as a
"fragrant space bedecked for love" that "shall now enclose you away from
the glare [*Duftender Raum, zur Liebe beschmückt, nehm' euch nun auf, dem
Glanze entrückt*]." As "Lohengrin embraces Elsa gently, he points to the
flower garden through the open window,"—as the stage directions put it—
and sings: "Don't you smell the sweets scents with me? O how beautifully
they bewitch the mind! They approach mysteriously through the breezes,
unquestioning I submit to their spell. [*Atmest du nicht mit mir die süßen
Düfte?/ O, wie so hold berauschen sie den Sinn!/ Geheimnisvoll sie nahen durch
die Lüfte,/ fraglos geb' ihrem Zauber ich mich hin*]." (The governess engaged
to teach the Wagner children in 1875–76, Susanne Weinert, noted in her
diary that Wagner frequently played and sang *Lohengrin*'s bridal song in
Wahnfried, mentioning just thereafter how she was once allowed to see
the fabrics used in Wagner's dressing gowns. "In the lower regions of the
house," she notes, "there were large boxes which shimmered with satin in
a mixture of colors, in pale pink, azure, and green." The housekeeper told
her that she made "dressing gowns and breeches into a negligee [*Schlafröcke
und Beinkleider zum Negligé*] for the master of the house. Weinert was particularly struck by a pea-green satin dressing gown richly garnished with
pink bows.)[38] Then in *Tristan* there is the "flowery bank" where "Tristan
sinks on his knees before [Isolde] and rests his head on her arm." Isolde's
penultimate lines in her Transfiguration are, moreover, drenched in perfumes: "Are these clouds of blissful scents?/ Look how they swell/nestling
around me/ should I breathe them, should I listen to them? Should I sip
them, dive beneath them/exhaling myself sweetly in their fragrance? [*Sind
es Wolken wonniger Düfte? Wie sie schwellen,/mich umrauschen,/soll ich ath-
men,/soll ich lauschen?/Soll ich schlürfen,/untertauchen,/süss in Düften/mich
verhauchen?*]." Then there are the lilac scents of the Second Act of *Die*

Meistersinger and the flowers and ribbons [*Blumen und Bänder*] which Magdalene gives to David in the Third Act, an act he likens to his lover stroking him and smiling at him blissfully [*streichelt sie mich/ und lächelt dabei holdselig*], and which he offers to Hans Sachs in the Third Act. Walther's Prize-Song itself contains a morning garden "lighted in a rosy glow, the air swelled from blossoms and perfume full of every joy [*Morgenlich leuchtend in rosigen Schein/ von Blüth' und Duft/geschwellt die Luft,/voll aller Wonnen*]." The stage directions for the Act III, sc. iii of *Siegfried* specify that "the cloud cover, becoming ever more delicate, has dissolved into a fine veil of mist of a pinkish coloration [*von rosiger Färbung*] and now disperses in such a way that the haze disappears completely in moving upwards. Even Klingsor's secret and sinister castle towers over "the most wonderful forest of flowering trees [*der wunderbarsten Blumenbaumwaldung*], out of which pour all around magically sweet birdsong and intoxicating aromas [*berauschende Wohlgerüche*]" (*BB*, 54).

Flower-Maidens

Within this magic realm—which one "approaches with anxious longing"—are the Flower-Maidens in *Parsifal*, who emerge out of a "rich, Arabian-style castle . . . enveloped in delicately colored veils casually [*flüchtig*] thrown over themselves," so that the scene of Parsifal's arrival in Act II fuses soft fabrics with delicate scents in a particularly rich combination. Consider the libretto and stage directions: Parsifal is full of wonder, having "never seen such a festooned race"—a true vision of beauty. Quite unlike Heine's Tannhäuser, Parsifal "wouldn't like to strike the Flower-Maidens but merely wants to play!" "I'll gladly do that," he says. *Das thu' ich gern.* The maidens aren't interested in money. "We play in the service of Love," and each tries to win Parsifal's favor. There stands Parsifal, "quietly serene in [their] midst," neither hearing their words nor inspecting their bodies, but entranced by their scent: "How sweetly you smell! [*Wie duftet ihr hold!*]" They admit it. They are nothing but "fragrance-emitting spirits" [*duftende Geister*] who "blossom for you in bliss." The Flower-Maidens desire only that their olfactory charms are found appealing. Indeed, "if you can't love and cherish us, we'll wilt and wither away."

For Wagner, the allure of their floral scents and "delicately colored veils" satisfies him only if the Flower-Maidens exhibit their incorruptibility in matters of seduction. Direct sexual overtures are forbidden. Nothing could be worse than an imitation of the frenzied revels of the Maenads in the "horrors of the Venusberg." At the *Parsifal* rehearsals in 1882, Wagner took pains to explain to his Flower-Maidens how to avoid the "passionate accents" engaged in by opera singers. Happily, Wagner "was instantly understood by [his] lady friends, and at once their rendition of the coaxing tunes expressed a child-like naiveté, which remained entirely remote from a provocative element of sensuous seduction, assumed in certain circles to have been the composer's intention" (*JA* X, 62). The Flower-Maiden scene pleased Wagner more than any other at the 1882 Festival and was at times the only music he could bear to sit through in its entirety:

> [Richard] feels so faint that he does not attend the performance, only appears during the intermissions, and then only hears the Flower scene all the way through, because its complete performance always refreshes him. (*CT* IV, 989)

At the eighth performance, on August 11, Wagner even called out a loud bravo from his box at the end of the Flower scene and was promptly "hissed" by the pious Wagnerians occupying the stalls.[39] What was irresistible was the maidens' pretence of innocence projected by their naïve vocal style and childlike costumes. United with an advanced chromatic idiom better suited to temptation than play-like purity, the scene translated a Wagnerian fantasy into vivid music and gesture.

It took another artist, Guy de Maupassant, to recognize Wagner's erotic attraction to floral aromas. Visiting the Hôtel des Palmes in Palermo a few years [*sic*] after Wagner had stayed there, de Maupassant was shown the room the composer had occupied. He opened the door of a mirrored wardrobe and was overwhelmed by "a powerful and delicious perfume . . . like the caress of a breeze blowing over a bed of roses." The proprietor told him that Wagner had stored his linen in the same wardrobe "after dousing it with *essence de roses*":

I drank in this breath of flowers, forgotten, captive, which was emitted by this piece of furniture, and seemed to discover a little of Wagner himself in this scent that he loved, of his desire, of his soul, in this trifle of secret and cherished habits which make up the intimate life of a man."[40]

Artists' intimate lives are always intertwined with their creations. As late as 1933, Thomas Mann can note with a sly if telling impunity in the *Sorrows and Grandeur of Richard Wagner:* "But who would fail to notice the satin contained some way or the other in Wagner's works?"[41] No doubt alerted to the question of the composer's sexuality following the republication of the Milliner letters in 1906, Mann treats the incorporation of Wagner's erotic desires in music as a matter of high aesthetic regard.

Kundry

If the Flower-Maidens evoke one side of Wagner's intimate desires, Kundry sits at the other end of the spectrum as the dominant woman who fancies herself both mother and courtesan. It is true that, in her ravaged pre-erotic transformation, she is, in Klingsor's words, a "primeval devil, rose [sic] of hell [*Urteufelin, Höllenrose*]" but it is far from clear that Wagner took that view of her. Once she changes costume after her encounter with Klingsor, she is, like the Flower-Maidens, an apparition from the Orient of the European imagination, "uncloaked from within a floral enclosure." She lies stretched out—as in a harem—on "a bed of flowers dressed in a lightly-veiled garment approximating the Arab style." The flowers in the first production in 1882 were, not surprisingly, "a bed of roses," as the critic Paul Lindau noted, and Kundry evoked "Frau Venus aroused to spine-tingling passion for her knight in the shell-encrusted grotto" (*GV* II, 34).[42]

Kundry's method of seduction depends, unlike that of Venus or the Flower-Maidens, on an extraordinary erotic crescendo. She begins by recalling a memory of seeing Parsifal suckled at the breast of his mother Herzeleide, a woman drenched in tears who covered him in caresses. "Embedded softly on tender mosses, she lulled him sweetly to sleep." But Herzeleide was troubled because of her husband's death and a fear of violence.

She wished only "to cradle and keep you far from the weapons of men's struggles and rages." Never did Parsifal spurn her embraces. "When her arm enfolded him, did he ever fear her kisses?" No, indeed not, though Kundry goes too far when she "inclines her head completely above his and fastens her lips onto his mouth in a long kiss." The moment of the most intense passion in the opera, shown in Chapter 3 to embellish the music of sexual desire as heard in *Tristan*, causes Parsifal to "start up with a gesture of the greatest fright." She has violated an erotic threshold, and causes the lad, suddenly aware of her sexual designs, to cry "O terrible grief" [*O furchtbare Klage*]. The word "terrible" recalls a dangerous side to Kundry's character. As Gurnemanz had recounted, it was a terribly beautiful woman [*ein furchtbar schönes Weib*] who had seduced Amfortas. In a letter to Judith Gautier from 1877, in fact, Wagner suggests the French word *terrifiante* [terrifying] to grasp the key aspect of Kundry's erotic power.[43] The dramatic peculiarity of Parsifal's reaction, then, which no one can fail to notice, depends more than anything else on a sympathy for male sexual fragility in the face of a fearsome beauty. In a sense, the composer had never been so honest in depicting the attraction to a strong woman along with the horrible thought that she might overpower him. It is an attraction to female domination that extends its spell until the moment the woman asserts herself as domineering "desirer," for at that moment, the wish to be enveloped, smothered in love is experienced as overassertive aggression, even violation.

James Gibbons Huneker

The kiss and its aftermath are unsettling, for the sexually inexperienced youth not only refuses the temptress but also turns his thoughts to the pain of another man. Even ardent Wagnerians broke with the composer over this alarming scene. Before hearing *Parsifal*, the American critic James Gibbons Huneker (1857–1921) had made a point of rebutting the charge that Wagner's music was indecent, writing that "the man whose pulses do not quiver during the second act of *Tristan* is as bloodless as a turnip and we'll have none of him." As a staunch defender of Wagner's erotics, for example, Huneker found it easy to praise Wagner's superiority as a "sensualist":

What is life itself, my virtuous master? Isn't it gross? Isn't love itself something shocking in its manifestations? Oh, you people who are so nasty nice that Goethe is coarse, Shakespeare shocking and Wagner sensual.[44]

Yet the relationship between Parsifal and Amfortas suggested to Huneker a creepy homoeroticism, and for this reason he repeatedly stresses in his essay that Parsifal is an "effeminate lad," "at no time a normal young man," "only an emasculate Siegfried."[45] Huneker, based in Paris in the 1890s writing for journals in London and New York, seems to have scoured obscure European publications for references to pederasty in the arts. He was impressed enough with the work of Oscar Panizza (1895) and Hanns Fuchs (1903) on "Wagner and homosexuality" to mention both of them in his criticism. Same-sexuality was, to be sure, a special sore point with Huneker, as he holds the distinction of having been the first to allude in print to Walt Whitman's so-called "effeminacy," and the "discovery" of same-sex leanings in Whitman—whom he knew personally—caused him to revise his initially positive assessment of *Leaves of Grass*. It was the same with his view of Tchaikovsky, which changed in 1899 the moment rumors about same-sexual proclivities began to circulate. Whereas in 1891 Tchaikovsky "is a strong man . . . who says great things in a great manner," Huneker began calling some of Tchaikovsky's music "truly pathological."[46] So it is not a surprise that Huneker was put off by "the psychology of Kundry's kiss and its repelling effect." Despite "the stirringly dramatic situation," one confronts "the morbid imagination of the poet who in his search for voluptuous depravity could mingle a mother's with a courtesan's kiss."[47] In private, he even coined a word to characterize his reading of the sexual deviance he heard in the opera: it was, he quipped to a friend in 1903, "Parsiphallic."[48] Huneker jumped to conclusions about Wagner's unusual erotics, and its effeminacy in particular. A man intoxicated with female domination who rejects the feminine vamp must be attracted to other men.

Paul Lindau, Max Kalbeck, and Paul Heyse

Anxieties about Wagner's sexual leanings and the ambiguous eroticism of his music preoccupy other writers as well, but it is striking how little these concerns have to do with the dominant image of Wagner today, that of the arch anti-Semite who smuggled Jewish caricatures into his operas and whose verbal attacks on the Jews heralded the genocide of the Second World War. It is true that political anti-Semites in Germany and Austria beginning in the 1880s saw Wagner as a leading mentor for their move-ment,[49] but it wasn't until after 1945 that the dominant portrait of Wag-ner as anti-Semite started to enter the popular imagination, and not until the 1970s that the topic dominated academic discourse. Given the iconic status of this portrait, it is all the more curious to discover how Wagner the deviant eroticist might—or might not—be related to Wagner the hater of Jews.

As surprising as it must be for anyone first exposed to Wagner in the late twentieth or early twenty-first century, the fact remains that the over-whelming majority of nineteenth-century writers, both virulent critics of Wagner as well as passionate advocates—Jewish as well as Gentile—refuse to see a serious threat in Wagner's anti-Judaism. Wagner's views may be offensive, of course, but, if anything, Wagner was to be pitied, not despised or excoriated, for his irrational hatred of Jews, which was, more than any-thing else, a sign of his own psychological disturbance: certainly Pusch-mann the psychiatrist takes this stand in his diagnosis. There are very few writers, in fact, who linked Wagner's attacks on *Judaism in Music* to an actual impending danger or even to an ominous cultural tendency. Of the many reactions to *Parsifal*, only two connect the opera with Wagner's anti-Semitism. Paul Lindau (1839–1919), a writer and critic who reviewed the *Parsifal* premiere in 1882 for the *Kölnische Zeitung*, saw the opera

> as the musical fulfillment of that program first articulated in one of Wagner's much discussed pamphlets, a program which can now be seen as an aesthetic precursor of a movement later transferred to the social and public life of the whole of Germany. So this latest work might well therefore be called "Christianity in Music." It is certainly not the Christianity of Sir Wolfram von Eschenbach who bears the shining armor of German knighthood in worldly joy coupled with piety . . . but the Christianity of the Spanish inquisitor who burns heretics while the pure voices of children praise divine mercy in sen-suous melodies and ring bells on high towers. (*GV* II, 32)

By "one of Wagner's much discussed pamphlets" Lindau—born to a Jewish father and married to a Jewish woman—means *Das Judentum in der Musik* but as an aesthetic precursor of political anti-Semitism, not as a causal agent. His aperçu certainly specifies the horrible "fulfillment" of Wagner's program, a return to the medieval Inquisition absent from *Parsifal*, but which is, he suggests, hidden behind the final Amens singing "Redemption to the Redeemer" at the opera's close. At the same time, Lindau could not conceal his delight at the music for the Flower-Maidens in Act II:

> The music which accompanies . . . the seductive chorus . . . reaches its highpoint and glows [*durchglüht*] throughout with a perfectly intoxicating melodiousness and the most voluptuous sensuality. There is a yearning, a desire, a languishing in it, both passion and lust— quite incomparable! . . . A more sensuously gorgeous and enticing tone painting of this depicted garden can scarcely be imagined. (*GV* II, 33)

Lindau was also enraptured by the Good Friday meadows—so no signs of inquisitors there!—which was one of the "pearls of the score," noting in fine humor that the location of the Good Friday Spell has been identified by Baedeker's travel guide and awarded two stars (*GV* II, 33). The ominous, even prophetic allusion to burning Jews at the stake has therefore to be seen in the context of the critic's composite assessment of the opera as an aesthetic accomplishment of the first rank.

Similar to Lindau, Max Kalbeck— Brahms's acolyte in Vienna—waxes rhapsodic in 1882 over some of the best music in *Parsifal*, Gurnemanz's narrative as well the Transformation in Act I, in a review from 1882 "written only a few hours after the first performance" (*GV* II, 172). In his detailed and serious engagement with the work, Kalbeck problematizes aspects of Wagner's libretto, including the character of the Redeemer and notes only in passing—if correctly—that *Parsifal* dispenses with the Jewish Jesus in favor of a Christian-German redeemer, "and those anti-Semites concerned about the state of the nation who have become weary of uncomfortable Protestant tolerance and brotherly love may wish to be thankful for Wagner's blond Christ" (*GV* II, 183). Despite their distaste for anti-Semitic overtones in *Parsifal*, neither Lindau nor Kalbeck can be said to have generated much heat about or interest in the subject, and it is a mistake to see them as especially preoccupied with anti-Semitism.[50] Neither do they adduce much evidence to support their claims.

For other artists and critics, the rejection of Wagner was tied to his immoral hatred of Jews, not to problems in the works. The writer Paul Heyse (1830–1914), born to a Jewish mother and later winner of the Nobel Prize for Literature, was morally offended by Wagner, and when in 1881 he broke temporarily with his friend Hermann Levi, son of a rabbi, it was over Levi's acquiescence in the matter of Wagner's anti-Semitism:

> Your artistic enthusiasm for the man whom I consider—despite every recognition of his unusual talents—a calamitous phenomenon [*eine unheilvolle Erscheinung*] should never have seriously come between us. . . . But when you confess that you are "addicted with body and soul [*mit Leib und Seele verfallen*]" to a man for whose personal behavior I feel a deep moral antipathy, a man for whom—supported by facts which you yourself don't dispute—I must deny that true aristocracy of spirit, that respect for the bonds between men, then the earth trembles beneath my feet. . . . How could the son of your admirable father surrender himself unconditionally [*auf Gnade und Ungnade*] to a man who seizes every opportunity to give vent to his fanatical hatred of members of your tribe [*Deine Stammesgenossen*]?[51]

Berthold Auerbach and Daniel Spitzer

Earlier, at the time of the republication of *Judaism in Music* in 1869, Berthold Auerbach (1812–1882), a Jewish writer and author of *Black Forest Village Tales* (1843–1854) whom Wagner actually mentions in his essay and who spent time with him in Dresden, was disturbed and outraged by the pamphlet, noting in letters to his cousin that Wagner "knows how to mix the true with the false, known falsehoods with lies, and for that reason the matter is all the more dangerous and poisonous."[52] Particularly galling was that Wagner "configured Felix Mendelssohn as the incarnation of Jewish music," since Auerbach recalled hearing Mendelssohn display "a distinct aversion to everything Jewish" when they were friends in

Dresden in 1845–1846. Auerbach even agreed in part with Wagner's dismissal of Mendelssohn's music: what was objectionable was creating a Jewish "nemesis" who "was actually a devout Christian" and denying "a creative spirit" to an entire "people who created the Bible upon which the whole world is built and developed till now and who knows for how much longer!" The danger in Wagner's writing was that it sought to turn back the clock and deny the cultural advances achieved by Jews and charted by Auerbach himself in *Das Judentum und die neueste Literatur* [*Jewry and Recent Literature*] (1836), which argued for complete Jewish integration into German culture.[53] More pernicious than Wagner's emotive cultural anti-Judaism, for Auerbach, were the views of Brahms's confidante, the physician and academic Theodor Billroth, who in 1875 argued on "scientific" grounds that Jews were constitutionally unfit for medical studies and against which Auerbach took a public stance.[54] (Billroth later recanted his anti-Semitism.)

Auerbach's outrage and Heyse's moral fervor are completely absent, however, from the writings of Daniel Spitzer, a self-identified Jew (later buried in the Jewish cemetery in Meran), who took, as we saw, a satirical rather than a psychiatric approach to Wagner's effeminacy, which prompted him a short time later, in fact, to pen a popular novella entitled *Verliebte Wagnerianer* [*Wagnerians in Love*] (Vienna, 1880), which makes fun of Wagner and the Wagnerians, even Jewish ones. In addition to Leonie, a love-sick Wagnerian who aspires to a Sieglinde-type tragic love affair, the novel features Max Goldschein, a Jewish Wagnerian, who is as much the butt of Spitzer's satirical pen as the Master himself. Goldschein is a forerunner of Thomas Mann's Siegmund Aarenhold in *Wälsungenblut*, and like Mann's protagonist is an aspiring but barren artist. He embosses the silk-lined volume of his *Schwanhilde: Grand Romantic Opera in Three Acts* before it contains a note of music, dresses in silk and Atlas satin trousers imitating the Master, and waits in vain for musical inspiration to strike. To help himself along, he reads Wagner's *Judaism* essay and gives up eating unleavened bread for Passover because he now believes in "Wuotan [*sic*], an old German god." Instead of fasting on Yom Kippur, Max "fasts on the days the Master has prescribed, and for years now no more melodies have passed my lips. I am *Ur*-German now, as if Moses hadn't led the Jews through the Red Sea but across the Teutoburg

Forest."[55] Although of negligible literary value, *Wagnerians in Love* makes it clear that Wagner's anti-Semitism was considered ridiculous rather than dangerous. Indeed, poking so much fun at Wagner's cross-dressing ensured that his politics were considered no more than a joke: Once the silk, satin, and rose scents were common knowledge, there wasn't much to link Wagner to the truly worrying political anti-Semites in Austria and Germany. Perhaps for this reason, Wagner's late Christian redemption writings were not much discussed by his Jewish and liberal critics: By this point he was considered a political crackpot, particularly as he was associated with no political party or movement, and his own circle included prominent Jewish figures such as Hermann Levi and Angelo Neumann. Even Heinrich Porges, a longstanding Bayreuth *aide-de-camp*, was a Jew by birth, as were visible Wagnerian academics such as Michael Bernays and Alfred Pringsheim, who later became Thomas Mann's father-in-law. Nor could visitors to Wahnfried fail to notice the tragic figure of Joseph Rubinstein, the live-in Russian-Jewish "court-pianist" entrusted with playing through Wagner's composition sketches, who entertained the family with Beethoven sonatas, Bach Preludes and Fugues, and Wagner transcriptions, all the while preparing to publish the piano-vocal score for *Parsifal*.

Max Nordau and Theodor Herzl

Even for the physician Max Nordau (1849–1923), author of the bestseller *Degeneration* [*Entartung*] of 1893, Wagner's anti-Semitism formed only a small part of a more pronounced hysteria that had given rise to a perverse Europe-wide movement of Wagnerism. The German hysteria, "partly abominable, partly ignoble and partly laughable," he writes, "manifests itself in anti-Semitism, that most dangerous form of the persecution-mania, in which the person believing himself persecuted becomes a savage persecutor."[56] Nordau was born Max Simon Südfeld to a Jewish family in Budapest—his father taught Hebrew and German—and used the pen name Nordau at the age of 13 when he published his first short story.[57] He later had his name changed in a court of law, though at what date is unclear. What is significant in the pseudonym is the change from the Jewish-sounding "Southfield" to the more Germanic, even Nordic appellation of

"North-meadow." Nordau later married a Gentile woman whom he successfully persuaded *not* to convert to Judaism.

Not "partly laughable" for Nordau were Wagner's "morbid erotics" that led "hysterical women [to be] won over to Wagner chiefly by the lascivious eroticism of his music, but also by his poetic representation of the relation of man to woman." Nordau certainly alludes to an innovative and fundamental component of Wagner's musical erotics when he tries to explain Wagner's allure to women. "Nothing"—he writes—"enchants an 'intense' woman so much as demoniacal irresistibility on the part of the woman, and the trembling adoration of her supernatural 'Frau' Venus, Brünnhilde, Isolde and Kundry have won for Wagner much more admiration among women than have Elizabeth, Elsa, Senta and Gutrune" (*ND*, 211). As for the composer himself, "There is another feeling that controls the entire conscious and unconscious mental life of Wagner, viz., sexual emotion. He has been through his life an erotic [*sic*] (in the psychiatric sense), and all his ideas revolve around woman" (*ND*, 180). Wagner, Nordau says, "suffered from erotic madness," that "leads coarse natures to murder for lust, and inspires 'higher degenerates' with works like *Die Walküre*, *Siegfried*, and *Tristan und Isolde*" (*ND*, 182). With Wagner:

> amorous excitement assumes the form of mad delirium. The lovers in his pieces behave like tom-cats gone mad, rolling in contortions and convulsions over a root of valerian. They reflect a state of mind in the poet which is well known to the professional expert. It is a form of Sadism. It is the love of those degenerates who, in sexual transport, become like wild beasts.

Although a medical clinician writing on degeneration, Nordau seems embarrassed to have to raise the topic of sex, and in an accompanying footnote, notes:

> In a book on degeneration it is not possible wholly to avoid the subject of eroticism, which includes precisely the most characteristic and conspicuous phenomena of degeneration. I dwell, however, on principle as little as possible on this subject, and will, therefore, in reference to the characterization of Wagner's erotic madness, quote only

one clinical work, Dr. Paul Aubry [who writes that]: "This derange-
ment [erotic madness] is characterized by an inconceivable fury of
concupiscence at the moment of approach." And in a remark on the
report of a murder perpetrated on his wife and children by an erotic
maniac—a professor of mathematics in a public school—whom Aubry had under his observation, he says, "*Sa femme qui parlait facile-
ment et à tous des choses que l'on tient ordinairement le plus secrètes, disait
que son mari était comme un furieux pendant l'acte sexuel.*" [His wife
who spoke effortlessly and of all the matters which ordinarily one
safeguards as the most secret, said that her husband was like a raging
madman during the sexual act.] (*ND,* 181–182)

To keep to the academic high road, Nordau sends his readers to another
"scientific" study, by Benjamin Ball on *Erotic Madness* [*La Folie érotique*],
published in Paris in 1891.

In every form of Wagnerian love, Nordau detected the sign of "an
erotically emotional degenerate nature." Wagner's music reveals a "most
reckless sensuality, a revolt of moral sentiment against the tyranny of appetite, the ruin of the higher man" (*ND,* 189–90). In an imagination,
moreover, that "surrenders itself to unbridled passion, [Wagner] . . . represents the ardent man wildly and madly abandoning himself to his appetite, without regard to the dictates of society." Wagner creates "distorted female characters like Venus, Sieglinde and Kundry, who can only
appeal to hysterical und oversexed women." Above all, it is the "shameless
sensualism" of Wagner's operas that perverts German audiences, who put
up with the immorality of Siegmund and Sieglinde, along with "the amorous whinings, whimperings and ravings of *Tristan und Isolde,* the entire
Second Act of *Parsifal,* in the scene between the hero and the flower-girls,
and then between him and Kundry in Klingsor's magic garden" (*ND,*
181). Oddly, they "seem to have no suspicion of the emotions by which
they are excited" and "without blushing crimson, sink into the earth for
shame" (*ND,* 181).

Although "Wagner is incontestably an eminently gifted musician" (*ND,*
197), Nordau concedes, "we know . . . that high musical talent is compat-
ible with a very advanced state of degeneration—nay, even with pronounced
delusion, illusion, and idiocy." "As the least intellectual of the arts," Nordau

notes, quoting the criminologist Cesare Lombroso, "It has been observed that the aptitude for music has been displayed almost involuntarily and unexpectedly among many sufferers from hypochondria and mania, and even among the really insane." He cites, among other cases, a mathematician attacked with melancholia who improvised on the piano; a woman seized with megalomania who "sang very beautiful airs, at the same time improvising two different themes on the piano"; a patient "who composed very beautiful new and melodious tunes," etc.; and he adds in explanation that those who are afflicted with megalomania and general paralysis surpass other mental invalids in musical talent, "and from the very same cause as that of their unusual aptitude for painting, viz., their violent mental excitation" (*ND*, 196–197). If Wagner's own "erotomania" isn't bad enough, to the extent that "the formlessness of the unending melody was exactly suited to the dreamy vagaries," his recitative-style and his "powerful orchestral effects produce hypnotic states" in the "weak brains" of his degenerated audiences, effects that "make no sort of demand on the mind," but allow listeners to emerge from the opera house "with a merely sensual feeling of having enjoyed a hot, nervously exciting tone-bath" (*ND*, 211). Obviously, that is a very bad thing, although Nordau's piquant descriptions and hyperbole were designed, above all, to sell copies of books (rather than contribute to scientific knowledge) much as the rants against the poor literary quality of the Bible in his bestselling *Conventional Lies of Our Civilization* (1883), written in an equally provocative style, claim merely "to be a faithful presentation of the [views of the] majority of educated, cultivated people of the present day."[58]

Only a few years later, Nordau adapted his critique of degeneration into his advocacy for the new movement called Zionism, which he led as second in command to Theodor Herzl. *Degeneration* had made Nordau famous, and by 1895, Herzl, whom Nordau had met in Paris a few years earlier, invited him to join the leadership of the Zionist movement.[59] Nordau's specific contribution, in his role as a student of psychology and critic of decadence, was to lay stress on the "development of sound bodies for those Jewish boys and girls whose Jewish hearts were not touched by the corrosion of assimilation, and upon whose strength of body and mind a Jewish future in the Jewish land would have to depend."[60] The slogan he devised for this attitude was "muscle-Judaism" [*Muskeljudentum*], which was to reverse "the fearful devastation which eighteen centuries of captivity have wrought."[61]

Nordau's image of the proud Zionist countered what he considered to be the traditional postures of Jewish weakness and submission. When anti-Semitism broke out in Europe of the 1880s—he noted in a speech given at the Second Zionist Congress—there were "a few isolated brave men who did indeed rise to their own defense. But the great majority hugged the walls, threw themselves down on their bellies, their eyes filled only with timid supplication." But worse than this, he continues:

> I even saw, to my unbearable shame . . . Jews with my own eyes, Jews who tapped their pockets and said: "The Aryans think they're better than we are and refuse us the dignity of men. What do we care? We're cleverer than they and shall make money on them." Shame and small profits, a humiliation into which one can dig down and bring up wealth—that seemed to them an acceptable relationship or even a hidden joke of fate.[62]

The rearing of a persistent anti-Jewish stereotype on the part of a Zionist leader—that of the sly petty businessman obsessed with money— may strike a dissonant chord, but contempt for the feeble opportunism of the rootless Jewish traveling salesman was common among the founding fathers of Zionism. Along with the fight against anti-Semitism, and the struggle for Jewish cultural regeneration, their politics depended on castigating the physical weakness and disgraceful moral cowardice of Jews, together with their pursuit of culture for profit.[63] An article by Herzl printed in the official Zionist newspaper in 1897 directly attacked the image of the "bad Jew" nicknamed *Mauschel* or "Yid," the derogatory term used to mock his mumbled and Yiddish-inflected speech:

> Yid is anti-Zionist. We have known him for a long time, and just merely to look at him, let alone approach or, heaven forbid, touch him was enough to make us feel sick. But our disgust, until now, was moderated by pity; we sought extenuating historical explanations for his being so crooked, sleazy, and shabby a specimen. Moreover, we told ourselves that he was, after all, our fellow tribesman, though we had

no cause to be proud of this fellowship. . . . Whenever he perpetrated some dirty deal, we tried to hush it up. When he compromised us all, we felt ashamed but kept silent.

Now at least the Yid has done something that merits praise—he has rejected us.

But who is this Yid, anyway? A type, my dear friends, a figure that pops up time and again, the dreadful companion of the Jew, one for the other. The Jew is a human being like any other, no better and no worse. The Yid, on the other hand, is a hideous distortion of the human character, something unspeakably low and repulsive. Where the Jew experiences pain or pride, the Yid feels only craven fear or twists his face into a sardonic grin. . . . The Yid is the curse of the Jews. . . .

And then came Zionism. Both Jew and Yid had to take a stand, and now for the first time, the Yid rejects our community. The Yid is anti-Zionist!. . . . This is one of the first and most beneficial consequences of the movement. We'll breathe more easily, having got rid once and for all of these people whom, with furtive shame, we were obliged to treat as our fellow tribesmen. . . . Watch out, Yid. Zionism might proceed like William Tell . . . and keep a second arrow in reserve. Should the first shot miss, the second will serve the cause of vengeance. Friends, Zionism's second arrow will pierce the Yid's chest.[64]

In line with Nordau's ideas on cultural vigor, Herzl's ideal elevates the Zionist over the miserable ragamuffin Jew so as to overcome his weakness and degeneracy. The fear of this enfeeblement was far more pressing than worrying about Wagner's anti-Semitism. For which music was chosen to accompany the opening ceremonies in Basel of the Second Zionist Congress in 1898? Why Wagner's *Tannhäuser* Overture, of course, which preceded excerpts by Halévy and Meyerbeer. All the musical numbers earned the assembled delegates' thunderous applause, although Herzl's secretary noted piously that anti-Semites might not have been "equally generous" in their reception of the work of the two Jewish composers. The symbolism of playing Wagner was not lost on either pundits or publicists, for a commemorative postcard issued after the Congress showed the figure of Siegfried against an Oriental [that is, Jewish] background.[65]

Apparently Nordau hadn't objected too strenuously to the inclusion of *Tannhäuser* to ennoble the Zionist mission because even he, in all his fulminations against Wagner, had admitted that "in his youth . . . he succeeded in creating some superb melodies." In *Tannhäuser*, for example, Wagner's power in melodic creation was more abundant, for the Venusberg music must be numbered among the composer's most "magnificent compositions," though its repetitions and dependence upon leitmotives "show precisely the peculiarly unmusical character of his genius" (*ND*, 201–203). So the upstanding Congress delegates—whom Herzl insisted should wear full dress and top hats—were in no danger of behaving "like tomcats gone mad" when the Bacchantic frenzy of the Venusberg music made its seductive appearance.

Herzl succeeded Daniel Spitzer as the leading book- and theater reviewer [*Feuilletonist*] at the *Neue Freie Presse* in Vienna, and surely knew of Wagner's letters to his milliner first published in that newspaper. He was also well aware of Wagner's views on the Jews because he resigned—and was also expelled—from the student fraternity Albia in 1883 after a Wagner-inspired event culminated in a speech by Hermann Bahr praising *Wagner-Antisemitismus*, thereby causing an uproar to which the police had to be called. Herzl missed the speech, and even though the University Senate made Bahr leave the university—he was subsequently also refused matriculation in Graz—Herzl resigned his fraternity membership in protest.[66] Yet nothing dimmed Herzl's enthusiasm for Wagner's operas, whose grandeur inspired the Zionist vision. In 1892, he bragged to his parents about the visit paid him by the Wagnerian soprano Anna Materna (1845–1918), whose concert he attended: Materna had premiered both Brünnhilde and Kundry at Bayreuth.[67] Then, during the 1895 opera season in Paris he made sure not to miss a single performance of *Tannhäuser* in Paris while writing his seminal work, *The Jewish State*. He later notes:

> I worked on [the book] daily until I was entirely exhausted; my recreation in the evening consisted in listening to Wagner's music, especially *Tannhäuser*, an opera that I heard as often as it was performed. Only on the evenings when there was no [Wagner] opera did I doubt the correctness of my ideas.[68]

A diary entry of the time also connects Wagner with the grand Zionist celebrations of the future:

> In the evening, *Tannhäuser* at the Opera. We too will have such mag-
> nificent auditoria—the gentlemen in tails, the ladies as luxuriously
> dressed as possible. Indeed, I want to make use of Jewish luxury, as
> everything else. I reflected again on the phenomenon of the crowd.
> There they sit for hours, crushed tightly together, motionless, their
> bodies in torment—and for what? For an imponderable . . . for
> sounds! For music and tableaux! I too shall encourage sublime pro-
> cessional marches to accompany [our] grand festivals.[69]

In debates with cultural Zionists such as Ahad Ha'Am, this view of future Zionist culture landed Herzl in trouble, but he never abandoned his Germanocentric aesthetic preferences. In his novel, *Altneuland* (1902), for example, which imagines an idealized life in the future Zionist state, Herzl, not surprisingly, names Wagner among the elect composers who will be played and sung in the Land of Israel.[70]

Whereas, for Nordau, Wagner's degenerate erotics overshadowed the dangers of his anti-Semitism, for Herzl, Wagner's ability to mesmerize audiences eclipsed the composer's racial prejudices altogether. Sensitive as he was to the dangers of European anti-Semitism, Herzl would have been amused to hear that Wagner's music bore anti-Jewish messages. In the shrill anti-Semitic politics of the 1890s he faced far greater menaces than inspirational operas treating medieval sagas and Norse myths. Besides, Zionism confronted its own sectarian enemies, and one reason Wagner was forgiven his anti-Judaism is that Herzl had founded an ideological enterprise on the rejection of the "repellent" Jew, who, in some surprising ways, replicates Wagner's negative stereotypes.

Otto Weininger

The worries about cultural debilitation connected to fears about one's own pathology are nowhere better expressed than in Otto Weininger, who is really the first author to connect Wagner's erotics with his anti-Judaism. A Wagner enthusiast, Weininger published his controversial *Sex and Character* in 1903 before taking his own life in Beethoven's Viennese apartment. For Weininger, the beginning of the twentieth century was a dangerous time:

> Our age is not only the most Jewish but the most feminine. It is a time when art is content with daubs and seeks its inspiration in the sport of animals; the time of a superficial anarchy, with no feeling for Justice and the State; a time of communistic ethics, of the most foolish of historical views, the materialistic interpretation of history; a time of capitalism and of Marxism; a time when history, life, and science are no more than political economy and technical instruction; a time when genius is supposed to be a form of madness; a time with no great artists and no great philosophers; a time without originality and yet with the most foolish craving for originality.[71]

Judaism, Weininger claims, is "saturated with femininity, with precisely those qualities, the essence of which I have shown to be in the strongest opposition to the male nature" (*WC*, 306). Richard Wagner, the greatest human being after Christ and the composer of *Parsifal*, "the greatest work in the world's literature" (*WC*, 344), stirred Weininger to grasp how one should overcome Judaism and womanishness. As a genius, Wagner in fact embodied these very two qualities, which is why he hated them. Of the many characteristics shared by the Jew and the Woman, Weininger claims that both

> are without extreme good and extreme evil, so they never show either genius or the depth of stupidity of which mankind is capable. The specific kind of intelligence for which Jews and women alike are notorious is due simply to the alertness of an exaggerated egotism; it is due, moreover, to the boundless capacity shown by both for pursuing any object with equal zeal, because they have no intrinsic standard of value—nothing in their own soul by which to judge of the worthiness of any particular object. (*WC*, 317)

By overcoming this mediocrity, Wagner, "the greatest anti-Semite," had allowed Judaism to be "the greatest help to him in reaching a clearer understanding of the extremes within himself in his struggle to reach *Siegfried* and *Parsifal*" (*WC*, 305–306).

In propounding the message of chastity in *Parsifal*, Weininger says—unexpectedly inverting Nietzsche's polemic—that Wagner rises above Judaism and eroticism toward a higher metaphysical love, humankind's only hope, much as Tristan and Isolde are united in death. For all his grand sweep of ideas—both Freud and Wittgenstein were very taken with him—Weininger had to dig deep into the hermeneutic mine to excavate these particular gems, which, like Nietzsche's, depend on assigning a philosophical "meaning" to Wagner's final opera.

Effeminacy and Jewishness

Wagner, to be sure, would have been less than best pleased to read of his own effeminate Jewishness, overcome or not. Interestingly, his own anti-Judaism shuns the association of (male) Jewishness with effeminacy. Indeed, he goes out of his way to avoid tarring the Jew as sexual deviant, even though this stereotype had persisted from medieval times. One still finds the myth in *Mein Kampf* (1923), where Hitler writes of the "satanic joy" with which

> the black-haired Jewish youth lurks in wait for the unsuspecting girl whom he defiles with his blood, thus stealing her from her people. With every means he tries to destroy the racial foundations of the people he has set out to subjugate.

For Hitler, the Jewish body itself evokes physical repellence:

> If the physical beauty [of German men] were today not forced entirely into the background by our foppish fashions, the seduction of hundreds of thousands of girls by bow-legged, repulsive Jewish bastards would not be possible.[72]

For Wagner, it is the "personality and manner [*Wesen*] of the Jews" that causes "instinctive repellence" (*SS* V, 67), especially the Judaized use of the German language and its translation into music: a Jewish sexuality doesn't come into it. Behind this debased approach to language lies the money-obsessed Jew who treats art works as cheapened commodities. The outward appearance of the Jew, Wagner writes in *Judaism in Music* (1850), "has something unpleasantly foreign" to it, and is such "an unpleasant sport of nature" that "we cannot think of any antique or modern character played by a Jew, whether it be a hero or a lover (*SS* V, 69–70). Indeed, Wagner underscores this point as "very important," adding that "a person whose appearance we must—not in this or that character but—in general find unsuitable for artistic representation [*Kundgebung*], we can't consider capable [*befähigt*] of the artistic expression of his manner [*Wesen*]" (*SS* V, 70). As the Jew can express "no true passion," he is barred from possessing sensuality, even an evil sensuality. Instead, he and his creative products are ridiculous and absurd. Listening to "Judaic works of music," Wagner writes, "often gives the impression that, for example, a poem of Goethe's were being declaimed in Jewish jargon" (SS V, 78).

Although Wagner might be credited with having devised a clever if defamatory simile—that Mendelssohn's music sounds like Goethe read in Yiddish—in fact, he was almost surely citing a notorious story from German theatrical history in which the failure of Jews to assimilate into German literary culture is parodied in a pseudo-Yiddish jargon. In the early part of the century, a Gentile actor named Albert Wurm specialized in comic Jewish roles and made a career of speaking in mock, "stage Yiddish" or *Jüdeln*—an ungrammatical use of German with Yiddish words thrown in. He starred, for example, in a farce called *Our Crowd* [*Unser Verkehr*] in which he played a crass Jewish parvenu with aesthetic pretensions, but he was also famous for a separate set piece in which he would declaim Schiller's heroic ballad, *The Diver* [*Der Taucher*], in stage Yiddish dressed in a silk gown while pretending he was a nouveau-riche Jewess, causing (at least some members of) his audience to dissolve into helpless laughter. Wurm's character tries hard to enunciate Schiller in her best High German, but amid the performance gets carried away and can't refrain from pronouncing words with a Jewish pronunciation—in *Judendeutsch*.[73] The act, which made Wurm famous, ensured that he fell afoul of the Jewish community in Berlin. As it happens, he was also convicted of sodomy, of which he had been accused by the mother of one of his lovers.[74] Having defended himself in a pamphlet exculpating his Jewish parodies, he was later attacked by the critic Ludwig Börne for revealing his "directionless passions and vacillating lusts as points of attraction [*richtungslosen Leidenschaften und schwankenden Begierden zum Anziehungspunkte*]," allusions to his publicized homosexuality.[75] Wurm's fate was to be known as a sodomite (shamed in public and named as such by the converted Jew Ludwig Börne) as well as an actor who made fun of Jewish assimilation. Instead of referring to Schiller in Yiddish, Wagner substitutes Goethe—both of them are interchangeable icons of Weimar Classicism—and thereby seems to reveal an awareness of the Börne essay (or at least Heine's mention of it), helping him to back up his view of Jewish music as laughable and corrupt, forever unable to shake off its Jewishness. Not insignificantly, perhaps, he mentions Börne by name in the final paragraph of *Judaism in Music* as the one example of a Jew who had overcome his Judaism, albeit through "sweat, anguish . . . and suffering." In suggesting, therefore, that Jewish music resembled a Yiddish rendition of classic German poetry, Wagner alluded to Wurm's performance as a metaphor for the debased Jewish perversion of a German classic, but he stopped short of mentioning the actor's sexual deviance when it would have offered an additional negative label with which to tarnish Judaism. A reference to Wurm's "silk dress" would, after all, not have been in the composer's interest.

Wagner, it turns out, had little interest in associating Jews with a sinister sexuality, and arguments suggesting otherwise are starved of convincing evidence.[76] When Hermann Levi was accused of having illicit relations with Cosima Wagner—certainly an instance, if ever there was one, of a traditional European prejudice rearing its ugly head—the composer failed to rise to the bait. A letter sent to Wahnfried in 1881 figures in many accounts of Wagner's humiliating treatment of his designated *Parsifal* conductor. An anonymous correspondent, one learns, had implored the Bayreuth Master to "keep his work pure" and not allow a Jew to conduct the Christian *Parsifal.* What was worse, the author of the letter insinuated that this same Jew was known to have taken liberties with the Master's wife. Levi himself put it more delicately in his own notebooks: that his "character and [his] relations to Wahnfried had been impugned in the most scandalous manner." Cosima recounted the story to her eldest daughter: "Poor Levi was so scandalously accused (and in connection with me!) that he could not get over it."[77] The charge of sexual impropriety stung Levi so profoundly that he left Bayreuth and tendered his resignation. How could he bear the awesome responsibility of conducting *Parsifal* if rumors were circulating that conjured up the most vile medieval slander about Jewish men? Wagner's reaction to the anonymous letter is revealing, no matter how he induced Levi to return to the fold. Cosima's diaries report the incident as follows:

Around midday [Richard] comes up to me, somewhat excited: "Here's a nice letter." I: "Something bad?" "Oh, you'll see." I read it, am astonished at first, but then agree with R[ichard]'s excited mirth. But when the letter is shown to the poor conductor he can't contain himself, it seems that such base things are new to him! (*CT* IV, 754)

For Wagner, the inflammatory letter was a defamatory piece of mischief, or *Schweinerei* as he put it in a letter to Levi, and for all Wagner's frequent and disparaging attacks on Jews, especially in his later years, the charge of their insidious sexuality didn't interest him.[78] Rather, it was the mad notion of the Jews' worldwide power that obsessed him, along with their "infiltration" into German culture and their putative command of the press and banking. As for the suggestion that Jewish men were effeminate, well this was a subject—given the public revelations about his own tendencies—that Wagner had good reason to avoid.

If there is a sad truth found in the readings of Wagner's "diseased" mind and music, it is that the diagnosticians—including Puschmann, Nietzsche, Nordau, and Weininger—fall back on the same categories of pathology that have branded the Jew and the effeminate as politically suspect and degenerate since the early nineteenth century. Ironically, then, to characterize Wagner this way is much the same as calling him a Jew or a limp-wristed male. Although one reaction to this morass of accusations might be to withdraw the understanding of music from philosophy and politics altogether, one might look at the matter another way: that philosophy and politics are far too important to depend on the "evidence" of mere music to argue their case. Just as it is foolish to read opera as serious philosophy, it makes little sense to treat music as deviant or as politically suspect. Not only do writers beholden to these metaphors miss the point of music; they often deny themselves (and us!) pleasure and stimulation. Only by dismissing a mind-set obsessed with cultural pathology can we savor Wagner's erotics, and only by disengaging them from politics can we assess what they meant for the artistic enterprise as a whole.

CHAPTER FIVE

Homoerotics

Paul von Joukowsky and Pepino

After lunch on February 25, 1881, Cosima and Richard Wagner quarreled about their friend Paul von Joukowsky (1845–1912) and his lover Pepino. "Incited by a miserable lovers' spat [*durch einen traurigen Liebschafts-Zwischenfall angeregt*]," Cosima declared their affair "ludicrous" [*albern*] but immediately regretted saying that. Richard took another view of the pairing. "It is something," he said, "for which I have understanding but no inclination [*Es ist etwas, wovon ich den Verstand dafür aber keinen Sinn habe*]. In any case, with all relationships what matters most is what we ourselves put into them. It is all illusion" (*CT* IV, 700–701). Joukowsky, a would-be painter and Russian aristocrat—whose father, the poet Vasilli Andreevich Zhukovskii, tutored Czar Alexander II—first met Wagner in January 1880 in Naples, where King Ludwig was funding ten months of a luxurious Italian sojourn while Wagner orchestrated *Parsifal*. Within a matter of weeks, Joukowsky became an inseparable family companion at the Villa d'Angri, and soon thereafter Wagner engaged him to design the sets and costumes for *Parsifal*. A pint-sized man with a goatee, the thirty-five-year-old Russian spoke fluent German as his native language—he was born in Germany to a mother from the German-Estonian aristocracy, though he grew up at the Russian court—and accompanied Wagner on the outing to Ravello where they "discovered" Klingsor's magic garden. He also tagged along to Siena, where the cathedral inspired designs for the Grail temple. So intimate was Joukowsky with the Wagners that he was assigned to take the eleven-year-old Siegfried on a tour of Umbria and Tuscany for several weeks. For the last three years of Wagner's life, Joukowsky rarely strayed from Wagner's side, moving to Bayreuth when the family returned to Germany. There he helped prepare the 1882 *Parsifal* performances, and joined the most intimate circle of Wahnfried. Not only did he travel to Berlin with Wagner (and Count Gobineau) for the *Ring* performances produced by Angelo Neumann, but he spent the next three Christmases with the family—in Bayreuth, Palermo, and Venice. The afternoon Wagner died, Joukowsky had lunched with the family, and only the day before, Wagner had arranged to relocate the artist's studio within the Palazzo Vendramin, where Joukowsky was present for the Master's Death in Venice.

For most of these three years, Joukowsky lived in an open same-sex relationship with a young Neapolitan folk singer named Pepino. Joukowsky at first passed Pepino off as his servant, but seems to have taken no special pains to disguise the intimacy of their liaison: he even later adopted Pepino as his legal "son."[1] Paul and Pepino must have been together for at least a year and a half when they met the Wagners in Naples because the couple attended the complete Munich *Ring* conducted by Levi in November 1878 (*GW* VI, 302). (Paul also attended the Bayreuth *Ring* in 1876 and used his Paris connections to wangle a reintroduction to Cosima, whom he had met socially in Munich.) According to Paul's memoirs, when he was invited to settle into the Villa d'Angri in mid-July 1880 to be closer to the Wagners, Pepino moved in with him (*GW* VI, 350).

Wagner was very taken with Pepino and praised his passionate singing as well his seductive charms. As Cosima described the first encounter:

> In the evening Herr Joukowsky introduces us to his servant, a Neapolitan folk singer, who delights us with his performing and his

passion; Richard admires among other things how he manages his breathing, and the things he sings are unique in their fiercely tender, cheerfully endearing and beguilingly sensuous manner [*verführerisch sinnlichen Art*]. But how I was stunned when the singer tries to recall the Rhinemaidens' theme (he has seen the *Ring*)! Richard plays it, and all the beauty of Nature is resurrected before us—the lusty animal we had in front of us now turned into an innocent human being! Pepino himself [is] very remarkable, solid, thickset, simple and proud—a lovely experience! (*CT* III, 483)

It dawned on Cosima only much later that Pepino was rather more than Joukowsky's servant, although given the gap in social class separating him from his master, she could hardly be expected to take such relationships seriously. At first she contented herself with the belief that Pepino was merely a devoted and grateful protégé. He delighted the Wagners once again, for example, when he sang on the occasion of Eva Wagner's thirteenth birthday in February 1880. Wagner played something from the *Ring* he thought Pepino would recognize, then accompanied him in the Bridal Chorus from *Lohengrin*, and Cosima remarked on "a lovely hour, wondering what will become of the passionate Pepino. Will he be able to endure this existence out of love for his master who rescued him from misery?" (*CT* III, 491). But even knowing about the bond between the master and servant, Cosima was troubled that Paul showed so little interest in marriage. After introducing him to a suitable young lady in Venice, she notes that "his reluctance to meet women is becoming ever more vehement, and he doesn't even bid farewell to the hospitable Hatzfeldt household" (*CT* III, 615). Cosima could not have meant a disregard for women in general, as Joukowsky was a suave and delightful social companion devoid of misogyny.[2] Rather, she was disturbed that Paul shunned eligible marriage prospects she had tried to arrange.

From the outset, Pepino was welcome in the Wagner household, sang the occasional duet with the Master, and for Wagner's birthday in 1880 even learned to sing Wagner's 1839 song *Mignonne, allons voir si la rose* [*sic*] (WWV 57) on a text by Ronsard, which Daniela von Bülow translated for Pepino into Italian (*GW* VI, 342). The children even insisted he join their Christmas pageant in 1880 as part of a *tableau vivant* they staged as a surprise for Papa. Next to Siegfried, who took the part of Jesus as a carpenter, the three younger Wagner girls were dressed as angels playing upon "early" musical instruments, while Daniela posed as the Virgin Mary. Pepino stood to the right of them, costumed as St. Joseph (*CT* III, 646). In the painting Joukowsky completed the next year for the Wagners, which re-created the *tableau vivant* from the previous Christmas, he thought it prudent to paint himself as St. Joseph rather than leave a permanent record of his young lover in association with two "holy" families. Yet Pepino also participated in social occasions with invited guests where Wagner would accompany him "to the great delight of those present," Cosima remarks (*CT* III, 643), though sometimes Pepino sang to his own mandolin accompaniment. The Wagners sympathized with his difficulties in adapting to life in Germany, and when Joukowsky told them that Pepino "felt homesick," they thought this reaction "only too understandable" (*CT* III, 624). Yet even after Cosima learned the truth about the relationship, she saw nothing wrong with Joukowsky's living arrangements or else would scarcely have allowed him to take Siegfried to Perugia and Orvieto: Pepino was sure to have gone along as well, if only as servant and porter to carry the luggage.

It was Joukowsky, though, whom Wagner considered his very own, calling him *Vetter Paul*—"Cousin Paul" (*GW* VI, 350), and even composing the opening motive of a "grand Joukowsky March" to the words "O! Paul!" for the painter's 38th birthday in January 1883 (*WWV*, 562). It was an affectionate friendship of an older man for a highly cultivated younger man of high birth who idolized Wagner's genius. But there seemed to be something else as well: According to Wagner, they both shared an unusual interest for soft things, as shown by a little play on words reported by Cosima on July 20, 1881 (*CT* IV, 766–767). Goethe's final chorus from the Second Part of *Faust* about the "eternal feminine" reads as follows:

Das Unbeschreibliche   *The incomprehensible,*
Hier ist es getan;   *now it is done.*
Das Ewig-Weibliche   *The eternally feminine*
Zieht uns hinan.   *draws us upwards.*

Speaking to Joukowsky one day, Wagner made a rather coarse pun on the Goethe verses, which has something of the following flavor in English. The first day it went like this:

Das Unbegreifliche,   *The inconceivable,*
Hier wird's getan,   *here it is done;*
Das angenehm weichliche,   *the pleasant and soft things*
Zieht man gern an.   *one likes to put on.*

The following day Wagner improves his play on words:

Das sanft Bestreichliche   *We've taken a fancy*
Hat uns getan,   *to strokable silk,*
Das angenehm weichliche,   *the softish and comfortable*
Zieht man gern an.   *worn by our ilk.*

(The word "silk" is added to the second translation to make an amusing rhyme: The German original only refers to "the softly strokable" and *weichlich* has an effeminate, rather than feminine, connotation.) Because Joukowsky is immune to women's charms, the joke makes clear that what binds the two men is their mutual appropriation of soft clothing, albeit suited to different erotic purposes: It was clever—and disarmingly re-laxed—of Wagner to refer to his satin fetish this way. At least Cosima thought so, because she writes the joke down without the slightest embar-rassment in a diary intended to be read by her children. What Joukowsky thought was another matter. Most likely he took it as a compliment to be taken into Wagner's confidence even if Wagner possibly misunderstood what attracted Paul. Given Pepino's sturdy build and outgoing character, it is unlikely that Joukowsky was interested in silk, and the anecdote may well say more about Wagner's presumed notions of a bond between his own eroticized cross-dressing and the feminized character of some men engaged in pederastic relationships.

It is clear that Wagner delighted in the company of a younger man so enchanted with him, someone with whom he could act in an unguarded manner. Yet Wagner was also extremely jealous of Paul. Each time

Joukowsky dared to leave Wagner's retinue, for example, there was a row, and the Master would punish him with a "comically hostile" [*scherzhaft schlecht*] reception upon his return (*CT* IV, 756). Richard "doesn't like it when those whom he feels belong to him go away"—Cosima notes in her diary in 1881– "and when he sees the roses blooming, he wants to show them to Joukowsky" (*CT* IV, 755).[3] Roses, indeed, because their fragrance could be enjoyed with a younger and homoerotically inclined acolyte, even one sexually involved at the same time with a younger man. After a trying afternoon in 1881, during which Wagner was driven nearly to "despair" coaching Hermann Winkelmann through Parsifal's duet in the Second Act, the composer relaxed in the evening with "Neapolitan songs sung by Pepino. Richard praises Pepino highly"—Cosima writes— "and tells me it's as if the Greek sky were opening above him" (*CT* IV, 786). Pepino was from Naples, not Athens, so the reference to Greece seems to suggest classical *Männerliebe* or Greek love, perhaps even Jupiter's rape of Ganymede, when the god, disguised as an eagle, swooped down to pluck up the handsome young man and ascend with him into the heavenly realm. This was one of those periods in Wagner's life—no doubt sparked by his affection for Joukowsky and Pepino—when his views on same-sex love were at their most accommodating.

Only when Pepino made excessive demands and exercised undue control over Joukowsky did Wagner begin to "pity" his friend (*CT* IV, 979). The liaison must already have been on shaky ground by October 1881, when Pepino actually refused to leave Bayreuth to travel south to Italy. Cosima's diary entry is telling: "Richard had a restless night, he bids farewell to our friend Joukowsky, whose servant Pepino prefers to remain here, out of fear of being left in Italy. We talk a lot about this strange case" (*CT* IV, 814). Pepino, it seems, was afraid that his lover would abandon him once he returned home to Naples, and he actually prevented Joukowsky from leaving Bayreuth with the Wagners. A year later, in October 1882, when the Wagners were in Venice, Joukowsky let them know he had "sent Pepino home," which "inspires Richard to write him a congratulatory message. . . . 'We heartily congratulate you,' and we all sign it" (*CT* IV, 1016). Joukowsky's memoirs suggest he felt a rather more affectionate remorse at Pepino's departure: He makes a point of saying that it was in Weimar that "I sent home my little Italian singer (Pepino) as he couldn't stand it any longer in Germany" (*GW* VI, 734). For a young Neapolitan from a modest background to have survived so long in such an unusual environment, Pepino had done rather well, as he lived together with Paul (mostly) in Wagner's proximity for more than two-and-a-half years, including the period of the 1882 Bayreuth Festival.

Around 1902, the English novelist and travel writer Norman Douglas (1868–1952) actually came face to face with Pepino—in fact, Peppino [*sic*], now bearing the nickname Zingariello or "little gypsy")—in Naples, where he was singing and playing the guitar (together with a "monstrously obese mandolin player") at the Scoglio di Frisio restaurant in Posillipo. Pepino was still "small and swarthy," but was, according to Douglas, "one of the few people who could extract something like music out of that hopeless instrument, the guitar, and his voice was still passable, though it had seen better days. These two were often kept singing their Neapolitan songs till late into the night."[4] Pepino claimed that Wagner had composed a fisherman's song for him in German, which the composer taught him to sing and which he sang for Douglas, who transcribed the tune (but not the words which he couldn't make out). Pepino was probably confusing the story of singing Wagner's *Mignonne* in Italian at the 1880 birthday celebration with a similar event at Wagner's 1882 birthday party, when, in appalling German, he sang a *Fischerlied* [a fisherman's song] that was actually composed by Engelbert Humperdinck (*WWV*, 565). But he was keen to assert his personal link to the great *maestro* and even dictated to Douglas a declaration about his time spent with Wagner in Naples and Bayreuth (though he exaggerated the number of years). According to Douglas, "he could barely sign his name." For reasons best known to Pepino (or perhaps to Douglas), there was no mention of Joukowsky.

Henry James

For the 1880s, the Wagners' attitude toward Joukowsky is extraordinary, as not everyone would have tolerated his liaison with an Italian boy from miserable circumstances. In fact, one of Paul's close friends didn't tolerate it at all. Henry James, it turns out, visited Joukowsky in Naples at the very time the Wagners occupied the Villa d'Angri and was shocked by what he found. James had met Joukowsky four years earlier in Paris, where the two were inseparable companions, frequenting the salons of Princess Ourusov and Pauline Viardot-Garcia, the longtime love object of Ivan Turgenev, himself a friend of Joukowsky's father's. Henry struck up what looks to be an intense romantic friendship with Paul in 1876, writing to his sister Alice in Boston that

> the person I have seen altogether most of, of late, is my dear young friend Joukowsky, for whom I entertain a most tender affection. He is one of the pure flowers of civilization . . . [and] is the most—or one of the most—refined specimens of human nature that I have ever known. . . . [H]e is much to my taste and we have sworn an eternal fellowship."[5]

The eternal fellowship did not, however, survive James's visit to Naples, and thereafter he broke off all relations for a few decades. Upon Joukowsky's suggestion, James booked a five-day stay at the pension in the Villa Postiglione where Joukowsky kept his studio and living quarters in Posillipo. There Joukowsky ran on at length about his passion for Wagner, a subject of little interest to James, who famously loathed music. He even turned down an offer to meet the Master, claiming there was little point because he didn't speak German, and Wagner spoke no French. (He was mistaken about Wagner's French.) But more distressing than having to hear about Wagner were Joukowsky's living arrangements, about which James writes elliptically, referring to "the manners and customs of a little group of Russians with whom the said friend—a Russian himself—is surrounded.[6] They are about as opposed to those of Cambridge [Mass.] as anything could well be—but to describe them would carry me too far" (*JL* II, 282–283). Hurrying away after three days to Frascati in the Lazio, James met up with some travelers whose admirable Englishness offered relief after the "fantastic immoralities and aesthetics of the circle I had left at Naples." Because he had failed to pay a call on the Wagners, the fantastic aesthetics must refer to Joukowsky's Wagnerism, while the immoralities can only mean the Russian friends along with Pepino, whose relationship Paul—surely aware of Henry James's own tendencies—made no bones about hiding. James wrote to his sister Alice that Joukowsky had always worshipped some figure of authority and had now found Wagner. Joukowsky, James wrote, was .

> the same impracticable and indeed ridiculous mixture of Nihilism and bric à brac as before. First he was under Turgenev, then the Princess Ourusov, whom he now detests and who despises him, then under H. J. Jr. (!!), then under that of a certain disagreeable Onegin . . . now under Wagner, and apparently in the near future that of Madame Wagner (*JL* II, 287–288).

Nothing in this story contradicts James's own subsequent homoerotic attachments, especially to the Norwegian sculptor Henrik Andersen. Writing in 1902 to his "dear, dear, dearest Henrik" from the Reform Club in Pall Mall, he enthuses:·

> The sense that I can't *help* you, see you, talk to you, touch you, hold you close and long, or do anything to make you rest on me, and feel my participation—this torments me, dearest boy, makes me ache for you, and for myself; makes me gnash my teeth and groan at the bitterness of things . . . I wish I could go to Rome and put my hands on you (oh, how lovingly I should lay them!) but that alas, is odiously impossible. . . . I return to Rye April 1st, and sooner or later to *have* you there and do for you, to put my arm round you and *make* you lean on me as on a brother and a lover . . . —this I try to imagine as thinkable, attainable, not wholly out of the question (*JL* IV, 225–226).

It seems probable that James ran away from Naples, not so much because of Joukowsky's immorality, but because, as someone with "pederastic" tendencies himself, James felt distress at the sight of the Russian's fearlessness in failing to conceal his more undiluted (as well as un-self-deluded) erotic attractions. After all, if the artist saw no reason to hide his relationship with Pepino from the Wagners, why, given what he knew or suspected about James, should he dissimulate around someone of his own generation and inclination? Only in 1908 did James try to reestablish contact with Joukowsky by asking a friend to enquire about him in Moscow, not realizing that Paul was in Weimar at the time.[7]

Compared with the strait-laced world of Henry James, the Wagner household must have seemed a haven of tolerance for someone like Joukowsky. Yet one reads little about how Wagner viewed same-sexuality; indeed, what role it played in his erotics generally. "Incited" by her husband into calling Joukowsky's liaison "ludicrous" and, realizing that this ran counter to Wagner's view, Cosima held her tongue. But the extent to which Wagner understood such matters remains to be clarified. What is certainly clear, as shown in Chapter 4, is that more than a few critics suspected he understood rather a lot.

Richard von Krafft-Ebing and Oscar Panizza

By the 1860s, homosexuality—though called by other names—had become an ever more pronounced topic in medical and cultural discourse, and there had been intimations of links between Wagner's music and homoeroticism already in mid-century, as mentioned in Chapter 1. As the fin de siècle drew near, though, the idea of Wagner's deviance related to "contrary sexuality" became ever more explicit. The French writer Joris-Karl Huysmans, for example, in a critical essay on *Tannhäuser* from 1880, wrote that Wagner's non-pagan, "Christian" Venus is an "allegory of Evil struggling against Good, symbol of our interior hell opposed to our internal heaven . . . [which] attracts and captures [a victim] like the most dangerous of the deities of Prudence whose name this writer can scarcely write down without trembling: *Sodomita Libido.*"[8] In case studies comprised of autobiographical statements Richard von Krafft-Ebing reported how Wagner's works appealed especially to "contrary sexuals." One subject tells how his tastes in art lean toward works with "refined feelings" and "strange passions." With music, it is the "nervous, excitable music of Chopin, Schubert, Schumann and Wagner which speaks to him most." Yet another subject, a thirty-seven-year-old technician from a large German city—who describes himself as "a rather powerful man with a good growth of hair and of a thoroughly masculine nature," though with feminine "sensitivity and feelings"—connects his Wagnerism directly to his sexuality:

As little as I'm interested in politics, all the more passionately do I love music, and am an ardent devotee [*ein begeisterter Anhänger*] of

Richard Wagner, a fondness I have noticed with most homosexuals. I find that this music in particular corresponds so well to our nature *(gerade diese Musik unserm Wesen so sehr entspricht)*.[9]

It was a fact of life, this fondness for Wagner by Uranians or Urnings [*Uringe*], the term coined by the campaigner for homosexual rights, Karl Ulrichs, and it was *Parsifal*, restricted until after the turn of the century to performances at the *Festspielhaus* in Bayreuth, which provoked the most intense response. By the 1890s, so great were the numbers of those whose passion for Wagner centered on *Parsifal* that the Festival administration had to inform its foreign clientele before the 1894 season that they could no longer guarantee seats for the "stage-festival-consecration play" unless patrons also booked tickets for *Tannhäuser* and *Lohengrin*.[10] In an essay from 1895, entitled "Bayreuth and Homosexuality," the novelist Oscar Panizza (1853–1921) spelled out what many had surmised, "that *Parsifal* offers spiritual sustenance for pederasts." No friend of same-sex love, Panizza was, on the other hand, less than a puritan.[11] His *Council of Love* [*Das Liebeskonzil*] from the same year had satirized the sexual repressiveness of his age through salacious representations of God, Christ, and the Virgin Mary, and for this he landed in a Bavarian jail for blasphemy. Amusingly, his article begins by decoding a personal advertisement in "southern Germany's most respected newspaper" in which a

young (foreign) bicyclist [from] a Christian background seeks similar companion from v. good household, up to 24 years old, for cycling holiday to Tyrol in month of August. Must be good-looking, and have distinguished manners and enthusiastic character. Offers must be accompanied by photograph, which will be returned at once. Write to "Numa 77," poste restante, Bayreuth. (*PH*, 71)

It was suggestive enough that the advertisement appeared just before the first of the season's *Parsifal* performances and listed the advertiser's address as "poste restante, Bayreuth." But the dead giveaway was the "catchword" at the end of the advertisement, "Numa," the pseudonym used by Ulrichs in the early 1860s to preach tolerance toward "love between Urnings." Coded references to *Parsifal*, Bayreuth, and homosexual rights therefore ensured that a young foreign cyclist met up with a suitable German lad with similar inclinations and interests.

It is not altogether a surprise that such an opera should have attracted adherents of same-sex love; after all, the libretto tells of a young man who shuns seductive maidens, refuses an offer of female sexual enlightenment, and joins a celibate knighthood. Panizza works through these themes before arriving at a conclusion that shocks even him. The character Parsifal, he writes, is *"nolens volens* homosexual," whether he wants to be or not (*PH*, 74). Furthermore:

> the source of his redemptive urge is "compassion," "pity," "longing" and "languishing," all of which qualities must be "pure" and "of the purest kind," that is, without taint of sensuality, in a word, the whole range of sublime emotions which we regularly find when Urnings vent their feelings. In *Parsifal* it is hinted that esoteric knowledge is vouchsafed to all who turn their backs on women: it is a specific knowledge acquired through pity. . . . Even the Urning occasionally mocks at the lower stage of humanity and its sensual animal passion: and he feels superior to others by virtue of his more refined behavior, his loftier outlook, and the knowledge which he keeps to himself. . . . In *Lohengrin* Wagner had followed his historical source, according to which Lohengrin was married and the father of children, and he had the Grail Knight fall in love with Elsa. . . . In *Parsifal*, by contrast, the hero and the community of Grail Knights are conceived entirely in homosexual terms. (*PH*, 74–75)

The main problem Panizza faced is why Wagner, not known as an Urning and the author of important works extolling opposite-sex erotics such as *Tannhäuser* and *Tristan*, should have become a pederast in his old age. To solve this conundrum, Panizza invokes Schopenhauer, who in an appendix to the "Metaphysics of Sexual Love" written for the third edition (1859) of *The World as Will and Representation* puts forth the theory that pederasty, which occurs in all ages and in all cultures, is Nature's way of ensuring the propagation of healthy offspring. Since semen from an old man may result in feeble progeny, he is aroused to feel sexual desire for a younger man with whom he cannot procreate. For Panizza, Schopenhauer's published views were a sign that the philosopher became homosexual "as a natural result of growing older," which would explain how Wagner also turned to pederasty in his later years, though, he hastens to add, "in a purely non-physical way."

Panizza is very interested, however, in citing the medical literature on the infrequency of carnal, that is, anal, intercourse between men, which explains why Urnings so often pursue a "spiritual" path in their sexual practices and aesthetic mores. (Perhaps Panizza changed his views by the time he spent an evening with Oscar Wilde in Paris in 1900, as reported by the American anarchist Emma Goldman.)[12] It is odd, though, that Panizza modeled same-sex relations on the love of an old man for a younger one, because in so doing, he forgot where he started. His two youthful *Parsifal* fans who head for the Tyrol on their bicycles are not only under the age of twenty-four but also surely in the peak of health. But neither pseudo-science nor Idealist philosophy will dim Panizza's enthusiasm:

> What we ourselves shall turn out to be like in old age, we do not know. But while we are young, we should remain healthy. And, as far as Wagner is concerned, the German nation—which will always remain young—should stick to the side of youth, to the healthy, sensual Wagner of *Tannhäuser*, and leave *Parsifal* to the blubberers, the penitents, and the esoteric and old. Be gone!—one could call out to them travestying a well-known passage—be gone! Be gone to the Mount of Venus *masculinus!*

To give *Parsifal* this homosexual reading only exposed the late Wagner's deviance so as to smear his unacceptable sexuality. At the same time Panizza identifies some legitimate issues motivating Wagner's erotics in his last opera.

The "healthy, sensual Wagner of *Tannhäuser*" would not at any rate have struck a consonant chord with critics of his decadence like Nordau, but with Panizza the threshold of an acceptable erotics within enlightened mainstream circles has shifted considerably. By the fin de siècle any eroticism might be sanctioned as long as it wasn't homoerotic. To be fair, Panizza begins by taking a liberal and "naturalist" view of homosexuality in which carnal desires, even heterosexual ones, cannot all be ascribed to functionality and the propagation of the species. "And yet," he writes, "homosexual intercourse between males is looked upon—except by the doctor and the philosopher—as the most reprehensible of all actions on earth. A quick and efficient murder is an act of heroism by contrast" (*PH*, 72). Only at the end of the essay does Panizza confirm the inherent unhealthiness of same-sexuality.

Hanns Fuchs and the "Homosexual in Spirit"

The first writer to reject a defamatory approach to Wagner's homoerotics was the German author Hanns Fuchs, whose book *Richard Wagner and Homosexuality* appeared in Berlin in 1903.[13] Fuchs had been writing various essays on same-sexuality in literature when the sexologist Magnus Hirschfeld commissioned him to write an essay on music and homosexuality. Hirschfeld, whose interpretation of Wagner's fetishistic transvestism was discussed in Chapter 4, founded the *Yearbook for Sexually Transitional Stages* [*Jahrbuch für sexuelle Zwischenstufen*] in 1899 and chaired the Scientific-humanitarian Committee [*das Wissenschaftlich-humanitäre Komitee*] devoted to the repeal of Paragraph 175 of the German criminal code (first promulgated in 1872), which punished sexual acts between men. Fuchs became so engrossed with Wagner that he decided to expand his study into a monograph that appeared in a series for the Berlin firm Barsdorf called *Studies in the History of Human Sexual Life*. Other titles in the series included *The Marquis de Sade and his Time*, *Sexual Life in England*, *The Occult and Love*, and *Love-Lives of Famous Uranians*. Fuchs, though a political radical, was scarcely a flag-waving partisan of recent homosexual literature. Although he later authored a "homophile" novel inspired by his book on Wagner,[14] he also wrote two other works of fiction for Barsdorf: a female domination novel, *Auf Dornenpfaden: ein Masochistischer Roman* (Berlin, 1904); and *Claire*, an epistolary novel about an aristocratic lady, who, "without foreknowledge of her tendencies, has masochistic desires and wishes to be dominated."[15] (Both novels, to be sure, include homoerotic subplots.) Only two years earlier he had criticized contemporary homosexual fiction for its naiveté:

German fiction already boasts an impressive number of homosexual books. The greater part of these, however, see it as their goal to

provoke the ire of heterosexuals. For they either contain an endless
lament on the frightful sufferings of poor homosexuals so as to touch
the hearts of lawmakers or they contain overweening and simple-
minded hymns of praise to homosexuality.[16]

Fuchs's special concern was to establish a literary context for the broader
category of Romantic friendship between men—*Freundesliebe* or *Männerliebe* in German—within which he could make sense of Wagner. He accepted the latest ideas about an essential homosexual identity based on
clinical diagnoses of deviant behavior, but he knew enough cultural history to realize that he needed a new category. The new category he called
der geistige Homosexuelle, the "homosexual in spirit"—another English
translation might be "the homophile"—which explains a number of artists
whose erotic lives confounded conventional social molds. Although Fuchs
was unaware of Wagner's silk and perfume fetish, his plausible reading of
the composer's unorthodox sexuality offers a useful complement to the
portrait presented thus far in this book. The subtitle of his work makes
clear in any case that his primary emphasis isn't biography but criticism,
wishing, as he did, to treat "the sexual anomalies" of Wagner's operatic
characters. Wagner's letters to Bertha Goldwag had been published in 1877,
as mentioned in Chapter 4, but hadn't been much mentioned in the press
during the intervening years. So even though Fuchs authored a female
domination novel, he did not detect related tendencies in Wagner's venera-
tion of Wilhelmine Schröder-Devrient or in his depiction of Venus. Only
in the account of Ortrud does he broach the subject in a useful way.

Fuchs avoids sensationalizing his subject and does not uncover a homosexual bogeyman hiding beneath Wagner's bed. Instead he situates Wagner among an historical panoply of artists for whom these feelings were
not alien. In so doing, his goal was to establish what influence "the specific sexual tendency had on their life and acts, and to see whether we can
identify traits in them which resemble those which [can be] summarized
as the 'spiritual side of homosexuality'" (*FH*, 16). He begins a survey of
historical evidence—such as Michelangelo's poems to Tommaso Caval-
ieri and Shakespeare's sonnets—which display the telltale signs of passionate Romantic friendships between men, where a soulful spiritualized
union overshadows an interest in satisfying carnal desires (*FH*, 16–25).

While an artist's infatuations never exclude the possibility of sexual con-course, the desire for sex does not define this kind of man, Fuchs says. Nor does he ask himself whether his love for a member of his own sex defines the kind of person he is.

Fuchs distinguishes between two erotic sensibilities, one homosexual and the other homophile, the first directed toward questions of sexual iden-tity and difference, and the second directed toward sentimental or "Ro-mantic" friendships that may or may not include a sexual component. As apart from pure homosexuals who are "driven to be sexually involved with persons of the same sex," there is a "second far more numerous class formed by those who, although they have relations with members of the opposite sex, and are therefore corporeally heterosexual, have the spiri-tual qualities, the tendencies, abilities, points of view, manners of think-ing, and views of homosexuals." That this is actually the view he endorses stems from a corresponding acquaintance who lived for years with a ho-mosexual as a young man, and, without being aware of it, admits he took on his values and manners, even though he wasn't sexually attracted to men. Within this second class, the "homosexuals in spirit," the essential divide lies between men who ignore their attractions and those

> who have a passionate need for [same-sex] friendship, and might, at least once in their lives, act on such desires in some sexual way. Kisses of the friend, indeed even mutual masturbation, need not be excluded here from those who have a passionate need for friendship. But with these sorts of people sexual union is a result of their togetherness, not its purpose. When a homosexual meets another person, and he finds this person sympathetic, he always thinks, even if quite secretly or even unbeknown to himself, how to reach this goal. With a person who yearns for friendship, this isn't the case, so that one mustn't gauge the performance of the sexual act by homosexuals and by intimate friends by the same measure. The homosexual in spirit, who confronts us so often in life, is also frequently found in literature. (FH, 65–66)

It is plain to see where Fuchs's own sympathies lie, for he views himself and those to whom he is attracted, not as Urnings, but as "homosexuals in spirit." Whereas he displays mere intellectual understanding for—or even condescension toward—pure homosexuals, it is the idealized communion of Romantic friendships that excites him, and causes him to describe their poetic formulations as "exceedingly beautiful [*wunderhübsch*]."

Homosexual Sensibilities in German Literature

In the poet August von Platen (1796–1835), Fuchs locates the pure homosexual sensibility, a man who views his loneliness as a result of unacceptable yearnings, from the fact that he is different from normal men and must suffer as a consequence. He cites as emblematic the poem entitled *An einen Freund* [To a Friend]:

Einsam und von Schmerz   *Lonely and with pain infused,*
   durchdrungen,
Sitzt der delph'sche Gott und sinnt,   *sits the Delphic god and muses,*
Er beweint den schönen Jungen,   . *he laments the handsome youth,*
Den geliebten Hyazinth.   *the beloved Hyacinth.*

Könnt ihm doch dein Bild   *Would your image to him appear,*
   erscheinen,
Das dir jedes Herz gewinnt,   *that every heart to you wins over,*
Traun! Er würde nicht mehr   *Trust me! He would no more*
   weinen   *mourn*
Um den schönen Hyazinth.[17]   *the beloved Hyacinth.*

Homophile writers around 1900 were critical of Platen's self-pity, which they found embarrassing and effeminate. This, for example, explains the views of Adolf Brand, Elisarion von Kupffer and others writing in the homophile publication *Der Eigene*, first issued in 1896. As against the empirical approach to homosexuality found in Hirschfeld's journal, which sought a special identity for "homosexuals," the organization called the *Gemeinschaft der Eigenen* [Community of the Particular] sought a return to Greek ideals and criticized scientific approaches which removed the aesthetics from same-sex eroticism.[18]

By contrast, it doesn't occur to the homophile to pity himself: His erotic repertoire is too broad for that. Johann Wolfgang von Goethe, according to Fuchs, is one such incarnation. For all that one knows about his female lovers, the poet "would not have been the all-embracing spirit he was, someone whom we admire and honor, had he not . . . experienced the power and omnipotent force [of same-sexual love] in his own body" (*FH*, 32). The second book (Chapter 12) of *Wilhelm Meisters Wanderjahre* (1829) serves to illustrate this sensibility, and in the cited episode, Wilhelm and a youthful fisherman go fishing and bathe together in the brook. As they dry themselves, Wilhelm is

> dazzled by a threefold strong sun, so beautiful was the human form which had never struck me before. The lad seemed to observe me with the same attention. Dressing quickly, we stood still baldly across from one another; our spirits attracted one another, and amidst the most fiery kisses we swore an eternal friendship.

The lad leaves, but promises ardently to meet Wilhelm the same evening:

> Night was falling as we neared the edge of the forest, where the young Friend had promised to wait for me. I strained my vision to the utmost so as to divine his presence; when I failed, I ran impatiently ahead of the slowly striding company, and ran through the bushes back and forth. I called, I was alarmed—he wasn't to be seen and didn't answer; I perceived for the first time a passionate pain, doubled and multiple.

Wilhelm learns that the young fisherman had in fact drowned with four other boys and goes to see his corpse laid out in the parish hall. He cries bitterly, throws himself on his friend's body, and rubs tears into it (which he had heard might revive someone close to death), but his prayers are in vain. He even wishes to resuscitate him mouth to mouth:

> In the confusion I thought to blow breath into him, but the pearly rows of teeth were shut tight, the lips upon which the farewell kiss still seemed to rest failed to stir the faintest sign of response.[19]

One finds passages of similar erotic intensity—some with more or less oblique references—scattered throughout Goethe's works—in *Faust*, in the *Roman Elegies,* in the *West-Easterly Divan,* in the *Venetian Epigrams,* in the *Letters from Switzerland,* in the essay on Winckelmann, and even in the *Erl-King*—yet only recently have critics come to take Goethe's homoerotics as signifying more than a fanciful triviality.[20] To his credit, Fuchs sees in Goethe a man for whom homoeroticism was "only a game of occasional sexual pleasure" (*FH,* 41), one that misses the deeper inclinations of the heart, such as one sees in Shakespeare's sonnets. It is curious how the tone in Fuchs's discussion of Goethe no longer implies the medical distancing of the Platen section; there is a condescension, even toward Goethe, for not reaching the heights of homophile comprehension scaled by other great artists. There follow long citations from Goethe's *Winckelmann* essay on heathens and friendship, especially the concluding passage on friendship, at which point Fuchs criticizes Goethe for suggesting that "one feels ashamed when we poets, historians, philosophers, speakers are overwhelmed with fables, happenings, feelings, attitudes of such [same-sexual] subjects and contents." Is this shame over Winckelmann, Fuchs asks, "not a quiet admission of a not exactly irreproachable sexuality?" (*FH,* 45). It is an odd criticism, for Goethe claimed Winckelmann reached the pinnacle of love in his own sexuality. Fuchs, it seems, wants his "homosexuals in spirit" to have a full understanding of their inclinations and to avoid any phobic responses to them.

Fuchs ends his contextual survey with Schiller, in whom he sees evidence of spiritual homosexuality in *Don Carlos,* in *Die Bürgschaft* [*The Hostage*] and in the famous poem entitled "Friendship" (1782) of which Fuchs cites strophes 3–5:

War's nicht dies allmächtige Getriebe,	*Was it not this mighty cosmos*
Das zum ewgen Jubelbund der Liebe	*which to endless bonds of love*
Unsere Herzen aneinander zwang?	*forced our hearts as one in triumph?*
Raphael, an *deinem* Arm—O Wonne!	*Raphael, on your arm—what joy!*
Wag' auch ich zur grossen Geistersonne	*Dare I take in joy and valor*
Freudigmutig den Vollendungsgang.	*to sunlit minds the final step.*

Glücklich! Glücklich! *Dich* hab ich gefunden	*Blessed! Blessed! Now I've found you,*
Hab aus Millionen *dich* umwunden,	*out of millions have entwined you,*
Und aus Millionen *mein* bist *Du*—	*out of millions are you mine*—
Lass das Chaos diese Welt umrütteln,	*let the chaos round this world rock,*
Durcheinander die Atomen schütteln;	*let atoms shake in confused turmoil;*
Ewig fliehn sich unsere Herzen zu.	*flee our hearts to one another.*
Muss ich nicht aus *deinen* Flammenaugen	*From your flaming eyes must I*
Meiner Wollust Widerstrahlen saugen?	*not suck the likeness of my lust?*
Nur in *dir* bestaun ich mich—	*Only in you am I astounded*—
Schöner malt sich mir die schöne Erde,	*Paints prettier the beauteous Earth for me,*
Heller spiegelt in des Freunds Gebärde	*more brightly Heav'n itself does mirror*
Reizender der Himmel sich.[21]	*in the gesture of my Friend.*

Fuchs might have mentioned that the italics of the original almost betoken a strong sensation of touching. Apart from some sentimental reminiscences about his school friends at the Karlsschule, there is, admittedly, little biographical evidence pointing to Schiller as a "homosexual in spirit." And yet, Fuchs asks, who wouldn't recognize from this poem and similar passages the most obvious manifestation of Romantic friendship? (*FH*, 72). Having shown that homophilia is easy enough to recognize, Fuchs turns to the life and works of Wagner so as to include him among the "homosexuals in spirit."

Fuchs develops his most striking argument from a review of Wagner's prose writings and his correspondence on the one hand, and from the peculiarities of his opera characters on the other. Within the revolutionary writings of 1849 is the essay *The Artwork of the Future*, in which Wagner—surprisingly—grounds the idea for a woman's selfless love in the unselfish devotion shown by male lovers in ancient Sparta:

This handsome naked man is at the core of everything Spartan: from genuine delight in the beauty of the most perfect human *male* body arose a *love between men* [*Männerliebe*] which pervades and shapes the whole configuration of the Spartan state. In its primitive purity, this love proclaims itself as the noblest and least selfish utterance of the human sense of beauty . . . for it teaches him to sink and merge *his entire self* in the object of his affection. And exactly to the same degree that a woman, in perfected womanhood, through love to a man and by sinking of herself within his being, has developed the manly element of that womanhood and brought it to a thorough balance with the purely womanly, and thus in measure as she is no longer merely a man's *lover* but his *friend*—can a man find fullest satisfaction in a woman's love. (*JA* VI, 110)

This affection is none other than that of Romantic friendship:

The higher element of same-sex love excluded the aspect of selfish pleasure. Nevertheless it not only included a purely spiritual bond of friendship, but [one] which blossomed from and crowned the sensuous friendship. This sprang directly from delight in the . . . sensuous bodily beauty of the beloved man; yet this delight was no mere sexual yearning, but a thorough abnegation of self into the unconditional sympathy with the lover's joy in himself involuntarily expressed by the joyous bearing prompted by his beauty. This love, which had its basis in the noblest pleasures of both eye and soul . . . was the Spartan's only tutor of youth, the never aging instructress of boy and man, the marshal of communal feasts and valiant forays, even the inspiring helpmate on the battlefield. (*JA* VI, 110–111)

As Fuchs puts it, "it is highly significant that both of the greatest German minds, Goethe and Wagner, juxtaposed same-sexual feelings of love next to heterosexual feelings of love; they concern themselves not with the purely homosexual but rather with the bisexual man who is able sensuously to love both man and woman" (*FH*, 137). Wagner makes another surprising reference to a homoerotic bond near the end of *Opera and Drama* (1851). There, treating the possibility of the poet and musician as "two persons," Wagner notes an ideal symbiosis between two men differing in age through which the younger man, closer to the instincts of real life, might help the elder realize his artistic aims better than himself. With this collaboration—Wagner's fantasy continues—"the most beautiful and noble love would blossom forth" in which "the bond of love" would be completely mutual, with both begetter and receiver feeling enriched by their shared aims (*SS* VII, 347-348).

Yet another fleeting, if undeveloped, reference to utopian love between men from about the same time is found in a fragment from Wagner's posthumous papers. It begins: "No individual can be happy before we all are, because no individual can be free before we all are":

> *Strength*—drive—will—enjoyment
> *Love*—drive: sexual love   Family love (the idea)
> *Love between men* [*Männerliebe*] (society)
> *Reason*—reduction of all ideas to nature (truth)
> Reason: measure of life
> *Freedom* (i.e. reality)
> The more independent and free, the stronger the love. . . . [22]

Ludwig II of Bavaria

One can imagine, as does Fuchs, the effect such passages in the Zurich writings had on an impressionable and isolated figure such as the homophile Prince Ludwig of Bavaria, who attended a performance of *Lohengrin* on his sixteenth birthday, and for the next three years immersed himself in everything connected with Richard Wagner. It is a fair guess—as Fuchs supposes—that Ludwig may first have encountered an exposition of Greek love in Wagner's writings:

> When Ludwig was 19 years old there was little to read on *Männerliebe*—it is probable that the first time he encountered the word was in the works of Richard Wagner. In most autobiographies of homosexuals the storm of feelings is mentioned in which the moment is conjured when the writer for the first time becomes aware—whether in books or in life—of homosexuality, when he

learns that he isn't the only one, whose world of feelings is so completely different from the greater part of humanity. Since royal children don't feel any different from conventional mortals, we can easily assert that Richard Wagner's views on Romantic friendship [*Männerliebe*] aroused happy . . . stimulation in the breast of the prince. . . . As soon as a homosexual in whatever way has learnt of the existence of his comrades in fate, he seeks to come in contact with them for easily understandable reasons, he aspires to approach them, to consort with them. It is easier for someone who moves within life's middle than it is for him who is close to the summit of society or is enthroned at its summit. (*FH*, 196)

This plausible reading may even help explain why, within four weeks of ascending the throne in 1864, the eighteen-year-old King Ludwig II sent his cabinet secretary von Pfistermeier to the fifty-year-old Wagner to invite him to Munich. Ludwig had naturally been attracted to the appeal—"Will this prince be found?"—which Wagner appended to his published text to the *Ring*. But what Ludwig II did—Fuchs points out—was far more than offer Wagner an annual pension or a home: He not only wished to promote his career but he also wanted a Friend, and wished to come close to Wagner's person (*FH*, 195). His notion of friendship fell squarely into the Romantic camp—some might prefer to call it Romantic camp!—inspired in part by his suspicion gleaned from Wagner's writings that the composer, like him, aspired to this high-minded calling.

Wagner was indeed capable of such a friendship, although at first he reacted more with amazement than anything else. Describing his first meeting with Ludwig to Mathilde Maier, he writes: "Our meeting yesterday was one great love-scene which seemed as though it would never end" (*SL*, 600). And to his confidante the poet and novelist Eliza Wille (1809–1893), he recounts that the young King is

so handsome and spirited, soulful and magnificent, that I feared his life must fade out like a fleeting godly dream in this beastly world. He loves me with the ardency and fervor of a first love; he has learnt and knows everything I have written and understands me like my own soul. He wishes me to remain at his side forever, to work, to rest, to perform my works; he wants to give me everything that I need to do this—I should complete the Nibelungs and he will have them performed just as I want it.[23]

The King's letters to Wagner from May 1864 until even after Wagner's departure from Munich in October 1865 blaze with the scorching heat of homophile passion. Here is one example (dated November 2, 1865) chosen from among scores of similar letters published in the *Königsbriefe*:

> My only friend! My ardent loved one! . . .
>
> I wish to struggle victoriously against all obstacles like a hero; I am completely your own, just let me show obedience.—Yes, we must speak to one another, I want to scatter all the stormy clouds, Love can overcome anything. You are the star that lights my life, und your glance always strengthens me wonderfully.—I burn for you, o my holy one! My adored one! I would be forever happy to greet my Friend here in eight days, o we have much to tell one another! Were I only able to banish the curse you spoke of, to send it back into the nocturnal depths out of which it arose! How I love, I love you my only one, my most cherished possession!—Sun of my life. . . . Is my beloved friend coming? I beg you, write soon! Never shall we be parted, I face the false beams of daylight . . . My inspiration and love for you are boundless!
>
> Once again I swear my loyalty to you unto death!
>
> Eternally, eternally
>
> Your Ludwig who burns for you
>
> (*KB* I, 203–204)

Wagner's letters are more muted in tone and passion, but equally crammed with pretentious prose, especially during the first year when *Tristan* was first performed. In April 1865, a few months before the premiere, Wagner writes:

Dear, dearest, magnificent Friend! . . .

Dear, Dear heavenly Friend! How you brighten my poor harassed existence. I feel so deeply, deeply satisfied and elevated through your love, through my—through our love! No words can express what this wonderful relationship between us means. Might I die—on the evening of my *Tristan*, with a last glance up to your eyes, with a last grasp of your hand!

Affectionate, blessed, divine Friend!

How deep, how deep is the bottom of our Love!

Suffering, but blissful—

Eternally yours

Richard Wagner (*KB* I, 86)

Wagner's responses might be thought opportunistic were it not for the fact that the composer confessed to all his intimates that his feelings toward Ludwig were genuine. A year before, in May 1864, he writes to Eliza Wille:

At last a love relationship [*ein Liebesverhältnis*] which doesn't lead to suffering and torments! That is how it is when I see this magnificent youth so before me. . . . . He stays mostly in a little castle in my proximity; in 10 minutes the carriage takes me to him. Our conversations are ravishing. I always fly to him as to a lover. (*WE*, 79)

A month later, in June 1864, he notes in another letter to Eliza:

Of my youthful King only still this one thing, that if I am really not utterly happy, this isn't his fault. You certainly still don't have a full picture of the glory of this relationship. That you'll obtain from me. In short, the masculine sex in my eyes has through this representative been completely rehabilitated. All this you'll come to see! (*WE*, 83)

At the same time, tired of having to manage his own household, Wagner writes both to Mathilde Maier and to the composer Peter Cornelius in May 1864, inviting them (separately) to set up house with him, as if he were waiting to see which offer were accepted first. To Cornelius he writes:

> Either you accept my invitation without delay, and settle down with me for the rest of your life's days in a kind of genuine domestic union with me. Or—you scorn me, and thus expressly repudiate my desire to bind you to me. . . . My present relationship with you torments me dreadfully; It must either become complete, or else break altogether. (*SL*, 608)

Wagner also writes in his loneliness to Heinrich Porges and to Mathilde Maier, to whose mother he makes an assurance that he will renounce sensuality and that the relationship will not be sexual: "I must aim, as carefully as possible, to find a relatively young woman whom I can trust to satisfy whatever needs I may have but which will in no way involve any further sensuality" (*SL*, 616). In a letter to Eliza Wille from May 1864 he notes: "Whether I could renounce the 'feminine' altogether? With a deep sigh I tell myself I almost wish it so!—A glance at [the King's] dear portrait helps me once again. Ah, this charmer, this youth [*Ach, dieser Liebliche, Junge!*]! Now he means more than anything to me, world, wife and child" (*WE*, 82). And then in October 1864:

> Yesterday when we had settled on the completion and performance of my Nibelungs I was so gripped by amazement over the miracle of this heavenly royal youth that I was near to sinking to my knees and worshipping him. (*WE*, 87)

Even to the more taciturn Hans von Bülow Wagner writes in June 1864:

> There is something godlike about him, something undreamt-of, something incomparably and gloriously beautiful that has come true and entered my life. . . . I have created this miracle, with my very own yearning and suffering, and a queen had to give birth to this son for me.— . . . But I shall send you a portrait of him. He is my genius incarnate whom I see beside me and whom I can love. (*SL*, 609)

And to Mathilde Maier he writes in March 1865:

> No one has proved of any lasting worth in the recent storm, except for
> me and the King. He is my only real friend,—and certainly the stars
> have destined him for me: he belongs to *me*, he *cannot* do otherwise,—
> and so—I belong to him. During this recent period, when his mother
> left no stone unturned in her efforts to tear him away from me, he did
> not bat an eyelid: he has survived every test with heavenly purity and
> loyalty.—His letters during these weeks have been utterly divine!—My
> dearest, I *must*, because he—*wills* it so! (*SL*, 639)

Infatuated with a young King who showered him with affection and Romantic friendship and—no small matter, this—offered him financial security, Wagner lurches into high poetic mode in a public poem dedicated to
Ludwig, which accompanied the print of *Die Walküre* the following year.
The protracted encomium tries (in vain) to imitate the high-flown style of
Schiller's own homoerotic verses in a manner that looked impossibly pur-
ple by the 1860s. Wagner's poem *To the Royal Friend* concludes:

So bin ich arm und nähre nur
   das Eine,
den Glauben, dem der deine sich
   vermählt:
er ist die Macht, durch die ich stolz
   erscheine,
er ist's, der heilig meine Liebe
   stählt;
doch nun geteilt, nur halb noch
   ist er meine,
und ganz verloren mir, wenn dir
   er fehlt.
So giebst nur Du die Kraft mir,
   Dir zu danken,
durch königlichen Glauben ohne
   Wanken.
(*SS* VIII, 2)

So poor am I and nurse one thought
   only,
the faith to which Your own is wed:

It is his power which makes me
   proud,
It's that which steels my holy love;

though now divided, half mine
   only,
quite lost to me if You lack faith.

So You alone give me strength to
   thank You,
through Royal faith that wavers
   not.

But even the identification of poetic hyperbole cannot supplant the extraordinary impression left by perusing the entire correspondence between Ludwig and Wagner, in which the diction of infatuated *Freundesliebe* spreads out over several volumes. Most intense, of course, is the initial period published in the first volume of the *Königsbriefe* which, all told, numbers 228 items—including letters, telegrams, and poems. Effusive terms of intimate endearment, sworn oaths of eternal loyalty, expressions of bottomless gratitude—these were the nurturing sustenance that fed a burgeoning love affair.

In a letter to the King from September 1865, Wagner even returns to his theoretical ruminations in *Opera and Drama*, seeing them as foreshadowing his ideal love with Ludwig:

> I suspected this highest possibility of [our] Love: near the end of *Opera and Drama*, I longingly pictured this relationship: the love which binds the older to the younger man. I said "older and younger man" and didn't say "father and son" because what is sexually natural could in no way have crossed my mind. I didn't say "teacher and pupil" for this implies "upper and lower" and I wanted complete equality; only therefore the divinely inspired difference in age [would do]. I rated the work of love between both these two as the true "Artwork of the Future." In the most sublime sense the ideal has been reached: here We stand!—only I have to confess that dizziness often still comes over me! Can this boundless happiness really have been granted me? (*KB* I, 170–171)

Rejection of Pederasty

Only one shadow stalked the horizon of ideal *Freundesliebe* for Wagner—that it must be kept apart from (indeed, must categorically reject) carnal sodomy. In a note found in Wagner's *Brown Book*, same-sexual intercourse is excoriated as perverse and foreign. Jotting down the following regarding "What is German" in April 1873, Wagner writes:

> We must understand a thing in *our* language if we want to understand it properly. (barbaros—un-German. Luther.) This is the sense

of a *German* culture. What we can never understand in any language about the Greek way, is what wholly separates us from it, e.g. their love—in—pederasty. (*BB*, 232)

Their homoerotics—those of the Greeks—must be sharply distinguished from *our* homoerotics, and in this statement one can most likely detect the perfectly understandable line Wagner drew between his awareness of classical same-sex love and his own configuration of *Freundesliebe*.

Given his "understanding" of same-sexual desires as reported to Cosima—though lacking the "inclination" to do anything about it—one can also begin to make sense of Wagner's fears for his younger Friends. In the case of Nietzsche, his putative self-abuse might have led to pederasty, whereas with Karl Ritter (discussed in Chapter 4) Wagner suspected that it had already done so, judging from two anecdotes in *Mein Leben* that allude to a dramatic work about Alcibiades and another "peculiar friendship [*sonderbare Freundschaft*]" with a German musician named Winterberger (*ML*, 520, 597). On the other hand, the issue of pederasty was mostly ignored when it came to Wagner's joy in cultivating the Friendship of Ludwig and Joukowsky, and only when it became threatening, as in Pepino's manipulation of Paul at the end of their relationship, did Wagner congratulate Joukowsky for breaking off the liaison.

Joukowsky's same-sex relationship wasn't perhaps the very first that Wagner approved, however. When visiting London in 1855, Wagner was charmed to meet a couple of men, Sainton and Lüders, both musicians who "lived together as man and wife," he reports in *Mein Leben* (*ML*, 531). Prosper Sainton (1813-1890) was a French violinist from Toulouse "with a fiery and naïve temperament," whose partner was a German from Hamburg, Carl Lüders, "a man with a dry yet agreeable temperament." Wagner found them so engaging that he ended up dining in this "unusual household [*eigentümliche Hauswesen*]" almost every evening. He was "very touched" by the story of how the two met and became lifelong friends. Lüders approached Sainton in a restaurant in Helsinki when he was indigent and stranded after playing a poorly paid concert, and asked whether "he were minded to accept his friendship" and half his worldly goods. Friendship, that is, rather than pederasty, made the story touching rather than incomprehensible, and Wagner enjoyed a warm reunion with Sainton and Lüders when he dined with them in London again in April 1877 (*GW* V, 350).[24] As for Wagner's own Romantic Friendships with men, so long as sexual intimacy played no role, he was prepared to travel quite some distance, as we've seen.

Signs of Romantic Friendship

Fuchs scours Wagner's opera librettos and poems for traces of intense *Freundesliebe* and has a fairly easy time of it. He finds "spiritual homosexuality" all across Wagner's oeuvre, beginning with *Die Feen*, but it is particularly concentrated in *Tristan* and *Parsifal*. Whereas "everyone knows," Fuchs writes, "that *Tristan* is the Song of Songs [*das Hohelied*] to sexual love," what people miss is that *Tristan* is also a "consecration of Romantic friendship [*Freundesliebe*]" as well (*FH*, 152). While the general public of his own day devalued such feelings, Fuchs was right to note that the frequency of homophile relationships—in which a sexual component remains unspecified—declined as medical and cultural definitions of the homosexual became more prominent. Even before an explicit discourse on homosexuality appeared, the cultural tide in German-speaking lands seems to have been turning against Romantic male friendships. As early as 1849, for example, Gottfried Keller (1819–1890) expressed his embarrassment over Schiller's homoerotic poetry, whose maudlin sentimentality distressed him. Keller writes:

> I must openly admit that Friendship doesn't fill any great gap in my life. There may have been a time when the great passionate and ideal friendships were justified, but they aren't, I think, any longer. It seems to me that at least among men it is becoming more and more inappropriate [*unpassend*] for two to want something so very special and exquisite between them; it is anti-social and misguided [*unbürgerlich und unpolitisch*]. . . . As for a relation to women it is rather different.[25]

Keller writes these lines in a letter to his female friend Johanna Kapp, intimating some vested interest in his repudiation of *Freundesliebe*, but his views suggest that the acceptance of erotic friendships with the opposite sex made sentimental attachments to men seem superfluous. A few years later, in 1855, Keller joined Wagner's social circle in Zurich where he heard Wagner read the completed *Tristan* poem in 1857. Apparently *Tristan* both bemused and tired him (*NL* II, 530). Perhaps it was, in part, Wagner's outdated panegyrics on *Freundesliebe* that put him off.

Brangäne

Compared with Keller, Wagner stands out as a man of the past by embedding his "special and exquisite" forms of sentimental friendships in *Tristan und Isolde*. For the erotic ethos of this opera gains a heretofore unheard-of intensity, not only because of the impossible Love-Death between Tristan und Isolde but also because even the minor characters, as Fuchs illustrates, are shown to be in love with one of the protagonists. Brangäne, for example, is far from a merely devoted and bungling servant. Her life "has only a single goal—the happiness of her mistress," which is why she has no choice but to switch the vials, supplying the Love potion instead of the Death philter (*FH*, 153). Her distressed diction betrays a desperate attachment, as when she "showers her mistress with pet names" in an attempt to placate Isolde after she curses Tristan:

O Süsse! Traute!	*My sweetheart! Beloved!*
Teure! Holde!	*Precious! Charmer!*
Gold'ne Herrin!	*Golden mistress!*
Lieb' Isolde!	*Dear Isolde!*

Four short lines—six exclamation points. The stage directions evoke a similar delirium. First Brangäne "flings herself upon Isolde with impetuous affection"—and then "gradually draws her to the couch." Fuchs treats only Wagner's poem, but the musical language also depicts this "unrestrained affection," blurring in the process Isolde's erotic suffering from Brangäne's own. Thereafter, as Brangäne hatches her plan to bind Tristan to her mistress with the love potion, we soon perceive her own erotic impulse in "conjuring up the power of love" from words, stage directions, but above all the music, often called Brangäne's Consolation. In fact, this leitmotive might best be dubbed *Freundesliebe*, which, as Brangäne's words make clear, is another form of love's power [*der Minne Macht*] that emerges directly out of the original pitch collection of the *Tristan* chord. (See Example 5–1.)

The complicated prehistory of this passage helps show that Wagner connected the music to the idea of sexless homoerotic love. In fact, Wagner composed this passage without tying it to any concrete words or ideas and only subsequently found a match to some verses in *Siegfried*. The music first occurs in Wagner's sketches in 1857 labeled *Im Asyl erstes Motiv 16 Mai*. As he writes to Mathilde Wesendonck several days later:

> The Muse is beginning to visit me: does it betoken the certainty of your visit? The first I found was a melody which I didn't at all know what to do with, till all of a sudden the words from the last scene of *Siegfried* came into my head.[26]

The words from Act III of *Siegfried* that came into Wagner's head occur just as Brünnhilde, shocked by Siegfried's sexual overtures, says: "My senses are confused, my knowledge is silent: must my wisdom vanish?" To which Siegfried replies: *Sang'st du mir nicht, dein Wissen sei das Leuchten der Liebe zu mir?* [Did you not sing to me that your knowledge would radiate your love for me?]. (In fact, the music for the verses in the ultimate version of *Siegfried*—the so-called World Inheritance motive—wasn't composed until 1864.) *Tristan* was actually much on Wagner's mind in 1857, and the composer found himself composing music for both operas at once, one reason why he ultimately abandoned his work on *Siegfried*. In fact, he found a far better use for his sketches in Brangäne's loving entreaty to her mistress.[27] What is clear is that Wagner associated the music—in an instinctive personal reaction—with a gentle erotic charge as he awaited a visit from Mathilde. It was, however, a charge with a nuance, as Wagner marks the sketch *Anmuthig*—"agreeable," or "charming,"—thereby revealing the particular shade of its character.

Even in the earliest sketch, one can see that the music embodies the sweet lyrical expression of two lovers in a particularly poignant way. Not only does the double counterpoint invert at the octave as the melodic first voice and subsidiary voice trade places, but there is a telling (and sensuous) overlap before the end of the weak notional fourth "beat" of the (hypermetrical) phrase, where the bass line interrupts and impatiently re-inaugurates the lyrical outburst in the form of the voice-exchange. The lilting reference to the waltz underlying this version of motive evokes a feminine grace, though Wagner—still thinking of music for *Siegfried*— also tried his hand at a version of the motive in a more "masculine" duple meter, a significant move because of the use he makes of it, as we shall see, in *Tristan*, Act III. The passage for Brangäne opens with the original pitches of the *Tristan* chord, and though the poetic-musical period is notionally in E♭, the sounding of *Freundesliebe* acts as a new imagined resolution to Desire in the key of G♭, where it ends with a conventional interrupted cadence.

Kurwenal

What is certainly more masculine is Kurwenal's love for Tristan, parallel to Brangäne's love for Isolde in the form of yet another adoring and trustworthy servant. So great is Kurwenal's loyalty to Tristan that it causes his death. When the ship arrives with Marke and Melot, he throws himself on the arrivals whom he takes for enemies, and sinks to the ground mortally wounded from the blows he has received from the defenders. Eight years earlier, in 1849, Wagner had already foreshadowed Kurwenal's selfless act in the *Artwork of the Future* when he wrote that the homoerotic bond between the Spartan lovers "knit the fellowships of love into battalions of war and military order that prescribed death-defying tactics to rescue the threatened lover or to exact vengeance if he fell in battle" (*JA* VI, 111). Kurwenal's affection unto death for Tristan offers a "classical" example of homophilia in sacrificing himself for his beloved in the precise terms Wagner had specified:

Tristan! Trauter!	*Tristan! Beloved!*
schilt mich nicht,	*Scold me not,*
daß der Treue auch mit kommt!	*so the faithful one may follow you!*

Kurwenal enunciates these lines as he dies, trying to take hold of Tristan's hand. "There he lies," Kurwenal sings to the King, "where I lie" (Act III, sc. iii).

Kurwenal's bond to Tristan presupposes the exclusion of women, in keeping with time-honored values of *Freundesliebe* between men. Most important to Kurwenal is that Tristan not denigrate himself before a woman:

Ein Herr der Welt	*A master of the world*
Tristan der Held!	*The hero Tristan!*
Ich ruf's: du sag's, und grollten	*I call it out: you say it, and even if*
mir tausend Frau Isolden!	*a thousand Dame Isoldes should*
	resent me!

(Act I, sc. ii)

As a paradigmatic Spartan companion-lover, Kurwenal serves as the ideal Friend to nurse Tristan in the Third Act, and, against the vassal's own wishes, "sends for the one female physician who can help his master."

Der einst ich trotzt',	*The one woman I once defied,*
aus Treu' zu dir,	*out of troth to you,*
mit dir nach ihr	*with you for her*
Nun muß ich mich sehnen.	*must I now crave.*

(Act III, sc. i)

The music Wagner crafts for Kurwenal's demise is rich in erotic allusions, though at the beginning of the incident, as Kurwenal "staggers, mortally wounded, before King Marke," the music of the Curse resolving to the *Tristan* chord might point to Marke as much as to Tristan's manservant. (See Example 5–2.) But the stage belongs entirely—if briefly—to Kurwenal as he clutches at Tristan's hand, gasping between his words as the orchestra plays a tragic, slow rendition of Silken Longing (first drafted in the version shown in Example 4–1). In the first statement of the motive in Act III, sc. i, Tristan, as mentioned in Chapter 4, "draws Kurwenal toward him and embraces him," and in the act of thanking the Friend, shares with him his ecstatic world. That Kurwenal's own music at his death alludes to Desire ensures that his erotic world—like that of Brangäne—is heard in conjunction with luckless Desire and the Love-Death of Tristan and Isolde. In the first scene, in fact, Tristan sings in martial praise of Kurwenal, calling him "my shield, my shelter in war and strife, always prepared to be at my side in joy and sorrow [*mein Schild, mein Schirm/in Kampf und Streit, zu Lust und Leid mir stets bereit*]." The intensity of these lines is fully echoed in the few stirring bars of martial music in which Wagner reconfigures the heroic fanfares of Siegmund's victory call [*Siegesruf*] from Act I of *Die Walküre*. It is also a kind of Spartan equivalent of Elsa's maidenly declaration of love to Lohengrin (Act I, sc. ii): "My shelter, my angel, my redeemer [*Mein Schirm, mein Engel, mein Erlöser*]." And even though Tristan believes that the compassionate Kurwenal cannot understand the full extent of Tristan's erotic misery—"this frightful yearning that sears me [*Dies furchtbare Sehnen, das mich sehrt*]," Wagner recalls Tristan's declaration of *Freundesliebe* in his hopeless longing at the moment of Kurwenal's death, now dragged down by the heavy-laden tones sounded in the bass register at half the tempo. It is difficult to see how else to decipher Silken Longing except as a brief but tragic commentary on Kurwenal's love for Tristan.

King Marke

As for King Marke, he is certainly the greatest of Wagner's homoerotic companions, as Fuchs makes clear from his inspection of the poem. Here is a man who loved Tristan so much that when his Queen died, he saw no need to remarry. Instead, he wished to turn over all his wealth to Tristan:

Dünkte zu wenig	*Did his thanks*
dich sein Dank,	*that what you acquired,*
Daß, was du erworben,	*seem too little for you,*
Ruhm und Reich,	*Glory and realm*
er zu Erb' und Eigen dir gab?	*which he gave to you as heir and owner?*
Da kinderlos einst	*He who was childless*
schwand sein Weib,	*when once his wife he lost,*
so liebt' er dich,	*loved you so much,*
daß nie aufs neu'	*that never again*
sich Marke wollt' vermählen.	*wished Marke to wed.*
(Act II, sc. iii)	

What torments the King is the pain that Tristan—not Isolde—inflicted on him, for he forgoes any mention of his wife's guilt. In the Third Act, when Tristan lies dead before him, he rejoices that Tristan—not Isolde—was innocent of intentional guile:

Da hell mir enthüllt,	*When clearly revealed to me*
was zuvor ich nicht fassen konnt',	*what till then I could not grasp,*
wie selig, daß den Freund	*how blessed, that I then found*
ich frei von Schuld da fand!	*the Friend free from blame!*

The Friend, indeed. And not necessarily a much younger friend either, for Wagner nowhere specifies King Marke's age at the time of the opera. In fact, "the sexual anomaly of King Marke would already have been felt many times before," Fuchs wrote, if stage directors had not insisted on making an old man of him "in contrast to [Wagner's] indications." What Fuchs—in addition to a few opera guides—didn't notice is that Marke sings to the same "homoerotic" orchestral leitmotive of *Freundesliebe* (shown in Example 5–1) that accompanied Brangäne as she sang to her mistress, but now in the more four-square and masculine duple meter, which Wagner originally conceived for *Sang'st du mir nicht* in *Siegfried*, Act III. Surely the traditional label of Brangäne's Consolation misses Wagner's point.

Of course, all these homoerotic desires end badly—death for Kurwenal, misery and unhappiness for King Marke and Brangäne. Yet none of these characters is deemed sick or perverse. To the contrary, their aspirations for love are noble and ennobling, for they reflect the mores of Romantic Friendship, values that Wagner esteemed in his own life, though it is fair to say that, apart from exceptional moments (such as his infatuation with King Ludwig II), he preferred to be the object of homoerotic devotion rather than its practitioner; preferred, that is, to play Tristan over Kurwenal. In the end—however one assesses his own personal motivations—the musico-dramatic acuity and sympathy Wagner brings to these characters evokes a sexual universe made all the more compelling by its multiple and overlapping sets of magnetic erotic attractions.

Parsifal

As for Parsifal's alleged homosexuality, Fuchs takes a more nuanced view than previous writers. He agrees with Panizza that in the scene with the Flower-Maidens, Parsifal doesn't "behave as one would expect from a female-loving nature-boy." "Such a type," Fuchs observes, "would surely devote his liveliest attention to the beautiful girls, and would quickly have chosen one so as to learn in her arms the joys of love. But what does Parsifal do? He remains quite indifferent. . . . [The Flower-Maidens'] caresses annoy him. But when the girls are not deterred and approach him ever more ardently, he becomes scared and wants to flee." Fuchs concedes to Panizza the point that Parsifal exemplifies only too well the kind of homosexual man "who moves very gladly in feminine circles, is happy to joke and laugh with women, indeed doesn't even shirk from trifling kisses and flees when more is demanded of him" (FH, 261). In the end, though, Parsifal lacks authentic homosexuality because he is captured so "fully and completely by Kundry's kiss."

> After receiving a kiss that is so thoroughly erotic as was the kiss which brought Kundry's and Parsifal's lips together, a homosexual would have pushed the woman away from him in an upsurge of revulsion: in Parsifal this kiss doesn't cause revulsion but rather an actual physical pain. (FH, 262–263)

This was, in fact, the one moment in the drama that mystified King Ludwig, who failed to understand what Parsifal gains from the kiss. In Wagner's prose draft written specially for the King in 1865, Ludwig read: "Transferred wholly into the soul of Anfortas [sic], he feels Anfortas's enormous suffering, . . . the unspeakable torments of yearning love" (KB, 57). The King, however, was puzzled:

> How the plot grips me!—Yes, this art is holy, the purest and most sublime religion. How I long for you: I can only be happy when I am with you!
> Beloved, we want to bear in mind our loyalty to the ideal which enthuses us, and to which the world will some day convert,—o how

I love you, my adored and saintly friend!—Only one question do I permit myself to direct to you regarding Parzifal [*sic*].—Why is our hero only converted by Kundry's kiss, why is it that only through it is made clear his divine mission? That only from this moment can he transpose himself into the soul of Anfortas, so as to grasp and feel with him the nameless torment! (*KB* I, 170)

Ludwig's question can be put in the form of a logical proposition. If Parsifal's ultimate quest is to experience the deepest empathy for another man's torment, surely he has no need of a woman's kiss to reach that goal. Wagner's answer to Ludwig (*KB* I, 174) is really no more than an elementary lesson in Christianity. The meaning of Kundry's kiss, he writes, is

a terrible secret, my beloved! You of course know of the serpent of paradise. . . . Adam and Eve became "knowing." They became "aware of sin." In this knowledge the human race had to atone in shame and misery until they were redeemed through Christ. . . . The kiss through which Anfortas [*sic*] lapsed into sin awakes in Parzival the full knowledge of that sin . . . and with lightning speed he says to himself as it were: "Ah! That is the poison from which he wastes away, him, whose complaint I haven't understood till now."

Wagner seems to have missed what lay behind Ludwig's question, for as someone who recoiled from a woman's embrace, the king would have been the last person to have learned about sin and compassion from Kundry's kiss. That is why Huneker and Panizza were quite wrong to call Parsifal a "homosexual." At best, he is no more than a "homosexual in spirit" or else Ludwig would have understood what the kiss meant.

The homoerotic component in Parsifal's compassion rather reflected Wagner's notion of Romantic Friendship, which is not at all opposed to a woman's meaningful kiss. For, as suggested in Chapter 1, Wagner crafted the scene a few days after the death of Schnorr von Carolsfeld, mimicking the histrionics of Schnorr's deathbed confession and incorporating his own deeply moved reaction. While still alive, Schnorr was, in Wagner's words to Ludwig, "utterly loyal in his love for me, and his tender-hearted docility in learning from my most gentle hints has once again completely enchanted me. [As Tristan] he—another *Ludwig*—will be perfect" (*SL* 640). Schnorr would make the perfect Tristan, in other words, because he was as much a Romantic Friend as was the king. The underlying biographical impulse after Schnorr's death entailed a reciprocal empathy, with Wagner enduring the tenor's suffering as much as Schnorr had grasped Wagner's own erotic torment by having sung the role of Tristan. No wonder, then—given such a confusing concatenation of motivations— that Kundry's seduction of Parsifal provokes such mystification and bemusement.

Wagner and his Romantic Friends

Fuchs's argument is flawed in many respects and his category of "a homosexual in spirit" is problematic, not least because he missed out on Wagner's satin and perfumes and other crucially relevant biographical sources. What he captures in his portrait of Wagner and his characters, though, is that, in same-sex infatuations, the question of who experiences which kind of desires is left intentionally vague. Hirschfeld, who commissioned Fuchs to write his book, rejected his inclusive notion of "homosexuality" because it was at odds with his own theory of sexual stages, all of which depend on classifications of sexual object choice. Hirschfeld was right to complain, moreover, that Fuchs ignored important components to Wagner's erotic impulse by not taking the letters to his milliner into account (*HT*, 165). But Fuchs may have been ahead of his time—perhaps even a bit ahead of our time—in arguing against one homosexual identity, and, by implication, against categories of sexuality that reduce erotic desires to a template of normative behaviors. Certainly a consideration of Wagnerian erotics—both in the composer's life and works—seems to complicate any simple delineation based on clear identities.

For this reason, it is useful to see the drift of Fuchs's discourse as suggesting—rightly—that Wagner resorted to a form of *Freundesliebe* in *Parsifal* because Romantic Friendship was a place free from the torment of erotic desire, a safe haven where the composer could experience compassionate love, the ideal dream of a selfless love he had been preaching since the 1840s, founded in part on an idealized attachment between Spartan lovers. One can see, for example, that all the homophile relationships,

though reciprocated, are fundamentally unequal in their pairing: Kurwenal loves Tristan more than Tristan loves Kurwenal, and the same goes
for Brangäne/Isolde, Marke/Tristan, Parsifal/Amfortas, and even Wol-
fram/Tannhäuser and Sachs/Walther. (Klingsor may enjoy a lustful moment when he ogles Parsifal—*Er ist schön, der Knabe* [He's handsome, that
lad]—but he certainly doesn't love him.) In Wagner's life as well, the
steady succession of special younger male friends all play different variants of a similar role. Karl Ritter, Hans von Bülow, Karl Taussig, Peter
Cornelius, Schnorr von Carolsfeld, King Ludwig II, Heinrich Porges,
Friedrich Nietzsche, Hermann Levi, and Joseph Rubinstein were more
infatuated with Wagner than he with them, and the biographical evidence
shows with some consistency that Wagner encouraged, even groomed,
each Romantic Friend to understand and fulfill his assigned role as the
adoring, self-sacrificing younger lover. As for the characteristic of good
looks that corresponds to Wagner's image of the ideal Spartan companion, perhaps only Ludwig II and Taussig fit the bill. There was always the
possibility of also dying in service, as did Schnorr von Carolsfeld, whose
cries on his deathbed quoted in Chapter 1 ("Oh! my Richard loved me!
How contentedly I die!") echo the role of Kurwenal this time, not Tristan,
with Wagner responding as Tristan: "My beloved!—I drove you to the
abyss!" (Taussig, whose luster never faded in Wagner's memory, died at
the age of twenty-nine before he had time to fall out with the Master.)

Yet when the younger man—even a Royal majesty—failed to live up to
the standard set for him, Wagner served notice and moved on. Such
was the case with Ritter, von Bülow, Cornelius, Nietzsche, and (to a
certain extent) King Ludwig. Three of the other four—Levi, Porges,
and Joukowsky—remained "in service" until the end and even beyond,
for they were among the twelve pallbearers at Wagner's funeral and carried out his wishes long after he lay in his grave. It may or may not be
relevant that, of these Friends close to Wagner at the end of his life, three
were either born or identified themselves as Jews—Levi, Porges,
Rubinstein—and at least three—Joukowsky, the King of Bavaria, and
Levi[28]—engaged in homophile relationships with men, though none of
them seems to have desired a sexual relationship with Wagner! If one
includes those who had fallen out with Wagner, then this number might

be supplemented by two more Friends: Karl Ritter and Friedrich Nietzsche. The boundaries aren't best drawn according to later categories of
"the homosexual" or "the heterosexual," either, because the Friends most
overtly passionate toward Wagner—Schnorr and Ludwig—fall on different sides of the modern binary divide. Nor does a Jewish identity or
background determine the quality of the Friendship—significant though
it must be thought in the case of Wagner. Angelo Neumann, the impre-
sario who produced the Berlin *Ring* cycle, was a Jew but not a Friend,
whereas Levi certainly was one, even once addressed by Wagner as his
alter ego or plenipotentiary.[29] In all these relationships, Romantic friendship and homoerotic attachments can be observed in the myriad ways
that Wagner encouraged and nurtured them.

Although there are exploitative aspects to every unequal relationship,
there is no need to moralize about Wagner's own domineering role, if
only because the devotee in each case firmly believed that he had gained
more from the emotional bond than had the composer. Idealized into
operatic characterizations and dignified with extraordinary musical depictions, Wagner's Romantic friendships can be seen—alongside his own
sexual pull toward both innocent and domineering women and toward his
soft fabrics and perfumes—as another pillar propping up his erotic edi-
fice. The homoerotic pillar is in some ways the most important, creating
as it does a refuge from the ravages of tormented heterosexual desire, an
obsession that had been exercising him since his earliest years. Above the
portal to his aptly named *Wahnfried*, as mentioned in Chapter 2, Wagner
placed a *sgrafitto* of great symbolic importance: The dominating sexuality
and tragic passion of the Schröder-Devrient figure are on the left side,
and the domesticated and loyal Cosima (flanked by Wagner's son and heir
Siegfried) is found on the right, but both women face inward toward the
imposing centerpiece, a magisterial image of Schnorr von Carolsfeld, one
of Wagner's loving male Friends loyal unto death, costumed as Wotan,
"the most tragic of all my heroes" (*SL*, 626). As Wagner wrote in his diary: "My friend? It is him I lose" (*BB*, 50). The link the composer forges
between a sentimental homoerotics and a pure asexual chastity helps explain why his final opera ends—conspicuously—with a flurry of "Amens"
floating above a homophile community in which compassionate love

prevails and erotic desires are forever stilled. It is the final representation of that desire for peace removed from the delights and travails of sexual love, a fitting complement and conclusion to a lifetime spent battling those very same wanton desires.

If Wagner's amorphous intentions motivating *Parsifal*'s erotics were somewhat hard to grasp—are still hard to grasp—it is because the taste for Romantic friendship was already in decline in his own day. Certainly we have become expert at naming people's sexual identities, but rarely notice how, in so doing, rather a few blossoming Friendships are nipped in the bud. The nineteenth century, for all its murky circumlocutions, its inequities and repressions, still nurtured these ambiguous relationships to a far more generous extent, though perhaps less routinely in opera than elsewhere. Whereas Verdi downplayed the patent homoerotics in Schiller's *Don Carlos*, for example, Wagner accentuated them in a significant way in *Tristan* and gave the theme a surprising new apotheosis in *Parsifal*.

What we learn from Wagner's homoerotics is that his passion for Romantic friendships fleshes out the composer's views on sex which, as we've already seen, involve an attraction toward other "forbidden desires" such as silk fetishism, cross-dressing, and female domination. It is easy to see, moreover, how Wagner's embrace of erotically unacceptable practices resulted in a self-knowledge that allowed him to cast a benign view over other people's less conventional sexual interests. As for other people's interests in Wagner, it is clear why the mere whiff of a marginal eroticism in his operas drew a huge contingent of those well aware of their own sexual marginality. All the same, Wagner stops short of making a definitive contribution to homoerotics in his last opera. For when Parsifal heals Amfortas's wound, he does so in an oddly ritualistic and impersonal manner. No words of compassion, no tears, no embrace accompany his gesture; the music tells us instead to bask in the miracle of a mystery play. Having clutched at a chaste version of homophilia to suggest a respite from erotic suffering, Wagner stands at a sympathetic but still safe distance from any greater engagement with these feelings, preferring instead an ecstatic fantasy of redemption. He was therefore right to tell Cosima that Greek love was something for which he "had understanding, but no inclination." If there is an erotic problem with *Parsifal*, it is not that the opera is too homosexual—as in the readings of Panizza and Huneker—but that it isn't homosexual enough. All the same, it was an act of artistic honesty to craft a work that gives shape to a dilemma embedded deep in the composer's own experience, and even the harshest critics of Wagner rarely accuse him of failing to do that.

Epilogue

Whatever one makes of the composer's intentions and actions, it is clear that Wagner's devotion to depictions of sexual desire was exceedingly unconventional, indeed unprecedented in the history of art. For as dazzling as is the music, as insightful the psychology, and as fascinating the unfolding of an aesthetic, Wagner's musical seductions bear little relation to traditional erotics. They depart strikingly from Shakespeare's sonnets with their fretful, manipulated lover, Goethe's *Werther* with its heavy dose of self-willed tragedy, or Ingres's *Bathers in a Harem* with its love of curvaceous flesh. Wagner suggests something altogether different: he is aware that sexual arousal is everywhere and takes a variety of forms; that its allure is often irresistible, and demands truthful artistic representations. At the same time, he inevitably falls into a desperate state that accentuates the torment of unfulfilled longing. In the end, he only wishes the dread feeling to go away. As against the diagnoses of cultural pathologists, there is no reason to pounce on this disposition as a symptom of grave illness or mental incapacity, for no amount of analysis is going to make

Wagner feel any better. What I have suggested is quite the opposite: that what is most remarkable in Wagner's erotics are precisely those aspects that are universal. One doesn't have to be a fan of rosy fragrances, satin dressing gowns, female domination fantasies, or homoerotically charged acolytes to rejoice in an aesthetic representation that gives form and substance to some of the most enduring preoccupations of humankind: those connected with sexual needs and attractions. During the course of a lifetime, who, after all, has not experienced the exhilaration of irrational desires, the hope of sex as a panacea for one's ills, the cruel ways sexual desires can torment, or the wish to rise above them? To come to terms with these themes as Wagner did, shaping them into a vivid musical and dramatic form, can hardly be thought deviant: They are far too common for that.

Yet as soon as Wagner's erotics were interpreted as signifying a coherent philosophy, a cultural practice, or—worst of all—an approach to politics, they immediately stood out as perverse, attitudes that called for serious censure. Had Wagner merely composed the music for operas or ballets, he might well have escaped this fate. But as someone all too eager to publicize his thoughts in feverish bouts of prolix prose, he must be held responsible, at least in great part, for the cultural havoc wreaked by his erotics. Wagner offered easy prey to critics who wished to formulate a case against him as diseased decadent, tarring him with negative stereotypes associated with effeminacy and "Jewishness." Curiously, for all of Wagner's famous public diatribes against the Jews and Judaism, he shunned the idea of a weakened Jewish sexuality to deflect attention away from his own attraction to some classically feminine pursuits. To point to Wagner or his music as diseased is just a more modern way to express discomfort with his erotics, which can scarcely be shown to cause great harm, and to the contrary—if one is willing to accept them—provide immense pleasure.

The enduring, if caricatured, image of Wagner today is that of Hitler's favorite composer,[1] a progenitor of National Socialism whose works are so drenched in violent race hatred and anti-Semitic vitriol that the only way they can be appreciated—if at all—is by excoriating the nasty man and begrudging him his occasionally beautiful music. Yet the moment tickets go on sale for a *Ring* cycle anywhere in the world, they are snapped up in a matter of days, suggesting that not everyone accepts the stereotype or allows it to interfere with an intense engagement with the music. It goes without saying that to read through Wagner's personal and public rants against the Jews is an extremely disturbing, even shocking, experience. (Neither, though, is it very pleasant to read Herzl's or Nordau's outbursts against "members of the tribe" of whom they don't approve.) But given the hounding out of Jews from Germany in the Nazi period and the subsequent attempt to murder the rest of them throughout Europe, it may be difficult for some to follow the thoughts contained in this book. Perhaps it was even wrong of me not to quote more of Wagner's mad and maddening political writings so no one forgets the context that sits so uncomfortably adjacent to the most captivating music and fulminating eroticism.

And yet, a look at the history of reactions to Wagner proves salutary precisely because it challenges Whiggish preoccupations obsessed with pointing accusingly to the political and ideological content of art. One may, of course, pontificate about musical complicity in prejudice and evil, in oppression and genocide, in death and destruction, or in insidious messages transmitted to unsuspecting aesthetes. One may also wish to censure composers for their self-centered nastiness and their noxious political views. If so, Wagner proves an easy target. But in so doing, critics have rarely staked out a coherent ethical position from which to throw stones. Have they articulated a vision of the world that contributes to the improvement of humanity? Is there a theory that ever satisfactorily integrates politics and aesthetics? More to the point: Does one gain much by rejecting Wagner and his music? Does one sleep more restfully by refusing Wagner? Possibly, but I'd gladly sacrifice those hours to savor musical experiences irreplaceable by any other art.

I've argued that the aesthetic accents and, to an extent, cognitive insights stressed in my account of Wagner's erotics make for some very memorable music. I've tried to link the music both intimately and unashamedly to Wagner's struggles, his erotic preferences, his aesthetic theories, his artistic projects and compositional techniques—but in some fundamental way it is never subsumed or subordinated by any one of these. Music clutches at life's *aperçus* in myriad ways, and the feelings it sparks are surely a product of metaphorical acts of imagination grounded in lived experience. One can hold arid debates on the problematic relations between composers' lives and their works, but in the end it is vital to draw on every bit of

evidence—internal, external, or contextual—to help explain musical insights that always eclipse a mere reflection of ideas, concepts, or philoso-
phies. In the case of Wagner's erotics, the span of metaphors is exceptionally wide-ranging, and the composer asked audiences to hear music in
ways they often found unpleasant, exhilarating, or both.

What one makes of these metaphorical leaps—how one judges their
significance as art—often changes over the course of a lifetime, reflecting a trajectory of altered circumstances and evolving views. Writing to
the Bayreuth scenic designer Emil Preetorius (1883–1973) in 1949 about
Wagner's "eroticism which had never before been exhibited in society,"
Thomas Mann asked: "Can you still manage to listen to the Paris Venusberg music? There are times when it is really unappetizing [*unappetitlich*]."
The author of the short stories entitled *Tristan* and *Wälsungenblut* goes on
to admit, at the age of 74, that

> the second act of *Tristan*, I now find, with its metaphysical web of ec-
> stasy [*Wonnesweben*], is for young people who don't know much about
> their own sexuality. But when I recently listened to the First Act
> again, I was completely overwhelmed. . . . All the same, I couldn't
> bear a complete *Tristan* any more.[2]

The propensity to change one's mind about Wagner's erotics extends even
to the composer's most damning critic, Friedrich Nietzsche, who—
paradoxically—began to waver in his view of Wagner as eroticist in a late
private letter about *Parsifal*. Nietzsche's published writings, including the
very last, bulge, as we saw, with insults damning this monument to sickness, this form of "Christianity cleaned up for female Wagnerians." So it
comes as a surprise to learn that it was only in January 1887 that Nietzsche actually heard the *Parsifal* Prelude performed by an orchestra for
the first time. The performance took place in Monte Carlo, and Nietzsche wrote a letter to his friend Heinrich Köselitz [Peter Gast] describing the experience:

> Apart from . . . the uses to which such music can or should be put,
> but rather posing the question purely aesthetically, has Wagner ever
> done anything better? The most sovereign psychological consciousness

and certitude with regard to whatever is said, . . . every nuance of feeling distilled into an epigram; . . . and finally, a sublime and extraordinary feeling, . . . a synthesis of emotional states, [formed] with such acuity and insight that it slices into the soul as with a knife. . . . Such artistry you only find in Dante, nowhere else. Has any painter ever before painted such a melancholy glance of love as has Wagner with the final accents of his Prelude? (*KSA* III, 5, 12)

For once, Nietzsche posed a "purely aesthetic" question about music, not quashing it with criticism and philosophy, and the insights that music offers are immediately apparent. A focus on the aesthetic allows us, in sum, to rescue Wagner from Nietzsche and from all the pathologists and ideologists who presuppose there is such a thing as healthy or politically responsible music. Wagner's is an aesthetic drenched in rich human experiences of every kind, especially erotic sensibilities and desires, and thus immune to the charge that it seeks to avoid culture, the body, or material reality.

All of us have blind spots, and Wagner's blind spot was his obsessive hatred of the Jews. But in matters erotic, his insights ran deep, even if they lacked systematic treatment. Hanns Fuchs concluded rather melodramatically more than a century ago that "Wagner's art will find enthusiastic adherents as long as people live who perceive their sexual lives as torment" (*FH*, 278). He has a point, though an exaggerated one. Perhaps the day will even come when erotic dissonances are outdated, though I tend to doubt it. Far more likely is that Wagner stumbled upon truths that celebrate the human condition, truths we love to hear repeated over and over again. For when thoughts of Eros no longer plague us, we might as well stop listening to music altogether.

Appendix: Musical Examples

Notes

Index

APPENDIX: MUSICAL EXAMPLES

EXAMPLE 2-1 *Das Liebesverbot* (Act II, sc. iv), No. 10, *Szene und Arie*

The Musical *Venusberg*

EXAMPLE 3-1 The Musical Venusberg

Musical *Venusberg* (cont.)

VOLUPTUOUS DANCE

JUBILANT SHOUTS

BACCHANTIC RAPTURE

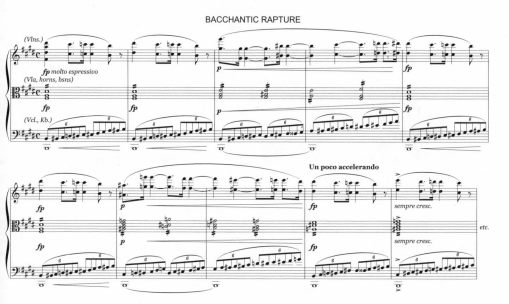

EXAMPLE 3-2.1

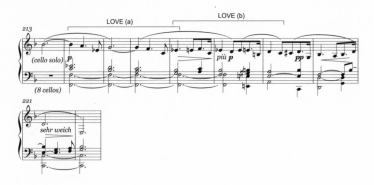

EXAMPLE 3-2.2

EXAMPLE 3-2 LOVE motives and their transformation in *Die Walküre* (Act I)

EXAMPLE 3-2.3

End of Act I

EXAMPLE 3-3 Half-diminished chords in TEMPTATION, *Lohengrin* (Act II, sc. i, mm. 38–52)

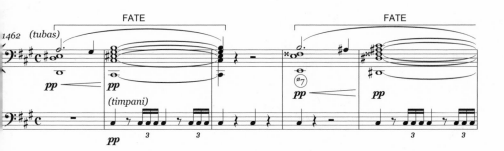

(She pauses and contemplates Siegmund from afar.)

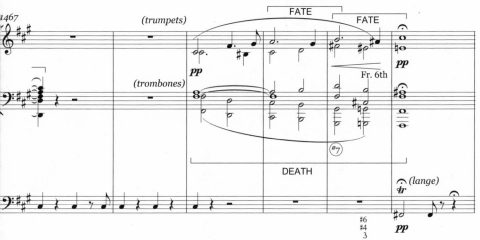

EXAMPLE 3-4 FATE and DEATH in *Die Walküre* (Act II, sc. iv, mm. 1462–1472)

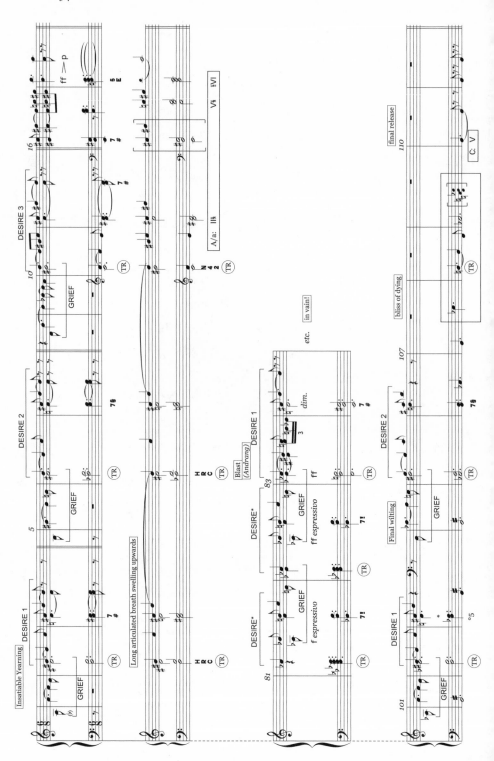

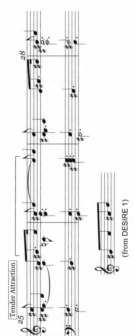

EXAMPLE 3-5 Paradigms in the *Tristan* Prelude

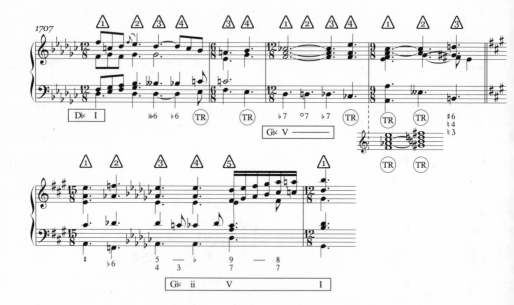

EXAMPLE 3-6 Post-*Tristan* voice-leading and hypermeter in the Quintet from *Die Meistersinger* (Act III, sc. iv, mm. 1707–1716)

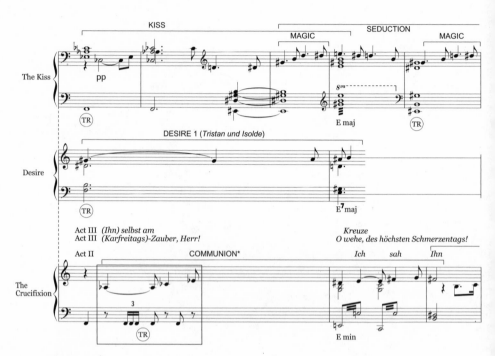

EXAMPLE 3-7 The Kiss (Act II) and The Crucifixion in *Parsifal* (Acts II and III) alluding to DESIRE in *Tristan*

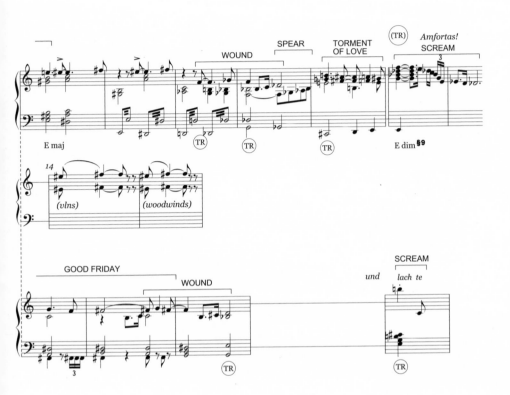

EXAMPLE 4-1 Silken longing—Sketch and voice-leading of a nameless leitmotive for *Tristan und Isolde*, Act III

EXAMPLE 5-1 FREUNDESLIEBE of Brangäne and King Marke—*Tristan und Isolde*, (Act I, sc. iii, mm. 872–885 and Act III, sc. iii, mm. 1590–1596)

EXAMPLE 5-2 Death of Kurwenal the "Friend", *Tristan und Isolde* (Act III, sc. iii, mm. 1535–1550)

NOTES

1. Echoes

1. Important exceptions to this neglect include Michael Tanner, "The Total Work of Art," in *The Wagner Companion*, ed. Peter Burbridge and Richard Sutton (Cambridge, 1979), 140–224; Dieter Schickling, *Abschied von Walhall: Richard Wagners erotische Gesellschaft* (Stuttgart, 1983); Dieter Borchmeyer, *Die Götter tanzen Cancan: Richard Wagners Liebesrevolten* (Heidelberg, 1992); *Richard Wagner und die Erotik: Erlösung durch Liebe*, Ausstellung des Richard-Wagner-Museums und der Bayreuther Festspiele, ed. Sven Friedrich (Bayreuth, 1995); John Tietz, *Redemption or Annihilation: Love Versus Power in Wagner's Ring* (New York, 1999); Anthony Winterbourne, *A Pagan Spoiled: Sex and Character in Wagner's Parsifal* (Madison, New Jersey, 2003); James Kennaway, *Musical Pathology in the Nineteenth Century: Richard Wagner and Degeneration* (PhD Diss. UCLA, 2004); and Roger Scruton, *Death-Devoted Heart: Sex and the Sacred in Wagner's Tristan and Isolde* (Oxford, 2004). Eroticism is treated insightfully by all these authors, although none is especially interested—as I am—in linking the reception of Wagner both to his musical representations and his own unusual sexuality.

2. Gustave J. Stoeckel, "The Wagner Festival at Bayreuth" [hereafter, *SF*], *The New Englander* 36 (1877), 276.

3. Max Kalbeck, "Richard Wagners Nibelungen: Erste Aufführung vom 13. bis 17. August 1876 in Bayreuth," *Schlesische Zeitung* (1876; Breslau, 1883), reprinted in Susanna Großmann-Vendrey, *Bayreuth in der deutschen Presse: Beiträge zur Rezeptionsgeschichte Richard Wagners und seiner Festspiele* [hereafter, *GV*], vol. 1 (Regensburg, 1977), 193. Positive reviews of the 1876 *Walküre* performances, on the other hand, while conceding that the scene prompts routine "accusations of a quite special immorality," note that the text adheres closely to the saga and that the characters are bred rather differently from the "boys and girls" who populate "our own educational establishments." V. K. Schembera, "Das Bühnenfestspiel zu Bayreuth," *Neues Wiener Tagblatt* (1876), reprinted in *GV* I, 139. Translations throughout this book are my own unless otherwise stated.

4. Bruno Walter, *Thema und Variationen: Erinnerungen und Gedanken* (Stockholm, 1947), 68.

5. Vernon Lee, "The Religious and Moral Status of Wagner," *Fortnightly Review* (1911), 868–885, esp. 868, 872–873, 879. See also Carlo Caballero, "'A Wicked

Voice': On Vernon Lee, Wagner, and the Effects of Music," *Victorian Studies* 35 (1992), 386–408.

6. Samuel Alexander in *Beauty and Other Forms of Value* (London, 1933), 127; Kenneth Clark, *The Nude: A Study of Ideal Art* (London, 1956), 6.

7. Arthur C. Danto, *Playing with the Edge: The Photographic Achievement of Robert Mapplethorpe* (Berkeley, 1996).

8. Here the less obvious reference to homoeroticism stems from the writings of Winckelmann, whose notions of the male nude as the apotheosis of Greek art influenced David and those like Ingres who worked in his studio. See Patricia Condon, "Ingres," *Grove Art Online*, www.oxfordartonline.com (accessed October 17, 2009).

9. For contrasting formulations of the debate, see Morse Peckham, *Art and Pornography: An Experiment in Explanation* (New York, 1971) and Peter Webb, *The Erotic Arts*, rev. ed. (1975; London, 1983).

10. Peter Webb, "Erotic Art and Pornography," in *The Influence of Pornography on Behaviour*, ed. Maurice Yaffe and Edward C. Nelson (London, 1982), 81.

11. *The Republic*, 3.399e, trans. Paul Shorey, in Plato, *The Collected Dialogues*, ed. E. Hamilton and H. Cairns, Bollingen ser. 71 (Princeton, 1961), 644.

12. Peter Wilson, "The *aulos* in Athens" in *Performance Culture and Athenian Democracy*, ed. Simon Goldhill and Robin Osborne (Cambridge, UK, 1999), 72–73; Alexandre G. Mitchell, *Greek Vase-Painting and the Origins of Visual Humour* (Cambridge, UK, 2009), 167-168.

13. Søren Kierkegaard, *Either/Or*, trans. David and Lillian Swenson (London 1944), 38, 57, 68, 109.

14. George Balanchine, "How to enjoy ballet," in George Balanchine and Francis Mason, *Balanchine's Complete Stories of the Great Ballets* (1954; New York, 1977), 744.

15. Peter Webb, "Erotic poetry," in *The Penguin Dictionary of Literary Terms and Literary Theory*, 4th ed., ed. J. A. Cuddon (London, 1998), 284.

16. Peter Webb, "Erotic Art," in *Grove Art Online*, www.oxfordartonline.com (accessed October 17, 2009); Eduard Fuchs, *Geschichte der erotischen Kunst*, 4 vols. (Munich, 1912–26). Fuchs (1870–1940) was a Marxist cultural historian and collector active in the Socialist and Communist movements. Later, during his years as an émigré in Paris, he became a friend of Walter Benjamin, who devoted an essay to him: "Eduard Fuchs, der Sammler und der Historiker," *Zeitschrift für Sozialforschung* 6 (1937), 346–381.

17. Eduard Fuchs, *Geschichte*, I, 128.

18. Jeffrey Kallberg, "Sex, sexuality," in *Grove Music Online*, www.oxfordmusiconline.com (accessed October 30, 2009).

19. Charles Baudelaire, "Richard Wagner et Tannhäuser à Paris" (1861), in *Sur Richard Wagner: Richard Wagner et Tannhäuser à Paris* (Paris, 1994), xxx–xxxiii, 15–16. See also Margaret Miner, *Resonant Gaps: Between Baudelaire & Wagner* (Athens, Georgia, 1995).

20. Richard Wagner, *Mein Leben: Jubiläumsausgabe* [hereafter, *ML*], ed. Martin Gregor-Dellin (Munich, 1963), 620.

21. Trans. by D. Kern Holoman in *Berlioz* (London, 1989), 543–544.

22. William Ashton Ellis, trans., *Richard Wagner to Mathilde von Wesendonk* [hereafter, *MWE*] (London, 1905), 210.

23. Baudelaire, *Wagner*, 53–54, 64, 35.

24. See Elliott Zuckerman, *The First Hundred Years of Wagner's* Tristan (New York, 1964), 83–122.

25. Cited in Dietrich Fischer-Dieskau, *Wagner and Nietzsche*, trans. Joachim Neugroschel (New York, 1976), 6.

26. Friedrich Nietzsche, *The Birth of Tragedy and other writings*, trans. Ronald Speirs (Cambridge, UK, 1999), 104, 123.

27. Friedrich Nietzsche, *Sämtliche Werke: Kritische Studienausgabe* [hereafter, *KSA*], ed. Giorgio Colli and Mazzino Montinari, 15 vols. (Berlin, 1980), vol. 1, 135.

28. See Georges Liébert, *Nietzsche and Music* [hereafter, *LN*], trans. David Pellauer and Graham Parkes (Chicago, 2004), 50.

29. Mildred Adams, ed., *Rebel in Bombazine: Memoirs of Malwida von Meysenbug* [hereafter, *MR*], trans. Elsa von Meysenbug Lyons (New York, 1936), 305.

30. Stewart Spencer, *Wagner Remembered* (London, 2000), 90.

31. Jürgen Lotterer, "Malwida von Meysenbug und die Musik," in *Briefe als Zeugnisse eines Frauenlebens: Malwida von Meysenbug und ihre Korrespondenzpartner*, ed. Hans-Peter Wehlt (Detmold, 2003), 185.

32. Malwida von Meysenbug, *Memoiren einer Idealistin und ihr Nachtrag, Der Lebensabend einer Idealistin*, 2 vols. (1898; Berlin, 1927), 344–345.

33. Richard Wagner, *Sämtliche Schriften und Dichtungen* [hereafter, *SS*], 16 vols., 6th ed. (Leipzig, 1911–1914), vol. 12, 346–347.

34. Édouard Schuré, *Le Drame Musical*, 2 vols. (Paris, 1875), vol. 2, 224–225, 226.

35. *Cosima Wagner's Diaries* [hereafter, *CD*], ed. Martin Gregor-Dellin and Dietrich Mack, trans. Geoffrey Skelton, 2 vols. (London, 1978), vol. 1, 761.

36. Édouard Schuré, *Souvenirs sur Richard Wagner: la première de Tristan et Iseult* (Paris, 1900), 38–43.

37. Édouard Schuré writing in the first issue of the *Revue wagnérienne* (1885–1886), 281, cited in Lucy Beckett, *Richard Wagner: Parsifal* (Cambridge, UK, 1981), 109.

38. Egon Voss, ed., *Richard Wagner: Dokumentarbiographie* (Mainz, 1982), 362–364.

39. Richard Wagner, *Das Braune Buch: Tagebuchaufzeichnungen 1865 bis 1882* [hereafter, *BB*], ed. Joachim Bergfeld (1975; Munich, 1988), 50. The entry is from August 24, 1865.

40. *König Ludwig II. und Richard Wagner: Briefwechsel* [hereafter, *KB*], ed. Otto Strobel, 5 vols. (Karlsruhe, 1936), vol. 1, 134.

41. Zuckerman, *Tristan*, 130–135.

42. Gabriele D'Annunzio, *Il trionfo della morte* (1894), anon. trans. in *Studies in Music*, ed. Robin Grey (London, 1901), 141, 143, 145.

43. Thomas Mann, "Tristan," *Die Erzählungen* (Frankfurt, 1975), trans. H. T. Lowe-Porter in *Stories of Three Decades*, (New York, 1936), 153–154.

44. I discuss the Wagnerian erotics of *Blood of the Volsungs* in "Music and Motive in Thomas Mann's *Wälsungenblut*," *Resounding Concerns, London German Studies* VIII, ed. Rüdiger Görner (Munich, 2003), 86–113.

45. Voss, *Dokumentarbiographie*, 409–410.

46. H. F. Chorley, *The Athenaeum*, London, December 18, 1852 as cited in Nicolas Slonimsky, *Lexicon of Musical Invective* [hereafter, *SM*] (New York, 1953), 222.

47. *Musical World*, London, June 30, 1855 as cited in *SM*, 226.

48. H. L. Klein, *Geschichte des Dramas* (Leipzig, 1871), vol. 8, 738–739, as cited in *SM*, 237.

49. O. Comettant, *Siècle*, Paris, March 8, 1886, as cited in *SM*, 245.

50. Louis Ehlert, "Das Bühnenfestspiel in Bayreuth," *Deutsche Rundschau* 9 (1876), as given in *GV* I, 182.

51. Karl Frenzel, "Die Bayreuther Festspiele," Berlin *Nationalzeitung* (1876) as given in *GV* I, 211.

52. Wilhelm Tappert, *Richard Wagner im Spiegel der Kritik* (1876; Leipzig, 1915), 91.

53. Berthold Litzmann, *Clara Schumann: Ein Künstlerleben nach Tagebüchern und Briefen* [hereafter, *LK*], 3 vols. (Leipzig, 1923), vol. 3, 326.

54. Clara Schumann—Johannes Brahms, *Briefe aus den Jahren 1853–1896*, ed. Berthold Litzmann (Leipzig, 1927), vol. 2, 59–60.

55. Eduard Hanslick, *Neue Freie Presse* (1873); W. F. Apthorp, *Boston Evening Transcript*, October 31, 1898; Louis Elson, *Boston Daily Advertiser*, February 25, 1904; J. A. Fuller Maitland in *Grove's Dictionary of Music and Musicians*, vol. 4, (London, 1908); Olin Downes, *New York Times*, November 29, 1935; all as cited in *SM*, 114, 212, 92, 192, 56.

2. Intentions

1. Richard Wagner, "Über das Weibliche im Menschlichen," in *Dichtungen und Schriften: Jubiläumsausgabe*, ed. Dieter Borchmeyer (Bayreuth, 1983) [hereafter, *JA*], vol. 10, 174.

2. Julius Kapp, *Richard Wagner und die Frauen: Eine erotische Biographie* (Berlin, 1912), ix; Julius Kapp, *The Loves of Richard Wagner*, auth. trans. (London, 1951), 9.

3. Kapp, *Loves*, 9.

4. For example, Paul Kühn, *Die Frauen um Goethe: Weimarer Interieurs* (Leipzig, 1910); Francis Gribble, *The Love Affairs of Lord Byron* (London, 1910); Karl Julius Schröer, *Goethe und die Liebe* (Radolfzell, 1922); and Clement Wood, *Byron and the Women He Loved* (Girard, Kansas, 1924).

5. Kapp, *Loves*, 255; Kapp, *Frauen*, 252.

6. Ernest Newman, *Wagner as Man and Artist* [hereafter, *NM*] (1914; London, 1924), 4.

7. Ernest Newman, *The Life of Richard Wagner* [hereafter, *NL*], 4 vols. (London, 1933, 1937, 1941, 1946).

8. Isolde sings the same line to Tristan just as he dies, but then Wagner is thinking of a more high-minded erotic style. *Nur eine Stunde,/nur eine Stunde/*

bleibe mir wach!, she exclaims over his limp body, begging him to stay awake for "just another hour" so she can "expire" with him.

9. On further textual references and relationships, see Dieter Borchmeyer, *Drama and the World of Richard Wagner*, trans. Daphne Ellis (Princeton, 2003), 18–28.

10. Richard Wagner, *Das Liebesverbot oder Die Novize von Palermo: Große Komische Oper in zwei Akten*, piano-vocal score by Otto Singer (Wiesbaden, 1922), 479–480.

11. Trans. adapted from *Richard Wagner's Prose Works* [hereafter, *PW*], trans. William Ashton Ellis, 8 vols. (1899; London, 1966), vol. 1, 396.

12. Ludwig Feuerbach, *The Essence of Christianity*, trans. George Eliot [Marian Evans] (1854; New York, 1989), 48, as cited in Mark Berry, *Treacherous Bonds and Laughing Fire: Politics and Religion in Wagner's* Ring (Aldershot, 2006), 189.

13. *Selected Letters of Richard Wagner* [hereafter, *SL*], trans. and ed. Stewart Spencer and Barry Millington (London, 1987), 180–181.

14. Richard Wagner, *Sämtliche Briefe* [hereafter, *SB*], ed. Gertrud Strobel and Werner Wolf, (Leipzig, 1967), vol. 5, 494–495.

15. John Deathridge suggests that the story "is probably a semi-conscious conflation of two separate events" in "Wagner: The formative years: 1813–32," *Grove Music Online*, www.oxfordmusiconline.com (accessed November 6, 2009). Klaus Kropfinger, however, argues that Wagner's memory was probably accurate. See Kropfinger, *Wagner and Beethoven: Richard Wagner's Reception of Beethoven*, trans. Peter Palmer (1974; Cambridge, UK, 1991), 32–33.

16. Hector Berlioz, *The Memoirs of Hector Berlioz*, trans. and ed. David Cairns (London, 1969), 399–400.

17. Cosima Wagner, *Die Tagebücher* [hereafter, *CT*], ed. Martin Gregor-Dellin und Dietrich Mack, 4 vols., rev. ed. (Munich, 1982), vol. 1, 419.

18. Alfred von Wolzogen, *Wilhelmine Schröder-Devrient: ein Beitrag zur Geschichte des musikalischen Dramas* (Leipzig, 1863), cited in *NL* I, 346.

19. Rupert Christiansen, *Prima Donna: A History* (London, 1984), 142. See also Carl Hagemann, *Wilhelmine Schröder-Devrient* (1904; Wiesbaden, 1947).

20. Richard Wagner, *My Life*, trans. Andrew Grey, ed. Mary Whittall (Cambridge, UK, 1983), 237; *NL* I, 347.

21. See Susan Rutherford, "Wilhelmine Schröder-Devrient: Wagner's theatrical muse," in *Women, Theatre and Performance*, ed. Maggie B. Gale and Viv Gardner (Manchester, 2000), 60–80.

22. Lilli Lehmann, *Mein Weg* (Leipzig, 1913), 72–73.

23. It is open to question whether these kinds of attractions and identities can be attributed to androgyny, as does Jean-Jacques Nattiez in *Wagner Androgyne: A Study in Interpretation*, trans. Stewart Spencer (1990; Princeton, 1993). Biographical considerations suggest more properly historical categories rooted in the "sensualist" discourse of the past.

24. To evade the censors, August Prinz (of the *Verlagsbureau*) made use of bogus foreign publishing houses: *Aus den Memoiren einer Sängerin* appeared under

the imprint of "Reginald Chesterfield, Boston" and *Galante Abenteuer der Sängerin Wilhelmine: nach vertraulichen Mittheilungen* [*according to confidential information*] of "Jules Flangarin" of Paris. Both publications are listed separately in Hugo Hayn, *Bibliotheca Germanorum Erotica: Verzeichniss der gesammten deutschen erotischen Literatur mit Einschluss der Uebersetzungen, nebst Angabe der fremden Originale*, 2nd ed. (Leipzig, 1885). Hayn thought the books appeared around 1862, though both are undated.

25. [Wilhelmine Schröder-Devrient], *Aus den Memoiren einer Sängerin* (1862; Munich, 1972). Guillaume Apollinaire brought out a French translation in 1913 (referred to briefly by *NL* I, 346n). Paul Englisch, in *Irrgarten der Erotik* (Leipzig, 1921), 92–93, showed—on textual and biographical grounds—how Schröder-Devrient cannot possibly have written the pornographic memoirs. Yet the issue of her authorship stuck, and an edition of the *Memoirs* appeared in a lavish illustrated edition of the "Eros-Gesellschaft" (Munich, 1920–1921) as volume 5 of "erotic masterworks of world literature." One can still obtain English translations of the *Memoirs* that name Wilhelmine Schröder-Devrient as the author.

26. Englisch, *Irrgarten*, 57.

27. Claire von Glümer, *Erinnerungen an Wilhelmine Schröder-Devrient* [hereafter, *GE*] (1862; Leipzig, 1904). The later edition issued in 1904 ignores the putative pornographic memoirs, and reveals (in the new preface) that Glümer's account, filled with quotations from letters and other documents, was authorized by the singer when she realized that because of ill health, she would be unable to complete her own reminiscences. According to Glümer, "as much as bequeathing an enduring keepsake of her aspirations and accomplishments was something close to her heart, she kept delaying the organization of her papers and review of her diaries: Even the preparatory work brought back too much half-forgotten pain and strife. When she finally began the description of her childhood, she became so severely ill that she wasn't able to carry on writing and, worried about her imminent death, entrusted me with the task which only she would have been able fully to manage." *GE*, 5–6.

28. Hagemann, *Schröder-Devrient*, 73–74.

29. Arthur Schopenhauer, *The World as Will and Representation* [hereafter, *SW*], 2 vols., trans. E. F. J. Payne (Clinton, Mass., 1958), vol. 2, 532.

30. *SL*, 345–347, 356–359. On Wagner's anti-Semitism generally, see the remarkable synthesis of perspectives in Thomas Grey, "The Jewish Question," in the *Cambridge Companion to Wagner* (Cambridge, UK, 2008), 203–218.

31. Ludwig Feuerbach, *Gedanken über Tod und Unsterblichkeit* (1830), in *Gesammelte Werke*, ed. Werner Schuffenhauer, 10 vols. (Berlin, 1981), vol. 1, 216.

32. Arthur Schopenhauer, *Die Welt als Wille und Vorstellung* (1819, 1844; 1859), in *Arthur Schopenhauers Werke in Fünf Bänden* (Zurich, 1988), vol. 2.

33. Arthur Schopenhauer, *Manuscript Remains*, 4 vols. (Oxford, 1989), vol. 3, 262. See also Bryan Magee, *The Tristan Chord: Wagner and Philosophy* (London, 2002), 170.

34. *Richard Wagner an Mathilde von Wesendonk: Tagebuchblätter und Briefe, 1853–1871* [hereafter, *MW*], ed. Wolfgang Golther (Berlin, 1910), 79. See also Joan T. Grimbert, *Tristan and Isolde: A Casebook* (London, 2002), 393.

3. Harmonies

1. Heinrich Heine coins the term in *Aus den Memoiren des Herrn von Schnabelewopski* (Chapter 7), in which he calls the Dutchman *den ewigen Juden des Ozeans*; that is, "the immortal" or "the eternal"—not wandering—"Jew of the Ocean." See Heinrich Heine, *Werke und Briefe in zehn Bänden* [hereafter, *HW*], ed. Hans Kaufmann (1961; Berlin, 1972), vol. 4, 79. Wagner uses the term *ewiger Jude* to refer to one aspect of his Dutchman in *A Communication to My Friends*, *JA* VI, 238. The French term for "the wandering Jew" was popularized in the nineteenth century by Eugène Sue's novel *Le Juif errant* (1845). In his 1865 prose draft for *Parzifal* [*sic*], Wagner associates Kundry with the figure of Ahasuerus, stating that her curse is "similar to the eternal Jew [*ähnlich dem 'ewigen Juden'*] in damning her to "always changing reincarnations." *BB*, 62.

2. Borchmeyer, *Drama*, 82.

3. *My Life*, 212–213.

4. Sven Friedrich, *Richard Wagner: Deutung und Wirkung* (Würzburg, 2004), 42.

5. Ludwig Tieck, *Werke in einem Band* [hereafter *TW*], ed. Richard Alewyn (Hamburg, 1967), 134.

6. *The Diary of Richard Wagner: The Brown Book, 1865–1882*, ed. Joachim Bergfeld, trans. George Bird (London, 1980), 47–48.

7. E. T. A. Hoffmann, *Die Serapions-Brüder* [hereafter, *HS*], ed. Walter Müller-Seidel and Wulf Segebrecht (Munich, 1976), 297.

8. Wagner, *My Life*, 212.

9. *Wagner Werk-Verzeichnis: Verzeichnis der musikalischen Werke Richard Wagners und ihrer Quellen* [hereafter *WWV*], ed. John Deathridge, Martin Geck, and Egon Voss (Mainz, 1986), 269.

10. Richard Wagner, *Dokumente und Texte zu* Tannhäuser und der Sängerkrieg auf Wartburg, *Sämtliche Werke*, vol. 25, ed. Peter Jost (Mainz, 2007), 48–49, 55.

11. See Carolyn Abbate, "The Paris *Tannhäuser* and the Parisian Venus," *Journal of the American Musicological Society* 36 (1983), 82.

12. *Tannhäuser*, Act III, sc. iii, mm. 368–373, as in Wagner's own 1845 keyboard arrangement edited in Richard Wagner, *Sämtliche Werke, Tannhäuser und der Sängerkrieg auf Wartburg: Klavierauszug* (Mainz, 1992), vol. 20, III.

13. I have omitted mention of various kinds of exciting if non-thematic filler music that lend to the *mise en scène* a heightened sensory awareness, along with the music of "wanton whirring and rustling" that symbolizes, as mentioned, "an unholy sensuous lust in a heightened state of sensual arousal."

14. G. Desrat, in his *Dictionnaire de la danse* (Paris, 1895), 72–75, claims that the can-can was a name given to a sort of "epileptic dance or *delirium tremens* [shaking madness] . . . marked by an originality that could be called spiritual" but very

far from the cheaply crude manner danced later at the Moulin Rouge. See also *International Encyclopedia of Dance*, ed. Selma Jeanne Cohen, "Can-Can" (Oxford, 1998), vol. 2, 52-53.

15. Wagner mentions in the same letter (April 10, 1860) that he wishes he had access to (Bonaventura) Genelli's (1798-1868) watercolors whose "mythological savageness is made very graphic." *MW*, 226-227. Genelli, born in Berlin, had painted a series of "Roman" frescoes in the Leipzig villa belonging to the Härtel family, and Wagner was probably seeking some visual stimulus for the retouching of his own erotic brushstrokes.

16. Richard Wagner, *Skizzen und Entwürfe zur Ring-Dichtung: mit der Dichtung Der junge Siegfried* [hereafter, *WS*], ed. Otto Strobel (München, 1930), 41.

17. The statements of Siegmund are each played a third higher so that their opening notes prefigure components of the harmony first underlying Love (a). Previously ravaged by the storm—his own motive is a synecdoche of the storm that opens the fiery Prelude to Act I—Siegmund now anticipates and is embodied in Love.

18. Holoman, *Berlioz*, 543-544.

19. Another passage (derived from Desire) is also labeled *zart* in the score, one which begins at m. 36 and again at m. 90. Wagner doesn't distinguish it in the prose program.

4. Pathologies

1. Thomas Grey traces a critical tradition dating back to Eduard Hanslick's *Vom Musikalisch-Schönen* (1854), which distinguishes between a properly "aesthetic" appreciation of music and a "pathological" mode of reception that values music as a drug. See "Wagner the Degenerate: Fin de Siècle Cultural 'Pathology' and the Anxiety of Modernism," *Nineteenth Century Studies* 16 (2002), 73-92, esp. 79-80.

2. Theodor Puschmann, *Richard Wagner: eine psychiatrische Studie* [hereafter, *PS*] (Berlin, 1873), 10. James Kennaway treats the Puschmann study and its critical reception in Chapter 3 of his doctoral dissertation, *Musical Pathology in the Nineteenth Century: Richard Wagner and Degeneration* (UCLA, 2004), 48-102.

3. Friedrich Nietzsche, *Der Fall Wagner: Ein Musikanten-Problem* (1888) [hereafter, *NW*], trans. Walter Kaufmann as *The Case of Wagner* in *Basic Writings of Nietzsche* (New York, 1967), 642.

4. Friedrich Nietzsche, *Briefwechsel: Kritische Gesamtausgabe* [hereafter, *NB*], ed. Giorgio Colli and Mazzino Montinari (Berlin, 1981), vol. III.6, 330 and vol. III.5, 458-459.

5. Sander L. Gilman, ed. with Ingeborg Reichenbach, *Begegnungen mit Nietzsche* (Bonn, 1981), 345. The translation is mine. The text of the interview is found in "Erinnerungen an Dr. Otto Eiser. Für das Nietzsche-Archiv aufgezeichnet von Prof. Lic. Dr. Eugen Kretzer" (unpublished manuscript deposited in Nietzsche Archive around 1913) in the private possession of Sander Gilman, also cited in Gil-

man, "Nietzsche, Bizet, and Wagner: Illness, Health, and Race in the Nineteenth Century," *The Opera Quarterly* 23 (2007), 247–264, esp. 256.

6. Laurentius, *Der persönliche Schutz: Aerztlicher Rathgeber bei allen Krankheiten der Geschlechtstheile die in Folge heimlicher Jugendsünden, übermäßigen Genusses in der geschlechtichen Liebe und durch Ansteckung entstehen* (1855; Leipzig, 1863).

7. See *Johannes Brahms: Life and Letters*, ed. and trans. Styra Avins and Joseph Eisinger (Oxford, 1997), 150–151.

8. Jean Stengers and Anne van Neck, trans. Kathryn Hoffmann, *Masturbation: The History of a Great Terror* (1998; New York, 2001), 105, 213–214.

9. Ibid., 133. In Germany, the work of Magnus Hirschfeld put forth the same idea slightly later.

10. Ibid., 130.

11. Wagner was not beyond making a joke of masturbation, trivializing rather than pathologizing it, as in a letter of 1851 to Ernst Benedikt Kietz (*SB* IV, 70): "So again you ran out of ink?—God, I'm so indifferent to ink just now! What we're now pursuing [*treiben*] with ink is no more than masturbation [*doch alles nur Onanie*]!" To characterize the practice as "wastage" suggests Wagner thought individual masturbatory acts trifling and ineffective, not dangerous or even shameful. Rather, it was chronic "self-abuse" that he thought led to homosexuality, organic disease, and dementia.

12. George Mosse, *Nationalism and Sexuality* (New York, 1985), 29. The eighteenth-century idea that masturbation caused homosexuality is still found in Richard von Krafft-Ebing, *Psychopathia sexualis*, trans. Charles Gilbert Chaddock (London, 1892), 188. The link was still being debated in the medical and psychoanalytic literature as late as Wilhelm Stekel's *Onanie und Homosexualität: Die homosexuelle Parapathie* (Berlin, 1917). The literature on the medical dangers of masturbation continues well past the mid-twentieth century, with the Kinsey Report (1948) the first to confirm that masturbation was a widespread, normal, and harmless practice.

13. Joachim Köhler suggests that Nietzsche's homosexuality was the key to what he calls *Zarathustra's Secret*, trans. Ronald Taylor (1989; New Haven, 2002). Cataloguing an impressionistic array of compelling if allusive historical facts—intense homoerotic friendships, a special fascination with Byron and August von Platen, a lack of documented sexual affairs with women, journeys on his own to Italy and Sicily, poems addressed to gondoliers—the evidence marshaled requires a more carefully argued case to tie Nietzsche's sexuality to his philosophy. Calling Nietzsche's tendencies "homosexual" falls short in any case of saying very much about his erotic disposition.

14. "Zwei Nietzsche Anekdoten," *Frankfurter Zeitung*, March 9, 1904 as printed in Gilman, *Begegnungen*, 163.

15. It is important to note that in the nineteenth century the color pink—the pale, flesh-tinted mixture of white and red called *rosa* in German—had not yet itself become associated exclusively with femininity and was still used to dress

baby boys, for example. It is rather Wagner's obsession with the strokable soft fabrics of silk and satin, along with styles of negligees copied from ladies' fashion magazines, which cement his identification with femininity. The composer makes a point of telling Judith Gautier that "*my* pink" is "very pale and delicate," so in no way robust or manly.

16. Ludwig Kusche, *Wagner und die Putzmacherin oder Die Macht der Verleumdung* (Wilhelmshaven, 1967), 94–98.

17. I treat the disparity between Wagner and his character Siegfried in "Siegfried's Masculinity," *The Wagner Journal* 4 (2010), translated as "Siegfrieds Männlichkeit," in *Wagner in der Diskussion*, ed. Tobias Janz (Würzburg, 2010).

18. *Richard Wagner and the Seamstress*, ed. Daniel Spitzer and Leonard Liebling, trans. Sophie Prombaum (New York, 1941), 37–38. Wagner's ink drawings for the lavish pink satin dressing gown and sash—actually four yards around—are reproduced in *SL*, 713.

19. *Puck: humoristisch-satyrische Wochenschrift*, ed. Constantin von Grimm (Leipzig), July 1, 1877, 205. I am grateful to the Herzogin Anna Amalia Bibliothek (Weimar) for permission to reproduce this illustration. Atlas is translated as "atlas (a silk or satin manufacture)" in Newton Ivory Lucas, *A Dictionary of the English and German and German and English Languages adapted to the present state of literature, science, commerce and arts*, 2 vols. (Bremen, 1868), vol. 2, 151.

20. Kusche, *Verleumdung*, 17.

21. Wagner's desire not to exhibit himself differed fundamentally, therefore, from Goethe's practice of greeting guests while dressed in shades of grey silk and satin, as reported in Eckermann's *Conversations*.

22. Ludwig Karpath, *Zu den Briefen Richard Wagners an eine Putzmacherin: Unterredungen mit der Putzmacherin Berta* (Berlin, 1906), 24–25.

23. Joachim Köhler suggests that the silk undergarments ordered at various times for Cosima were for Wagner himself, but the evidence is ambiguous. See *Richard Wagner: The Last of the Titans*, trans. Stewart Spencer (2001; New Haven, 2004), 586.

24. *Lettres à Judith Gautier par Richard et Cosima Wagner*, ed. Léon Guichard (Paris, 1964), 194.

25. Kapp, *Frauen*, 43; Kapp, *Loves*, 36.

26. Spitzer, *Seamstress*, 9.

27. Ferdinand Praeger, *Wagner as I knew him* (London, 1892), 251–252. Despite Praeger's many proven fabrications, Wagner admits in a letter to Klindworth in 1857 that while in London "they met comparatively often . . . because, given my passionate and earnest nature, what I sought above all else from this particular relationship was to satisfy a need of mine to let myself go in a nonchalant sort of way, and a desire for homely relaxation. What I seek on such occasions is comfort, and I am easily won over by helpfulness and flexibility" (*SL*, 369). The notion of "comfort" is certainly consonant with a shopping trip for silk shirts in London's Regent Street.

28. Stewart Spencer, "Wagner and Gaetano Ghezzi," *The Wagner Journal* 1:1 (2007), 18–32.

29. Ibid., 27.

30. Wagner's letters to Cyriax are edited and translated by Barbara Eichner and Guy Houghton in "Rose Oil and Pineapples: Julius Cyriax's Friendship with Wagner and the Early Years of the London Wagner Society" [hereafter, *EC*], *The Wagner Journal* 1:2 (2007) 19–49.

31. *Gazzetta di Venezia*, February 15, 1883, cited in Stewart Spencer, "'Er starb,—ein Mensch wie alle': Wagner and Carrie Pringle," in *Bayreuther Festspiele 2004*, ed. Peter Emmerich (Bayreuth, 2004), 76.

32. Lehmann, *Mein Weg*, 125.

33. Carl Maria Cornelius, *Peter Cornelius: Der Wort- und Tondichter*, 2 vols. (Regensburg, 1925), vol. 1, 403.

34. Curt von Westernhagen, *Richard Wagner: sein Werk, sein Wesen, seine Welt* (Zurich, 1956), 528.

35. Agnès Masson, *Le Travestissement: Essai de Psycho-Pathologie sexuelle* (Paris, 1935).

36. Richard von Krafft-Ebing, *Psychopathia Sexualis* (1886; trans. ed. London, 1906) 276–277, cited in Valerie Steele, *Fetish: Fashion, Sex and Power* (New York, 1996), 147–148.

37. Magnus Hirschfeld, *Die Transvestiten* (Leipzig, 1910), trans. Michael Lombardi-Nash as *The Transvestites: The Erotic Drive to Cross-Dress* [hereafter, *HT*], (Amherst, NY, 1991), 158–170.

38. *Richard Wagner Briefe: Die Sammlung Burrell*, ed. John N. Burk (New York, 1950), 576. Weinert provides further descriptions of silk furnishings at Wahnfried and in Wagner's thinking-room [*Denkzimmer*], 568–571. English translation in *Letters of Richard Wagner: The Burrell Collection*, ed. John N. Burk (New York, 1950), 436.

39. See also Wagner's letter to Ludwig II, August 1882, translated in *SL*, 926, which calls the Flower scene conducted by Levi "probably the most masterly piece of direction in terms of music and staging that has ever come my way." The entry for September 6, 1882 (*CT IV*, 999) notes that Wagner "had loudly called 'Bravo' at every performance over the top of the whole audience."

40. Guy de Maupassant, *La vie errante* (Paris, 1890), 63.

41. Thomas Mann, "Leiden und Grösse Richard Wagners," in *Leiden und Grösse der Meister* (Berlin, 1935), 147.

42. The rapture of a woman ensconced in flowers was also part of the plan for *Die Sieger* [*The Victors*]. As Wagner wrote to Marie Wittgenstein in 1857, Savitri, "while waiting for Ananda in the second act, rolls in the flowers in utter ecstasy, absorbing the sun, the words, the birds and the water—everything—the whole of nature in her wanton pleasure" (*SL*, 365). And speaking of costumes for *Das Rheingold*, in a letter to Hans Richter in 1869, Wagner notes that "as goddess of flowers and fruit," Freia, a symbol of youth and love should be similarly characterized (*SL*, 752).

43. *Lettres à Judith Gautier*, 71–72.

44. *Musical Courier* 35 (1897), 20, as quoted in Arnold T. Schwab, *James Gibbons Huneker: Critic of the Seven Arts* (Stanford, 1963), 104.

45. James Gibbons Huneker, "Parsifal," *Overtones* (1904), 97, 96.

46. Malcolm Brown, "Tchaikovsky and Anglo-American Criticism" in *Queer Episodes in Music and Modern Identity*, ed. Sophie Fuller and Lloyd Whitesell (Urbana, 2002), 142–143.

47. Huneker, "Parsifal," 97.

48. Schwab, *Huneker*, 147.

49. See Hartmut Zelinsky, *Richard Wagner: Ein deutsches Thema* (Berlin 1983), 50–56.

50. Lindau made a point of commissioning a review of *Parsifal* for his journal *Nord und Süd* in 1889 during the only season between 1882 and 1894 when Felix Mottl, a Gentile, conducted the work instead of Hermann Levi. There are more than a few cultural ironies in the assessment of Mottl, about whom Paul Marsop writes, "there is something nervous, unreliable, womanlike about him. . . . The drama which leads onto all the heights and depths of life requires a conductor like the Munich Court Capellmeister Hermann Levi, and Mottl isn't such an artist, though he might become one." Cited in Frithjof Haas, *Zwischen Brahms und Wagner: Der Dirigent Hermann Levi* (Zurich, 1995), 337.

51. Julia Bernhardt, *Der Briefwechsel zwischen Paul Heyse und Hermann Levi: Eine kritische Edition* (Hamburg, 2007), 115–116.

52. Jens Malte Fischer, *Richard Wagners* Das Judentum in der Musik: *Eine kritische Dokumentation als Beitrag zur Geschichte des Antisemitismus* (Frankfurt, 2000), 245–247. Fischer also documents other Jewish reactions to Wagner's anti-Jewish pamphlet.

53. See Nancy A. Kaiser, "Berthold Auerbach: The Dilemma of the Jewish Humanist from 'Vormärz' to Empire," *German Studies Review* 6 (1983), 399–419.

54. Ibid., 417.

55. Daniel Spitzer, *Verliebte Wagnerianer* (Vienna, 1880), 97–98. I'm grateful to Thomas Grey for presenting me with a first edition of this novel.

56. Max Nordau, *Degeneration* [hereafter, *ND*] (1893; London, 1895), 209.

57. Anna and Maxa Nordau, *Max Nordau: A Biography* (New York, 1943), 21.

58. Max Nordau, *Die conventionellen Lügen der Kulturmenschheit* (Leipzig, 1883), Preface to first edition.

59. In a short autobiographical statement from 1909, Nordau notes that "I myself experienced an assimilationist phase from which I emerged only with the greatest effort and moral exertion. . . . Only with the growth of anti-Semitism was the consciousness of my duties to my people awakened in me. . . ." Max Nordau, *Zionistische Schriften* (Berlin, 1923), 484–486.

60. Anna and Maxa Nordau, *Biography*, 126.

61. Nordau, *Schriften*, 72. A subsequent short piece from 1900 for the Jewish Gymnastic Association was entitled *Muskeljudentum*; Nordau, *Schriften*, 424–426.

62. Anna and Maxa Nordau, *Biography*, 154.

63. Sander Gilman, *Jewish Self-Hatred: Anti-Semitism and the Hidden Language of the Jews* (Baltimore, 1986), 298.

64. *The World*, October 15, 1897 as quoted and trans. in Ernst Pawel, *The Labyrinth of Exile: A Life of Theodor Herzl* (London, 1990), 345–346. In Amos Elon,

Herzl (New York, 1975), 251–252, *Mauschel* is translated as "Kike." The original article was reprinted in *Theodor Herzls Zionistische Schriften*, ed. Leon Jellner (Berlin, 1920), 172–176.

65. Elon, *Herzl*, 259.

66. The letter is reproduced in Zelinsky, *Thema*, 51. See also Alex Bein, *Theodor Herzl: Biographie* (Vienna, 1934), 66–67. Hermann Bahr, who became a well-known writer and novelist, was subsequently expelled from the University in Czernowitz for anti-Semitic agitation, though he later worked as a theater director for Max Reinhardt [born Maximilian Goldmann] in Berlin.

67. Theodor Herzl, *Briefe und Tagebücher*, 7 vols. (Berlin, 1983), vol. 1, 496.

68. Bein, *Herzl*, 98.

69. *Theodor Herzls Tagebücher, 1895–1904*, 3 vols. (Berlin, 1922), vol. 1, 39. See also Steven Beller, "Herzl's Tannhäuser: The Redemption of the Artist as Politician," in *Austrians and Jews in the Twentieth Century: From Franz Joseph to Waldheim*, ed. Robert S. Wistrich (London, 1992), 51.

70. Theodor Herzl, *Altneuland* (Leipzig, 1902), 302.

71. Otto Weininger, *Sex and Character* [hereafter, *WC*] (1903; London 1906), 329.

72. Adolf Hitler, *Mein Kampf* [Munich, 1923], trans. Ralph Manheim (1943; Boston, 1999), 325, as cited in George M. Frederickson, *Racism: A Short History* (Princeton, 2002), 119–120.

73. See Jacob Katz, *Out of the Ghetto: the Social Background of Jewish Emancipation, 1770–1870* (Cambridge, MA, 1973), 86. See also, G. R. Philon, *Ueber die Juden auf Veranlassung der Posse* Unser Verkehr (Königsberg, 1825), who saw *Unser Verkehr* from a Christian perspective as the most petty and hateful expression of anti-Judaism.

74. See Gilman, *Self-Hatred*, 156–160, 414–415.

75. *Ludwig Börne's Gesammelte Schriften*, 3 vols. (Leipzig, n.d.), vol. 2, 86.

76. Marc A. Weiner, *Richard Wagner and the Anti-Semitic Imagination*, 2nd ed. (Cambridge, UK, 1997) sees *Parsifal's* Flower-Maidens and their enticing floral scents (which so delighted Wagner) as "constructions of anti-Semitic stereotypes" (238), in this case of stinking Jews. Given Wagner's love of floral scents, this interpretation flies in the face of the biographical evidence.

77. *Cosima Wagners Briefe an ihre Tochter Daniela von Bülow*, ed. Max von Waldberg (Stuttgart, 1933), 215.

78. I discuss the primary sources for the incident in "Hermann Levi's shame and *Parsifal's* guilt: A critique of essentialism in biography and criticism," *Cambridge Opera Journal* 6 (1994), 125–145, esp. 127–131. Since Glasenapp bowdlerized the word *Schweinerei* (far from an obscenity) as "*Sch—*," Wagner was misunderstood as having characterized the affair by the word *Scheisse* in most published accounts in English and German, as in, for example *SL*, 914.

5. Homoerotics

1. Pepino is listed as "servant of Joukowsky" in Carl Friedrich Glasenapp's *Das Leben Richard Wagners in sechs Büchern* [hereafter, *GW*], (Leipzig, 1896–1911) vol. 6, 823, while Newman (*NL* IV) calls him Peppino [*sic*] Joukowsky.

2. Adelheid von Schorn, with whom Joukowsky lived (in a platonic relationship) from 1886 until 1890, and then again from 1907 until his death in 1912, writes warmly about his friendship and character in *Zwei Menschenalter: Erinnerungen und Briefe aus Weimar und Rom* (Stuttgart, 1920), 332–333, 373–374. See also Malwida von Meysenbug's late memoirs, *Lebensabend einer Idealistin* (Stuttgart, 1898), 149.

3. Wagner enacted a similar scene of feigned pouting when Joukowsky arrived in Venice, having spent the autumn in Weimar painting Liszt's portrait instead of remaining at Wagner's side. But the composer was genuinely elated to have Joukowsky back in his entourage, telling him prophetically: "Friend, we've now been through fire and water with you. It's only death that can still separate us now" (*GW* VI, 732–734).

4. Norman Douglas, *Looking Back: An Autobiographical Excursion* (New York, 1933), 271–273.

5. Henry James, *Letters* [hereafter, *JL*], ed. Leon Edel, 4 vols. (London, 1975), vol. 2, 49–50. See also Peter Brooks, *Henry James goes to Paris* (Princeton, 2007), 43, who argues that Henry was clearly "in love" with Joukowsky in Paris. (In the literature on James, Paul's surname is sometimes given as Zhukovsky. His given Russian first name and patronymic—Pavel Vasilievich—are rarely found in the literature.)

6. It is unclear who these Russians were. Leon Edel (*HJ* II, 289) jumps to the conclusion that James apparently found Joukowsky "in a veritable nest of homosexuals," but James's visit to Naples took place in early April 1880, and Joukowsky states in his memoirs—quoted extensively in Glasenapp—that his Russian sister from Wiesbaden (Frau von Wöhrmann), along with his German brother-in-law and nephew, had been living with Paul and Pepino in the Villa Posiglione for an extended visit since the beginning of March (*GW* VI, 332).

7. Brooks, *Paris*, 37–44 notes (44) that "James was back in occasional friendly correspondence with Zhukovsky [*sic*] a couple of decades later."

8. Joris-Karl Huysmans, "L'Ouverture de *Tannhäuser*," in *Croquis parisiens* (1880; Paris, 1955), 201–202.

9. Richard von Krafft-Ebing, *Psychopathia sexualis* (Stuttgart, 1893), 251, 291–293.

10. Cited in Oscar Panizza, "Bayreuth und die Homosexualität," in *Die Gesellschaft: Monatsschrift für Literatur, Kunst und Sozialpolitik* 11 (1895), 88–92; English trans. as "Bayreuth and Homosexuality" [hereafter, *PH*], *Wagner* 9 (1988), 71–75.

11. Isolde Vetter discusses Panizza's essay and the possibility that "his attitude to homosexuality was marked by equally conflicting feelings" in "Aspects of *Parsifal*," *Wagner* 9 (1988), 69–71.

12. Emma Goldman, *Living my Life*, 2 vols. (New York, 1931), vol. 1, 268.

13. Hanns Fuchs, *Richard Wagner und die Homosexualität: mit besonderer Berücksichtigung der sexuellen Anomalien seiner Gestalten* [hereafter, *FH*] (Berlin, 1903). It is important to distinguish Hanns Fuchs from Eduard Fuchs, author of the *History of Erotic Art* cited in Chapter 1. The final chapter of Hanns Fuchs's book (treating *Parsifal*) is translated by John Urang in "Parsifal and Eroticism in Wagner's Music," *The Opera Quarterly* 22 (2006), 334–344.

14. Hanns Fuchs, *Eros zwischen euch und uns* (Berlin, 1909). Mitchell Morris summarizes the plot of the novel in "Tristan's wounds: On Homosexual Wagnerians at the Fin de Siècle," in Fuller, *Queer Episodes*, 271–292. See also Mitchell Morris, "Homosexuality and the Manly Absolute: Hanns Fuchs on Richard Wagner," *The Opera Quarterly* 22 (2006), 328–333.

15. Advertisement on back flyleaf of Fuchs, *Wagner*. He later wrote a cultural study of Masai social practices in Kenya, *Sagen, Mythen und Sitten der Masai nach der Masaisprache und dem Englischen* (Jena, 1910), in which homosexuality does not figure.

16. Hanns Fuchs, "Die dichterische Verwertung der Homosexualität," as cited in James W. Jones, *The "Third Sex" in German literature from the turn of the century to 1933* (PhD thesis, University of Wisconsin-Madison, 1986), 33. See also the article on Fuchs by Joachim Münster, in *Lexikon homosexueller Belletristik*, ed. Dietrich Molitor and Wolfgang Popp (Siegen, 1988), as cited in Wolf Borchers, *Männliche Homosexualität in der Dramatik der Weimarer Republik* (PhD dissertation, University of Cologne, 2001), 22.

17. August Graf von Platen, *Lyrische Blätter* (Leipzig, 1821), 47.

18. Harry Oosterhuis, *Homosexuality and Male Bonding in Pre-Nazi Germany* (Abingdon, UK, 1991), 3, 50–51.

19. Johann Wolfgang von Goethe, *Wilhelm Meisters Wanderjahre* (1829; Zurich, 1949), 295, 297, 299.

20. See, for example, Alice Kuzniar, ed., *Outing Goethe and his Age* (Stanford, 1996) and Karl Hugo Pruys, *Die Liebkosungen des Tigers: Eine erotische Goethe-Biographie* (Berlin, 1997).

21. Friedrich Schiller, *Sämtliche Werke*, ed. Gerhard Fricke and Herbert Göpfert, 3 vols. (Munich, 1958), vol. 1, 91–92.

22. Richard Wagner, *Nachgelassene Schriften und Dichtungen* (1895; Leipzig, 1902), 141; see also *PW* VIII, 368 where Ashton Ellis translates *Männerliebe* as "love toward men."

23. Eliza Wille, *Erinnerungen an Wagner* [hereafter, *WE*] (1894; Munich, 1935), 75.

24. In 1860—at the age of forty-seven—Sainton had married the famous English contralto Charlotte Dolby—thirty-nine-year-old at the time—but he continued to live with the pianist Lüders, as Samuel Clemens [Mark Twain] met them (without Sainton's wife) in London in 1874, and heard a similar story about their life-long friendship. According to Clemens, they were "two white haired gentlemen 60 years old" who were "good natured old fellows." Sainton boasted that Lüders, an indigent pianist, had been taken into his "house as one of the

family & there he has remained every day from that day to this—five-and-thirty years!" That would mean they had been together since 1839 (when Sainton had indeed been on tour, including a period in the Nordic countries, and hadn't had a family) and that Wagner's story about their meeting in Helsinki in *Mein Leben* was plausible. Sainton's brother-in-law George Dolby recounted how, during the Franco-Prussian War, "it was something gorgeous to see those two old men get into a frenzy & blackguard & abuse each other like fishwomen until they were exhausted, and then kiss as fondly as two children & go off to bed." *Mark Twain's Letters*, ed. Michael B. Frank and Harriet Elinor Smith (Berkeley, 2002), vol. 6, 8–9. It is possible that their friendship was Romantic without being sexual, but according to Glasenapp (*GW* III, 470), Karl Klindworth, who socialized with Wagner, Berlioz, Sainton, and Lüders in London in 1855, made a point of identifying Lüders as Sainton's *Pylades*, whom Lucian described in *Amores* as the lover of Orestes.

25. Letter to Johanna Kapp in Jacob Baechtold, *Gottfried Kellers Leben* (1894; Berlin, 1903), vol. 2, 215, as cited in Lilli Jung, *Dichterfreundschaft und ihr romantisches Eigengepräge* (Saalfeld, 1934), 11. Keller's letter continues: "Oh dear, what a boring sermon! It's as if I'm exaggerating, not everything is true. To emphasize: Keller thinks differently about women as a part of social life!"

26. See John Deathridge, "Wagner's Sketches for the 'Ring': Some recent studies," *Musical Times* 118 (1977), 386; and also Robert Bailey, "The Method of Composition," in *The Wagner Companion*, ed. Peter Burbridge and Richard Sutton (New York, 1979), 317–327, where there is a transcription of these musical sketches for *Siegfried* and *Tristan*, along with the translation of Wagner's letter and a detailed commentary.

27. In *CT* III, 142, an entry from 1878, Cosima reveals that the World Inheritance motive set to the passage in *Siegfried* was originally intended for the Buddha in *Die Sieger* [*The Victors*], presumably when he gains a new insight about the stilling of sensual desires. Wagner describes this moment in a letter to Mathilde Wesendonck from 1858, speaking of how this insight marks the Buddha's final progress toward a state of supreme enlightenment. A woman, now understood compassionately, could be accepted into the "community of the saintly" as long as she also renounced sensuality as a component of her love for a man. See *WB*, 57–58. The musical depiction of this idea apparently occurred to Wagner in 1864 as he was sketching out ideas for this never-to-be-completed opera based on a Buddhist legend. The link to Siegfried shows how Buddhist renunciation of sexual desire figures in the idealized and far from erotic arousal of Siegfried in the Act III duet with Brünnhilde. See Dreyfus, "Siegfried's Masculinity."

28. See *Johannes Brahms im Briefwechsel mit Hermann Levi, Friedrich Gernsheim, sowie den Familien Hecht und Fellinger*, Brahms-Briefwechsel VII (1910; Tutzing, 1974), 178–179; and Dreyfus, "Levi," 136, in which I quote and translate the homoerotic letter Levi sent to Johannes Brahms.

29. Ibid., 131.

Epilogue

1. See Pamela Potter, "Wagner and the Third Reich: Myths and Realities," in *The Cambridge Companion to Wagner*, ed. Thomas S. Grey (Cambridge, UK, 2008), 221–234.

2. Thomas Mann, *Briefe 1948–1955* (Kempten, 1965), 1714–1715.

Index

Abbate, Carolyn, 249n11
Andersen, Henrik, 183
Apollinaire, Guillaume, 248n25
Auerbach, Berthold, 159–160

Bach, J.S., 161
Bahr, Hermann, 255n66
Bailey, Robert, 258n26
Balanchine, George, 13–14
Ball, Benjamin, 163
Baudelaire, Charles, 17–23, 24, 25, 27, 128, 134
Beethoven, Ludwig van, 3–4, 53, 56, 60, 161, 169
Beller, Steven, 255n69
Bellini, Vincenzo, 2, 56, 57, 60
Benedictus, Louis, 143
Benjamin, Walter, 244n16
Berg, Alban, 39, 48
Berlioz, Hector, 36, 257n24; mystified by Tristan Prelude, 21, 101; and Schröder–Devrient's stage histrionics, 54
Bernays, Michael, 161
Billroth, Theodor, 160
Binet, Alfred, 149
Bisexuality, 15, 195–196. See also Homoeroticism, male, and homosexuality
Bizet, Georges, 36; Nietzsche's praise of, 122–123
Borchers, Wolf, 257n16
Borchmeyer, Dieter, 75, 243n1, 247n9
Brahms, Johannes, 4, 38, 39, 132, 158, 160; Nietzsche's diagnosis of his weak erotic nature, 128–129; interest in Wagner's silk obsession, 136; recipient of homoerotic letter from Hermann Levi, 258n28
Brand, Adolf, 191
Brooks, Peter, 256n5

Büchner, Georg, 48
Bülow, Daniela von, 177–178
Bülow, Hans von, 30, 57, 200, 214
Byron, Lord, 42, 251n13

Caballero, Carlo, 243n5
Callas, Maria, 58
Can–can, 86, 88, 249n14
Caravaggio, 13
Chaillon, Charlotte, 142
Charcot, Jean-Martin, 149
Chaucer, Geoffrey, 14
Chopin, Frédéric, 35, 36, 109, 184
Clark, Kenneth, 7
Clemens, Samuel [Mark Twain], 257n24
Condon, Patricia, 244n8
Cornelius, Peter, 147, 214; invited to set up house with Wagner, 199–200
Cyriax, Julius: supplier of rose oil for Wagner, 145–146, 253n30

D'Annunzio, Gabriele, 32
Danto, Arthur, 7
David, Jacques-Louis, 244n8
Deathridge, John, 247n15, 258n26
Debussy, Claude, 17, 39
Degas, Edgar, 36
Diminished seventh chord, 49, 76, 86, 87, 92, 98, 102
Dolby, Charlotte, 257n24
Donizetti, Gaetano, 46, 109
Douglas, Norman: chance meeting with Pepino, 181
Dujardin, Édouard, 23

Edel, Leon, 256nn5,6
Effeminacy, 122, 127, 128, 137, 156, 160, 179, 191; and Jewishness, 130, 170–173
Eiser, Otto: on Nietzsche's rift with Wagner, 130–132, 147–148, 250n5

Eichner, Barbara, 145, 253n30
Ellis, Havelock, 132
Ellis, William Ashton, 42, 257n22
Elon, Amos, 254n64
Epiktetos, 9
Erotics: in antiquity, 7, 9–10, 16–17,
    244n12; and sensuality, 17, 55, 58
Erotics, musical, 10, 12–13; and religion, 3,
    5–6, 18, 22, 36, 59, 79–80, 187, 211;
    nature of, 6–7; compared to visual
    arts and literature, 7–10, 14–15; and
    pornography, 8–10, 12, 39, 58–59,
    71, 244nn9,10; invisibility of, 11, 91,
    112
Erysipelas [Gesichtsrose]. See Wagner,
    Richard; skin condition

Female domination, 54, 57, 188–189, 213,
    216, 222; of Tannhäuser by Venus,
    90–91; of Parsifal by Kundry, 1
    55–156
Fetish, silk and satin. See Silk and Satin
    Fetish
Feuerbach, Ludwig, 50–51, 62–64, 68, 71,
    93–95
Fragrances. See Roses, rose scents and
    perfumes
Fuchs, Eduard, 14–15, 244n16
Fuchs, Hanns, 156, 213, 222,
    257nn13,14,15,16; on literary context
    for Romantic friendship, 188–197;
    on Romantic friendship in Wagner's
    works; 204–205, 207, 209–211

Gautier, Judith, 23, 61, 140–141, 145;
    supplies Wagner with pink satin and
    rose oils, 143–144, 147, 251n15;
    Kundry's erotic power explained to,
    155
Genelli, Bonaventura, 250n15
Genet, Jean, 9
Ghezzi, Gaetano, 142
Gilman, Sander L., 250n5, 254n63, 255n74
Glasenapp, C. F., 42, 255n78, 256n1, 257n24
Glümer, Claire von: on Wilhelmine
    Schröder-Devrient, 59, 248n27
Gobineau, Arthur Count de, 176
Goethe, J. W. von, 42, 51, 65, 156, 246n4,
    257n20; erotic styles in, 14, 218; in
    Wagner's view of "Judaic" works of
    music, 171–172; Wagner's joke on
    "the eternal feminine," 178–179;
    homoeroticism in works by,

        191–193, 195; and silk dressing
        gowns, 252n21
Goldman, Emma, 187
Goldwag Maretschek, Bertha: provides
    satin garments and furnishings for
    Wagner, 136–140, 189
Greek love. See Homoeroticism, male, and
    homosexuality
Grey, Thomas, 248n30, 250n1, 254n55,
    259n1

Ha'Am, Ahad, 168
Haas, Frithjof, 254n50
Halévy, Fromental, 60, 166
Half-diminished chord, 98, 101–102, 114,
    232. See also Tristan chord
Hanslick, Eduard, 7, 250n1
Heine, Heinrich, 172; erotic episode
    avoided in Wagner's Flying
    Dutchman, 74; erotics and sado-
    masochism in Tannhäuser-Lied, 82,
    90, 152; on the Flying Dutchman as
    "eternal Jew," 249n1
Herzen, Alexander, 25, 26
Herzl, Theodor: as Wagnerian, 164–168,
    220, 254n64, 255n66
Heyse, Paul, 159, 160
Hirschfeld, Magnus, 191, 251n9, 253n37;
    on Wagner's fetishistic transvestism,
    149–150, 188; commissions text
    on music and homosexuality,
    188, 213
Hitler, Adolf, 170, 219
Hoffmann, E.T.A: source for Tannhäuser,
    82–83
Homoeroticism, female, 14, 56–57, 60, 101,
    205–207
Homoeroticism, male, and homosexuality,
    8, 11, 14, 20, 51, 101, 128, 133, 156,
    175–217, 219, 244n8, 251nn11,12,13,
    256nn,5,6,7,11
Houghton, Guy, 253n30
Humperdinck, Engelbert, 181
Huneker, James Gibbons, 155–156, 212, 217
Huysmans, Joris-Karl, 184

Ibsen, Henrik, 36
Ingres, Jean Auguste Dominique, 7, 8, 147,
    218, 244n8

James, Henry, 181–184, 256nn5,6,7
Jewish Wagnerians, 23, 38, 39, 57, 77, 118,
    143, 147, 159, 161, 164–168,

168–170, 172–173, 176, 200, 214,
  215, 220, 253n39, 254n50, 254n64,
  255n66, 255n78, 258n28
Joachim, Joseph, 38, 132
Jones, James W., 257n16
Joukowsky, Paul von, 56, 175–184, 203,
  214, 256nn1,2,3,5,6,7

Kalbeck, Max, 4–5, 158–159
Kallberg, Jeffrey, 15–16
Kapp, Johanna, 204
Kapp, Julius, 42–43, 44, 128
Katz, Jacob, 255n73
Keller, Gottfried, 204–205, 258n25
Kennaway, James, 121, 243n1, 250n2
Kierkegaard, Søren, 10–12, 15
Kietz, Ernst Benedikt, 251n11
Klindworth, Karl, 26, 252n27, 257n24
Köhler, Joachim, 251n13, 252n23
Köselitz, Heinrich, 133, 221
Krafft-Ebing, Richard von, 148, 149,
  184–185, 251n12
Kretzer, Eugen, 131
Kropfinger, Klaus, 247n15
Kupffer, Elisarion, von 191
Kusche, Ludwig, 137–139
Kuzniar, Alice, 257n20

La'Mert, Samuel, 132
Laube, Heinrich, 45
Lawrence, D.H., 9
Lee, Vernon, 5–6
Lehmann, Lilli, 57; remarks on Wagner's
  pink satin lining, 147
Lehmann, Marie, 57
Lehrs, Samuel, 77
Leitmotives, musical, 6, 83–88, 97–98, 100,
  101–102, 105–106, 114, 115, 122, 127,
  142, 167, 205–207, 209, 210,
  250nn17,19
Lesbian sex and love, 14, 20, 60, 130. See
  also Homoeroticism, female
Levi, Hermann, 38, 39, 118, 159, 161,
  172–173, 176, 214, 215, 253n39,
  254n50, 255n78, 258n28
Liébert, Georges, 245n28
Lindau, Paul, 154, 157–158, 254n50
Liszt, Franz, 39, 51, 62, 63, 70, 84, 100,
  256n3
Lombroso, Cesare, 164
Löw, Marie: plays Juliet to Schröder-
  Devrient's Romeo, 57
Lucas, C. T. L., 83

Lüders, Carl, 203–204, 257n24
Ludwig II of Bavaria, King, 32, 61, 136,
  139, 175, 253n39; Romantic
  friendship with Wagner, 196–202,
  210, 214; fails to understand
  Kundry's kiss, 211–212

Magee, Bryan, 248n33
Maier, Mathilde, 197, 199, 200, 201
Mallarmé, Stéphane, 23, 148
Manet, Édouard, 8
Mann, Thomas, 161, 221, 246n44;
  Wagnerian erotics in *Tristan* and
  Wälsungenblut, 32–33, 160; allusion
  to Wagner's satin fetish, 154
Mapplethorpe, Robert, 7, 9
Masturbation, 17, 105, 148, 190, 251n12;
  Wagner's anxieties regarding,
  130–134; Wagner's joke about,
  251n11
Maupassant, Guy de: discovery of
  Wagner's perfume fetish, 153–154
Mendelssohn, Felix, 84–85, 159–160, 171
Mendès, Catulle, 23
Meyerbeer, Giacomo, 166
Meysenbug, Malwida von, 24–27, 37, 256n2
Michelangelo, 7, 189
Millington, Barry, 248n30
Miner, Margaret, 244n19
Monteverdi, Claudio, 2
Morris, Mitchell, 257n14
Mosse, George, 251n12
Mottl, Felix, 254n50
Mozart, W.A., 2; Kierkegaard's "musical
  erotic" in *Don Giovanni*, 10–11
Münster, Joachim, 257n16

Nattiez, Jean-Jacques, 247n23
Neumann, Angelo, 161, 176, 215
Newman, Ernest, 43–44, 53
Nietzsche, Friedrich, 6, 115, 148, 170; early
  enthusiasm for *Tristan und Isolde*,
  23–24; Wagner's erotics as a
  sickness, 38, 117, 121–135, 173, 221;
  unwitting positive identification of
  Wagner's erotics, 127–128; supplied
  Wagner with silk underwear, 135,
  136, 140; Wagner's presumption
  about masturbatory practices of,
  203, 250n5; Wagner's Romantic
  friend, 129, 214; late change of heart
  about *Parsifal*, 221–222; sexuality of,
  251n13

Nijinsky, Vaslav, 17
Nordau, Max, 38; on Wagner's erotic
    madness, 161–165, 168, 173, 187;
    conversion to Zionism, 164–167,
    220, 254nn59,61

Panizza, Oscar, 156, 184–188, 211, 212,
    256nn10,11
Peckham, Morse, 244n9
Pederasty, 19–20, 51,120, 127–128, 179,
    180, 183, 191, 196–197, 216; result of
    masturbation, 132, 133, 203, 251n12;
    Huneker's preoccupation with, 156;
    Panizza's view of *Parsifal* and,
    185–187; Wagner's rejection of
    carnal sodomy in, 202–204. *See also*
    Homoeroticism, male, and
    homosexuality
Pepino: lover of Paul Joukowsky, 175–184,
    203, 256nn1,6
Perfumes. *See* Roses, rose scents and
    perfumes
Philon, G.R., 255n73
Pink, color, 135–143, 145, 146, 147, 148,
    150, 151, 152, 251n15, 252n18
Platen, August von, 191, 193, 251n13
Plato, 9
Poe, Edgar Allan, 134
Porges, Heinrich, 147, 161, 200, 214
Potter, Pamela, 259n1
Poussin, Nicolas, 88
Praeger, Ferdinand, 141, 252n27
Preetorius, Emil, 221
Pringsheim, Alfred, 161
Prinz, August, 58, 247n24
Pruys, Karl Hugo, 257n20
Purcell, Henry, 2
Puschmann, Theodor, 119–121, 123, 157,
    173, 250n2

Renunciation of sexual desire, 43, 64, 71,
    79, 95, 99, 102, 110–112, 200, 258n27
Richter, Hans, 253n42
Ritter, Karl, 51, 131, 132, 203, 214, 215
Röckel, August, 63, 93, 95, 99
Romantic friendship, 182, 189, 197,
    257n24, 258n25; importance in
    Wagner's life, 60, 197, 202–203,
    213–216; literary context for, 189,
    191–195; in Wagner's works,
    204–205, 207, 208–209, 210, 241
Roses, rose scents and perfumes, 61, 81,
    110; in Wagner's works, 91, 110,

152–154, 177, 255n76; in Nietzsche's
    critique of Wagner; 127, 135; in
    Wagner's life, 135–138, 141,
    143–146, 180; and Wagner's skin
    condition, 148
Rossini, Gioachino, 2
Rosy mists, 85, 90, 151, 152. *See also* Pink,
    color
Rubinstein, Joseph, 161, 214
Rutherford, Susan, 247n21

Sacher-Masoch, Leopold von, 58
Sainton, Prosper, 203–204, 257n24
Same-sex love. *See* Homoeroticism,
    male, and homosexuality
Sand, George, 35
Satin fetish. *See* Silk and Satin Fetish
Sayn-Wittgenstein, Carolyne von, 27, 111
Schiller, Friedrich, 51, 171–172, 193–194,
    201, 204
Schnappauf, Bernhard, 144
Schnorr von Carolsfeld, Ludwig, 31–32,
    60–61, 212–213, 214–215
Schopenhauer, Arthur, 61–69, 70, 94, 95,
    99, 100, 102, 123; metaphysics of
    sexual love, 25–26, 51, 61–62, 65,
    68–69, 70–71, 186–187; link
    between music and sexual love,
    65–67; on pederasty, 186–187
Schorn, Adelheid von, 256n2
Schröder-Devrient, Wilhelmine, 53–56,
    59–60, 73, 74, 77, 189, 248n27;
    inspiration for Tristan and Kundry,
    56–58; image on portal to Wahn-
    fried, 60–61, 215; spurious
    authorship of a pornographic novel,
    58–59, 247n24, 248n25
Schubert, Franz, 184
Schumann, Clara Wieck, 59–60, 85; rejects
    sexual madness of *Tristan*, 37–39,
    101, 118
Schumann, Robert, 38, 78, 84–85, 97, 184
Schuré, Édouard, 28–30
Shakespeare, William, 13, 14, 26, 45, 48,
    56, 156, 189, 193, 218
Silk and satin fetish, 61, 112, 135–150, 151,
    154, 160–161, 171–172, 178–179,
    189, 208, 209, 213, 216, 219, 240,
    251n15, 252nn18,19,21,27, 253n38
Spencer, Stewart, 245n30, 247n23, 248n30,
    252n28, 253n31
Spitzer, Daniel: exposes Wagner's silk
    obsession, 135–140, 167, 252n18,

254n55; satirical novella *Verliebte Wagnerianer*, 160–161
Steele, Valerie, 148
Stekel, Wilhelm, 149
Stoeckel, Gustave, 2–4, 12, 98
Strauss, Richard, 16, 39
Strobel, Otto, 96
Sue, Eugène, 249n1

Tappert, Wilhelm, 35
Taussig, Karl, 214
Tchaikovsky, Pyotr Ilyich, 39, 156, 254n46
Tieck, Ludwig, 80–81
Tissot, Samuel Auguste, 132
Titian, 13, 88
Transvestism. *See* Wagner, Richard; cross dressing of
Tristan chord, 248n33; chief marker of *Tristan* erotic, 101–102, 106–107, 108, 142, 205–208; in Paris *Tannhäuser*, 110–111; in *Die Meistersinger*, 112–113; in *Götterdämmerung*, 113–114; in *Parsifal*, 115
Tristan Prelude, 17, 18, 21, 23, 27, 66, 102–108
Turgenev, Ivan, 182
Twain, Mark. *See Clemens, Samuel*

Ulrichs, Karl, 185

Verdi, Giuseppe, 2, 35, 216
Vetter, Isolde, 256n11
Viardot-Garcia, Pauline, 182

Wagner, Cosima Liszt, 20, 29, 42, 54, 55, 56, 57, 58, 60–61, 71, 100, 111, 116, 119, 142, 146, 153, 172–173, 175–177, 178–179, 180, 184, 203, 215, 216, 258n27; and Wagner's silk obsession, 140–141, 143, 144, 252n23
Wagner, Eva, 177
Wagner, Minna Planer, 74, 141
Wagner, Richard: and sensualism [*Sinnlichkeit*], 3–4, 5, 19, 27, 33–35, 36, 38, 40–41, 45–46, 51, 52, 118, 124, 133–134, 163; and fragrances, 4, 34, 83–84, 85, 91, 110, 143, 145, 147, 151, 152, 153, 180, 255n76; musical leitmotives, 6, 83–88, 97–98, 100, 101–102, 105–106, 114, 122, 127, 142, 167, 205–207, 209, 210, 250nn17,19; erotic crescendos,

12, 99, 105–107, 108, 109–110, 154; cross–dressing of, 15, 135–144, 146–151, 161 171–172, 179, 216; as philosopher, 36, 41, 43–44, 52–53, 62–64, 65, 69–71, 99, 123–124, 126, 128, 170, 173, 219, 248n33; against libertinage, 49–50, 52, 76–77, 88, 89, 95; on love and friendship, 52–53; anti-Semitism of, 62–63, 71–72, 117–118, 119, 133, 143, 157–161, 168, 169–174, 177, 219, 220, 222, 248n30; and the Wandering Jew, 76, 115, 249n1; pleasure in the pain of abstinence, 112; praise of Spartan same-sexual love, 120, 180, 194–196, 203, 207–208, 213–214, 216, 257n22; views on modern homosexual love, 120, 175–180, 202–204; skin condition, 139, 141, 148; fabric and perfumes in the operas of, 151–154; works' appeal to women, 162–163, 169. *See also* Roses, rose scents and perfumes
Wagner, Richard: Works
Die Feen, 52, 204
Das Liebesverbot, 1, 40, 45–49, 52, 73, 110, 120, 225
Rienzi, 54, 56, 73, 74
Der fliegende Holländer [*The Flying Dutchman*], 1, 18, 33, 43, 47, 49, 52, 54, 56, 89, 103, 114, 116, 249n1; and Wagner's musical erotics, 73–77; and renunciation of sexual desire, 111
Die Sarazenin, 77
Tannhäuser, 1, 2, 17–18, 20, 21–23, 43, 49, 51–52, 54, 73, 77–92, 96, 103, 104, 116, 118, 128, 151, 152, 184, 185, 186, 249n13; Venus inspired by Schröder-Devrient, 60, 77; symbolic importance of Venus, 77–80; its protagonist's passivity, 89–90; reconciliation between spirituality and sensuality, 78–80; erotic depiction of the *Venusberg*, 83–91, 97, 100, 101, 108, 112, 153, 167, 226–227; Venus in Paris version, 110–111, 221
Lohengrin, 18, 19, 21, 30, 43, 49, 59, 92, 93, 101–102, 103, 114, 120, 123, 125, 151, 177, 185, 186, 196, 209
Siegfrieds Tod, 92–94
Der junge Siegfried, 93–95

Wagner, Richard: Works *(continued)*
  Der Ring des Nibelungen, 1, 2, 63, 92–95,
    114, 176, 177, 197, 219
  Das Rheingold, 93, 95, 97, 102, 114, 123,
    145, 253n42
  Die Walküre, 40, 64, 93, 100, 102, 106,
    108, 114, 123, 201, 209, 243n3; those
    shaken by its erotics, 2–4, 35, 120,
    162; Thomas Mann's erotic travesty
    of, 33; musical erotics in Act I of,
    95–99, 228–231; love duet con-
    trasted with Parsifal, Act II, 116
  Siegfried, 64, 93, 94–95, 114, 152, 162,
    206, 210, 252n17, 258n26
  Götterdämmerung, 99, 113–114
  Tristan und Isolde, 1, 2, 33–35, 43, 76, 88,
    99–112, 114, 142, 151, 240, 246n8,
    258n26; reactions to its erotics, 5, 6,
    7, 15–16, 26, 28–30, 31–35, 37–38,
    118, 120, 155, 162, 163, 186; Prelude,
    17, 18, 21, 23, 27, 66, 102–108,
    234–235; Nietzsche's view of, 23–24,
    121, 125, 128, 134; erotic prose
    program to Prelude, 27–28, 65–66,
    102–108; Isolde's erotic ecstasy in,
    29, 57, 89, 100, 109–110, 113, 151,
    205, 246n8; links to Schopenhauer's
    metaphysics of sexual love, 60, 70,
    99; Brangäne's love for Isolde in,
    101, 205–207, 208, 210, 214, 241;
    Kurwenal's love for Tristan in, 101,
    207–209, 210, 214, 242; King
    Marke's love for Tristan in, 101,
    209–210, 214, 241; links to Parsifal,
    115, 155; Romantic friendship in,
    204–210, 213, 214, 216
  Die Sieger [The Victors], 99, 253n42,
    258n27
  Die Meistersinger, 1, 2, 43, 52, 69, 92;
    erotics in, 112–113, 115, 151–152,
    237

Parsifal, 1, 30, 31–32, 43, 49, 78, 86, 128,
    157–158, 169–170, 176, 185–186,
    204, 214; Kundry's kiss in, 2, 27, 32,
    47, 57, 115–116, 154–155, 163;
    Flower-Maidens in, 27, 82, 86, 115,
    116, 152–154, 158, 163, 211, 255n76;
    unacceptable erotics of, 30, 126–127,
    130, 185–186, 216–217; Klingsor in,
    49, 115, 118, 126, 145, 152, 163, 176,
    214; Kundry as Wandering Jew in,
    76; sexual identity of Parsifal in,
    152, 154–156, 186, 211–213, 216
Wagner, Siegfried, 60, 176, 178, 215
Walter, Bruno, 5
Watteau, Antoine, 13
Webb, Peter, 9
Weiner, Marc A., 255n76
Weinert, Susanne, 151, 253n38
Weininger, Otto, 168–170, 173
Wesendonck, Mathilde, 42, 70, 71, 76, 89,
    96, 111, 142, 206, 258n27
Whitman, Walt, 156
Wilde, Oscar, 187
Wille, Eliza, 197, 199, 200
Wilson, Peter, 9
Winckelmann, Johann Joachim, 193,
    244n8
Winkelmann, Hermann, 180
Wittgenstein, Marie, 253n42
Wolzogen, Alfred von, 54
Wurm, Albert, 171–172

Yiddish language, 165, 171–172

Zelinksky, Hartmut, 254n49, 255n66
Zhukovskii, Pavel Vasilievich. *See*
    Joukowsky, Paul von
Zhukovskii, Vasilli Andreevich, 175
Zionism, 164–168
Zola, Émile, 148
Zuckerman, Elliott, 245nn24,41